Erratum

The map included on p. x of this volume does not purport to be an accurate representation of the political boundaries of the Republic of India. It is intended merely to show readers unfamiliar with India the location of the states.

The State of India's Democracy

A *Journal of Democracy* Book

•

BOOKS IN THE SERIES

Edited by Larry Diamond and Marc F. Plattner

Electoral Systems and Democracy (2006)

Assessing the Quality of Democracy (2005)
(Edited by Larry Diamond and Leonardo Morlino)

World Religions and Democracy (2005)
(with Philip J. Costopoulos)

Islam and Democracy in the Middle East (2003)
(with Daniel Brumberg)

Emerging Market Democracies: East Asia & Latin America (2002)
(Edited by Laurence Whitehead)

Democracy after Communism (2002)

Political Parties and Democracy (2001)
(Edited by Larry Diamond and Richard Gunther)

The Global Divergence of Democracies (2001)

Globalization, Power, and Democracy (2000)
(Edited by Marc F. Plattner and Aleksander Smolar)

The Democratic Invention (2000)
(Edited by Marc F. Plattner and João Carlos Espada)

Democratization in Africa (1999)

Democracy in East Asia (1998)

Consolidating the Third Wave Democracies (1997)
(with Yun-han Chu and Hung-mao Tien)

Civil-Military Relations and Democracy (1996)

The Global Resurgence of Democracy, 2nd ed. (1996)

Economic Reform and Democracy (1995)

Nationalism, Ethnic Conflict, and Democracy (1994)

Published under the auspices of
the International Forum for Democratic Studies

The State of
India's
Democracy

Edited by Sumit Ganguly,
Larry Diamond, and Marc F. Plattner

The Johns Hopkins University Press
Baltimore

9 8 7 6 5 4 3 2 1

Chapters 7, 10, and 12 in this volume appeared in the April 2007 issue of the *Journal of Democracy*. For all reproduction rights, please contact the Johns Hopkins University Press.

The Johns Hopkins University Press
2715 North Charles Street
Baltimore, Maryland 21218-4363
www.press.jhu.edu

Library of Congress Cataloging-in-Publication Data

The state of India's democracy / edited by Sumit Ganguly, Larry Diamond, and Marc F. Plattner.
    p. cm. — (Journal of democracy book)
    Includes bibliographical references and index.
    ISBN-13: 978-0-8018-8790-1 (hardcover : alk. paper)
    ISBN-13: 978-0-8018-8791-8 (pbk. : alk. paper)
    ISBN-10: 0-8018-8790-9 (hardcover : alk. paper)
    ISBN-10: 0-8018-8791-7 (pbk. : alk. paper)
    1. Democracy—India. 2. Civil society—India. 3. India—Politics and government—1947– I. Ganguly, Sumit. II. Diamond, Larry Jay. III. Plattner, Marc F., 1945–

    JQ281.S73 2007
    320.954—dc22

                               2007018293

A catalog record for this book is available from the British Library.

CONTENTS

IV. The Economy

ACKNOWLEDGMENTS

This is our nineteenth *Journal of Democracy* book, but it is the first that concentrates on the politics of a single country. Yet India, whose population far exceeds that of entire regions to which we have devoted previous studies (Africa, the Middle East, the postcommunist world), is certainly a worthy candidate for this kind of close attention. As it marks its sixtieth year of independence, India is becoming an ever more important object of study for scholars of comparative democracy. It has long stood out as a remarkable exception to theories holding that low levels of economic development and high levels of social diversity pose formidable obstacles to the successful establishment and maintenance of democratic government. In recent decades, India has proven itself capable not only of preserving democracy, but of deepening and broadening it by moving to a more inclusive brand of politics. Political participation has widened, electoral alternation has intensified, and civil society has pressed more vigorously for institutional reforms and greater governmental accountability.

Moreover, with economic reform, India has now begun to achieve notable improvements in economic growth that promise to upgrade the living standards of its citizens, strengthen its institutions, and make it an increasingly prominent player on the world stage. Yet political scientists still have not devoted to this country the kind of attention that its significance warrants.

With these considerations in mind, the *Journal of Democracy* was pleased to accept a suggestion from Sumit Ganguly, Rabindranath Tagore Professor of Indian Cultures and Civilizations and professor of political science at Indiana University–Bloomington, that we collaborate in convening a small conference on democracy in India. The meeting was held at the University's India Studies Center in Bloomington in April 2006. The richness of the discussions there prompted us to consider a more ambitious undertaking, and after enlisting Professor Ganguly as a coeditor, we resolved to produce a collection of essays on Indian democracy.

Professor Ganguly played a key role in identifying the subjects to be covered and the authors to be invited, and he deserves the largest share of the credit for whatever merit this volume may possess. He wishes to acknowledge the following for their help in supporting the conference: the Department of Political Science, the Dean of the College of Arts and Sciences, the Office of International Programs, and the Office of the Vice-Provost for Research at Indiana University–Bloomington; the Embassy of India in Washington, D.C.; and Tata and Sons in Arlington, Virginia. And he is grateful for the assistance provided throughout the project by Tim Callahan, assistant director of the India Studies Program, and Scott Nissen and Leila Zakhirova, both doctoral students in the Department of Political Science.

Due to other pressures on our limited space, we were able to publish only a handful of the essays that follow in the April 2007 issue of the *Journal of Democracy*. This meant that the *Journal* staff had to do a great deal of additional labor to prepare the remaining essays for publication in this volume. Thus we are exceedingly grateful to Phil Costopoulos, Sarah Bloxham, Sumi Shane, Zerxes Spencer, and Eric Kramon for their outstanding editorial work. Sarah also took charge of production, and she did a splendid job of readying the book for publication, without missing a deadline.

Finally, we cannot help repeating our thanks to those we have so often thanked in earlier volumes: The Lynde and Harry Bradley Foundation for its continuing financial assistance to the *Journal*; the Board of Directors of the National Endowment for Democracy and its president Carl Gershman for their unswerving support; and Henry Tom and his colleagues at the Johns Hopkins University Press for both their professionalism and their good cheer.

—Marc F. Plattner and Larry Diamond

INTRODUCTION

Sumit Ganguly

The emergence and persistence of Indian democracy are theoretical and historical anomalies. Early theorists of democracy argued that this form of government not only required but was generated by certain social and economic requisites—none of which India possessed.[1] More recent analysts have claimed that particular levels of economic development are crucial for the perpetuation and consolidation of democracy.[2] India's rapid and successfully consolidated transition to democracy during the years following British withdrawal in 1947—a transition accomplished despite acute and widespread poverty as well as deep and numerous social cleavages—raises doubts about this claim's validity. India has also managed to make its democratic experiment work even though the annual per-capita income of its citizens still remains under US$1,000, a level of economic development that is considered poorly conducive to the maintenance and consolidation of democracy.[3]

The historical origins of India's democracy also present an important puzzle. Contrary to popular belief, the British did little or nothing to promote the growth of democratic institutions in India. Instead, Indian nationalists from the late nineteenth century onward successfully appropriated liberal-democratic principles from the United Kingdom and infused them into the Indian political context. Under the towering influence of Mohandas K. Gandhi in the 1930s, these beliefs and principles were disseminated to a broad swath of India's population via the Indian National Congress (Congress party), the leading nationalist political party. As this was occurring, the British colonial regime was losing few opportunities to thwart or at least contain the growth of democratic sentiment and practice in India.[4] Indian nationalists can justifiably claim that each step toward self-rule and democratic governance was the result of sustained and unrelenting political agitation by Indians against authoritarian colonial rule.[5]

It can be argued that India's transition to and sustenance of democracy have been the fruits of both *structure* and *contingency*. The dominant strand of the nationalist movement had been democratic. In keeping

STATES AND TERRITORIES OF INDIA

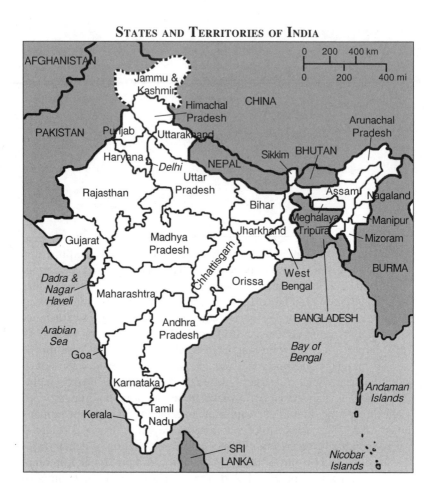

with that spirit, the framers who drew up India's constitution in 1950 adopted a democratic structure that sought to represent the views of the many rather than the opinions of the few.[6] Yet the role played by contingent factors—the great "wild cards" of history—cannot be dismissed. Indian democracy, and with it the world, will always owe a huge debt of thanks to particular nationalist leaders such as Gandhi and Jawaharlal Nehru, the first prime minister. They and their colleagues not only shucked off the dead hand of colonialism but also fostered a nationalist movement and a political elite that have shunned the authoritarian temptation.[7]

That is not to say that Indian democracy's record since the British exit in 1947 has been unblemished. On the contrary, that record is distinctly mixed. And yet there can be little question that, despite myriad challenges, India has managed to achieve democratic consolidation. Any dispassionate assessment will run through a familiar litany: the adoption and maintenance of a system of universal adult franchise from the outset; mostly free and fair elections; regular alternation of the parties in power as a result of those elections; a range of viable political parties across a wide ideological spectrum; an open and vibrant press; an apolitical and professional military; and a fiercely independent judiciary.

These achievements are reflected in the annual ratings of India by Freedom House since 1972. With the exception of the period of emergency rule from 1975 to 1977, India was rated continuously as a Free state from 1972 through 1990, with scores of 2 on political rights and 3 on civil liberties (on the 1 to 7 scale, with 1 being most Free). Then, as a result of rising ethnic, religious, and political violence, including the assassination of former prime minister Rajiv Gandhi, India was downgraded to Partly Free status for the first seven years of the 1990s, with a score of civil liberties stuck at 4 during this period (and political rights worsening from a 2 to a 4 from 1993 through 1995). With the electoral alternation that brought a new political party to power in 1998, Freedom House judged that India had returned to its Free status, with scores of 2 on political rights and 3 on civil liberties, and it has maintained these scores for the last nine years.

Moreover, the federal structure that India's constitutional dispensation enshrines has often shown a remarkable capacity for innovation. As early as 1956, the array of states inherited from British India was reorganized along linguistic lines; as recently as 2000, the new state of Jharkhand was carved out of the northern state of Bihar in order to meet demands for regional autonomy. India's fitful embrace of the market since 1991 will, in all likelihood, continue to reinforce the logic of federalism. As the national government sheds its voluminous regulatory powers, states will be able to pursue more innovative economic policies and pursue diverse strategies of economic development. India's language policy also constitutes a striking success of its federal structure. By means of the three-language formula,[8] the country has fended off the kinds of fratricidal conflicts that led to the 1971 breakup of Pakistan and continue to wrack Sri Lanka.

As the Table on page xii shows, within the context of its democratic framework, the Indian state has contributed to measurable improvements in the quality of life of its citizenry. In 1990, for example, the overall literacy rate for men stood at 62 percent; in 2004 it had risen to 73 percent. Similar figures for women also registered a marked improvement, from 36 percent in 1990 to 48 percent in 2004. Changes in other areas are even more dramatic. Between 1980 and 2004, without any resort to coercion, the population-growth rate fell from 2.25 percent to 1.43 percent.[9] Similarly, overall life expectancy at birth has shown considerable improvement, increasing from 54 to 63 years between 1980 and 2004. The UN Development Programme's Human Development Index (HDI), which captures the net effect of these changes, rose from

TABLE—INDIAN SOCIOECONOMIC INDICATORS

INDICATOR	1975	1980	1985	1990	1995	2000	2004
Human Development Index (UN Development Report)	0.413	0.439	0.477	0.515	0.548	0.577	0.611
GDP per capita (in year-2000 dollars)	215	224	261	318	374	454	548
Literacy Rate (men)	—	—	—	62%	—	—	73%
Literacy Rate (women)	—	—	—	36%	—	—	48%
Literacy Rate (total)	—	—	—	49%	—	—	61%
Population	613,459,008	687,331,968	765,147,008	849,515,008	932,179,968	1,015,923,008	1,079,721,216
Population Growth Rate (annual percentage)	2.28	2.25	2.04	2.02	1.78	1.68	1.43
Mortality rate, infant (per 1,000 live births)	124	113	97	80	74	68	62
Female life expectancy at birth (years)	—	54	57	59	62	64	64
Male life expectancy at birth (years)	—	54	57	59	61	62	63
Total life expectancy at birth (years)	—	54	57	59	61	63	63

Source: World Bank

0.413 to 0.611 between 1975 and 2004. A democratic state could have done even more to improve the material conditions of its citizenry, but these achievements cannot be dismissed as trivial.

In addition, amid intense contestation and debate, India's programs of affirmative action (or "positive discrimination") have made both symbolic and substantive progress toward breaking the "mind-forged manacles" (to borrow William Blake's evocative phrase) of caste and caste-based discrimination. These are also notable achievements in a vast country that began its democratic career burdened with low literacy, extraordinary ethnolinguistic diversity, highly uneven economic levels of development, widespread poverty, and serious external threats to its territorial integrity.

Yet even if one sets aside the more polemical critiques of Indian democracy, there is no denying its shortcomings.[10] The country's performance in protecting the rights of ethnic and religious minorities has been flawed; the government has shown scant regard for civil and personal rights when suppressing secessionist movements; the efficacy of many of India's public institutions remains questionable; and its achievements in the area of development are at best disappointing, as the quarter of all Indians who still live below the poverty line might attest.

Would an alternative form of governance be more appropriate for India? The country did, in fact, experiment with a brand of authoritarianism under Prime Minister Indira Gandhi in the late 1970s. The results of this brief undemocratic interlude proved unsatisfactory in many ways, and the Indian electorate resoundingly rejected it in the 1977 national elections.[11] Since then the country has witnessed the decline of the once-dominant Congress party and the rise of a plethora of regional parties; coped with a major economic crisis that came to a boil by the end of 1990; and confronted the specter of resurgent Hindu nationalism. Of these, the rise of Hindu chauvinism perhaps poses the greatest threat to democracy's well-being. An extraordinary pluralism of religious beliefs, practices, and identities has long been a basic feature of life on the subcontinent. Any failure or abandonment of India's secular dispensation would sound the death knell of democracy as well.[12] Such threats and difficulties notwithstanding, the constitutional structure of democracy in India remains robust.

More to the point, democracy is now the only game in town. The key tenets of democracy are woven firmly into the warp and woof of India's political culture.[13] No political party can expect to make serious headway without a fundamental commitment to democratic procedures. Debate in Parliament may have become less civil and more contentious now that a fuller range of India's social and economic diversity is represented there, but all parties accept the concept of a loyal opposition. Furthermore, India's poor and illiterate participate in national and state-level elections with gusto. Indeed it is worth reiterating that it was the

Indian public which resoundingly rejected Indira Gandhi's authoritarian experiment in the late 1970s.

Challenges and Prospects

Sixty years after independence and fifty-seven years after the adoption of its constitution, how has Indian democracy fared? What are the principal challenges that it confronts? What are the prospects for fuller democratic consolidation? The successful consolidation of Indian democracy has a range of implications. From a theoretical standpoint, India's democratic consolidation challenges the current expert consensus that some "floor" level of economic growth is needed before democracy can consolidate. The policy relevance is equally significant: The continuing success and deepening of democracy in such a large, polyethnic, unevenly developed country could have a potent demonstration effect on prospects for democratic governance elsewhere in the developing world.

Discussing every one of the numerous conceivable challenges that Indian democracy confronts as it enters the new millennium is far beyond the scope of a brief introductory essay. Three areas, however, do stand out by virtue of the significance that they hold for the future working of Indian democracy: human rights, institutional efficacy, and secularism.

Human rights. Despite the considerable success of the Indian state in holding free and fair elections, sustaining a free press, and dramatically expanding the franchise, the abuse of coercive state power remains a grave problem. All too often, such power is used arbitrarily against the poor, minorities, and those who dare to challenge the state's writ. The police, as a recent tragedy dramatically underscored, evince scant regard for the rights of the poor and dispossessed.[14] All too often, a person's class status has too much to do with how and even whether the police respond. Furthermore, police abuses are more pronounced in poorer states such as Bihar or Uttar Pradesh, where standards of accountability are sorely lacking. The evidence from such states of rampant deaths in police custody underscores the gravity of this ill.[15]

The state's willingness to uphold human rights has come under the greatest strain whenever it has had to deal with substantial challenges to its authority. In its efforts to suppress secessionist movements (whether in the Himalayan state of Jammu and Kashmir to the north, Tamil Nadu in the far south, Punjab in the northwest, or Assam in the far east), the central government in New Delhi has resorted to a panoply of draconian legislation that enables it and its agents to act with virtual impunity. Particularly worth discussing are two laws which together have substantially corroded personal rights and civil liberties, especially under conditions of widespread political instability and institutional duress.

The first is the Armed Forces Special Powers Act (Jammu and Kashmir) of 1990. This law was enacted in order to help deal with the longstanding ethnoreligious insurgency in Kashmir, India's only Muslim-majority state and long the bone of contention in a bitter territorial dispute with Pakistan. The act was meant to grant the Indian military and other security forces as much leeway as possible to conduct counterinsurgency operations without fear of punishment. Among other disturbing features, this act permits Indian security forces to use extensive coercive powers (including deadly force) when acting in good faith in the conduct of counterinsurgency operations. Under the aegis of this sweeping legislation, security forces sometimes resorted to deliberate extrajudicial killings.

The second law that opened the door to systematic human rights abuses was the March 2002 Prevention of Terrorism Activities Act (POTA). Passed in the aftermath of the September 11 attacks in New York and the 13 December 2001 suicide assault on the Indian Parliament building in New Delhi, POTA had a nationwide reach which surpassed that of the Armed Forces Special Powers Act, as the latter law applies only to particular states. Individuals arrested under POTA were legally denied access to the writ of *habeas corpus*. The legislation also included significant speech restrictions that led to its use as a weapon in political vendettas.

It is perhaps a testament to the growing strength of India's civil society and the concomitant regard for democratic norms that the Congress party–led United Progressive Alliance (UPA) government, which came to power in May 2004, felt compelled to repeal POTA in September 2004. Nevertheless, insist human rights activists, POTA's two-year existence saw the law repeatedly misused in a blatantly partisan and arbitrary manner, often as part of efforts to punish minorities and political opponents. Although it is comforting that POTA, under severe public criticism, was eventually overturned, the mere fact that the Indian state was willing and able to encroach upon individual rights and civil liberties with such impunity constitutes a disturbing comment on the state of India's democracy.

Institutional efficacy. Indian democracy can be justifiably proud of the success of many of its institutional arrangements. It has a vigorously free press, robust political parties, a working (if terribly overburdened) judiciary, and an apolitical military. In recent years, the state has even created new institutions to cope with rising challenges. In 1993, for example, the government of Prime Minister P.V. Narasimha Rao responded to criticisms from home and abroad about its human rights record in the insurgency-wracked state of Jammu and Kashmir by creating the National Human Rights Commission (NHRC). Critics at first dismissed the NHRC as little more than a token body, yet since its inception it has increasingly asserted institutional autonomy, several times forcing the government to account for its actions or omissions regarding issues as varied as squalid prison conditions and violations of laws banning child labor.

At the same time, other institutions that had fallen into disuse have shown renewed vigor. For example, the National Election Commission (NEC), once a glaring failure at its mission of conducting elections free of intimidation or fraud, has over the past two decades become a robust and highly effective body. No government or politician dares publicly to challenge its prerogatives. Regardless of which individual holds the office of chief election commissioner, the writ of the NEC is now mostly beyond question or reproach.

The revitalization of the NEC began under the aegis of a senior former civil servant, T.N. Seshan. Using the powers vested in the Commission, Seshan began the Herculean task of cleaning out the Augean stables of an electoral process increasingly beset by corruption, violence, and the plottings of criminal elements. Not surprisingly, Seshan quickly became a hero to legions of exasperated Indian voters and the scourge of many a venal politician. His successors cannot touch him for dramatic flair, but in their own quiet way they enforce an evenhanded regimen of consistent procedures and fair regulations. The continuation of Seshan's innovations suggests that they were not the refulgent yet transitory attainments of one strong-willed man, but rather solid achievements that bespeak a lasting improvement in the conduct of elections. Thus despite the decline and decay of a number of institutions, the renewal of other constitutionally mandated bodies such as the Supreme Court and the Election Commission bodes well for the future of Indian democracy.

These two examples provide much hope and comfort to champions of Indian democracy. The state of other key institutions, however, generates much concern and distress. Even though Parliament, for example, has long ceased to be an Anglicized, upper-caste–dominated institution and is now a genuinely representative body, its day-to-day functioning has shown acute signs of decline. An important and perceptive 2006 study has underscored the significant shortcomings that plague this highest of all Indian representative bodies.[16] This study found, for instance, that actual days of sitting—in other words, the time that Parliament spends deliberating over laws—have been dropping steadily, and are now only a third of what they were in the 1950s, even though travel and communication are far easier today than they were in the India of a half-century ago. Worse still, a dramatic increase in adjournments means that less official business than ever before can be conducted.

The precipitous decline in procedural norms has also had an important impact on substantive outcomes. The authors of the 2006 study underscore the impact of this decline on fiscal discipline. In recent years, a distracted, neglectful Parliament has passed federal budgets with little or no scrutiny, thereby contributing to alarming deficits. The refusal of this apex body to honor basic norms of professionalism in the conduct of the people's business constitutes a most disturbing failure of one of the central institutions of Indian democracy and bodes ill for the future.

Secularism. Institutional debility is not the only disturbing aspect of India's democracy. Certain key norms and principles that have undergirded Indian democracy are also at risk. One of them is the vital dimension of Indian secularism, the future of which is under threat. Ironically, secularism must face attacks from both left-wing intellectuals and right-wing ideologues. The left has attacked secularism on the grounds that it lacks an organic basis in a fundamentally religious society. Leftist intellectuals such as Ashis Nandy contend that secularism is a colonial imposition without indigenous roots. Consequently, they contend, an ethic of religious tolerance may be more appropriate than secularism in the Indian context. Nandy argues that an ethic of religious tolerance embraces religion in both the public and private spheres while accepting religious pluralism. Such an ethic requires the state to respect all faiths, but it differs from both Western and Indian concepts of secularism, which insist upon a strict separation of church and state.

The other challenge comes from right-wing Hindu ideologues, such as Ashok V. Chowgule, who make two separate arguments against secularism. First, they contend that Hinduism is not merely a religion but an entire cultural ethos that pervades Indian life and society; consequently, a secular order is well-nigh impossible in India. Second, they argue that secularism, as practiced in India, has amounted to little more than the "pampering" of minorities and is therefore "pseudosecularism."

It is somewhat difficult to pinpoint the sociopolitical antecedents of the left-wing critique of secularism. The only plausible explanation is that most of the left-wing critics also have some deep distrust of modernity and adhere to some postmodern agenda. The origins of the right-wing critique are easier to identify. These critics believe that a unified India depends on an organic vision of Indian society that is rooted in the Hindu *Weltanschauung*. This concern, in turn, emanates from a deeply felt sense of insecurity about India's status in the world, the uncertain cultural leanings of some of its elites, and the increasing assertiveness of its once-dispossessed but now-assertive minorities.[17]

Given the country's multireligious character, the demise of secularism would seriously compromise democracy by consigning a significant share of the populace—mainly belonging to religious groups outside the Hindu majority—to second-class status. This normative concern aside, the dismantling of the secular edifice could also unravel the social compact between the Indian state and minority populations that number in the hundreds of millions (India's Muslim community alone is thought to contain as many as 150 million people). If minorities were to become targets of systematic, legalized discrimination, would their

sense of loyalty to the Indian state survive the mistreatment? A fraying
of social bonds could in turn fuel movements of subnational self-asser-
tion or even secessionism should minority populations come to feel
lastingly disenfranchised.

It is important to underscore that the founders of the Indian state
were committed to a vision of civic nationalism.[18] Nevertheless, even at
the time of independence and partition, a forerunner to today's Bharatiya
Janata Party (BJP), the Hindu Mahasabha, was opposed to the creation
of a secular state. Large sections of the Hindu Mahasabha, seeking an
entry into the electoral arena, joined the Bharatiya Jana Sangh, founded
shortly after independence by a Bengali politician, Shyama Prasad
Mukherjee. Until the 1989 national elections, the heavily upper-caste
Hindu nationalists constituted an extremely limited force in parliamentary politics because of their small numbers. In that year, however, they
became more formidable, winning more than an eighth of the seats in
the Lok Sabha (Parliament's lower house). A decade later, they won a
parliamentary plurality and managed to forge a coalition government at
the national level.[19]

During their time in office, BJP leaders sought systematically to alter
the terms of political discourse in India. While professing a commitment to secularism, they argued that the Congress and other political
parties had simply appeased religious minorities in pursuit of electoral
gains. This charge had some merit, but the BJP was less interested in the
principled correction of abuses than it was in finding political cover for
a wholesale dismantling of the secular order enshrined in the constitution. The Hindu nationalists' hostility to secularism became evident in
a number of different arenas, ranging from a systematic attempt to alter
history and social-science textbooks to the party leaders' willingness to
countenance widespread state-sanctioned violence against Muslims,
especially during bloody disturbances that rocked the western state of
Gujarat (then one of three BJP-run states in India) in February 2002.[20]

In the April and May 2004 national elections, for complex reasons
that included a poor choice of electoral allies and complacency about
the benefits of rapid economic growth, the BJP suffered an electoral
rout. The Congress-led coalition that returned to power has reaffirmed
its commitment to secularism and has reversed many antisecular BJP
policies. Yet it would be premature to dismiss the challenge that the
BJP and its extraparliamentary allies (popularly referred to as the Sangh
Parivar or "family group" and composed of the Bajrang Dal, the Vishwa
Hindu Parishad, and the Rashtriya Swayamsevak Sangh) pose to secularism. Their electoral defeat in 2004 has led them to reexamine their
political strategies, but their commitment to an antisecular agenda remains intact. Whether or not the BJP can make a significant electoral
comeback will, in considerable measure, depend upon whether the Congress party reaffirms its commitment to principles of secular governance

without resorting to sleight-of-hand favoritism toward certain minorities when electoral imperatives so demand.[21] Too many compromises by Congress will provide the BJP with fresh ammunition for its charge that Congress and its allies "pamper" minorities, especially Muslims.

Given the country's multireligious currents, an Indian democracy gone adrift from its moorings in secular neutrality would soon come to grief on illiberalism's rocky shores.[22] It might maintain the trappings of procedural democracy, but would lose one of its cornerstones—namely, the protection of minority rights.

Portents of Hope?

Arenas such as the three problematic ones discussed above are far from the whole story. The essays that follow, taken together, offer important support for the proposition that in some ways the Indian experiment in democracy is faring very well indeed and shows signs of continuing vitality. These reservoirs of strength and life are connected to the political effects of a viable party system; a generally robust electoral process; an expanding electorate; a flexible federal structure; an independent higher judiciary; the growth of civic movements dedicated to uncovering and fighting corruption; the persistence of a free press; and the generally positive consequences of economic liberalization. Yet ethnic and religious violence continue to stalk the land, the institutions and mechanisms of law enforcement are often partisan and callous, and stark regional economic differences characterize the recent spurt in economic growth. It is impossible to gloss over these tangible shortcomings of India's otherwise impressive democratic record.

The present study of Indian democracy has four parts. The first deals with politics, the second with the state, the third with society, and the final section with the economy and its sociopolitical effects. The opening chapter, by E. Sridharan and M.V. Rajeev Gowda, traces the evolution of India's party system since independence and its impact on democracy. Sridharan and Gowda deftly explore and assess a number of competing (and complementary) explanations for the survival of India's democracy and then proceed to examine the trajectory of the once-dominant "catchall" Congress party. They then explain the reasons for its fragmentation and the concomitant rise of regional political parties. They conclude that the end of Congress's dominance and the fragmentation of the party system have stopped short of undermining the basic power-sharing characteristics of the system, and indeed have contributed to democratic consolidation.

Steven Wilkinson's chapter neatly segues into the question of India's electoral performance. His chapter is woven mostly around the complex reasons for the BJP coalition's unexpected defeat in the 2004 national elections. He debunks three popular explanations that highlighted the deleterious effect of economic reform on the poor, a backlash against the BJP's antisecular practices, and the growth of anti-incumbent sentiment. Instead, he opts for a tactical explanation and contends that the particular choice of electoral alliances largely explains the apparently anomalous electoral outcome. He then turns to a careful examination of the overall integrity of the electoral process and suggests that, on balance, it remains mostly free and fair. His summary judgment is that "India has a generally effective and impartial electoral system, especially so when we compare it to its neighbors, but also for that matter if we compare it to the politicization of boundary demarcation and the proliferation of different ballot and registration systems that have made recent elections in the United States controversial."

Obviously, as Wilkinson's chapter shows, India's leadership can take justifiable pride in having sustained a viable electoral democracy. The country's record in containing ethnic and religious violence, however, has been far from exemplary, as Rajat Ganguly argues in considerable detail. Interestingly enough, Ganguly shows that sharp departures from India's established constitutional and democratic procedures and norms constituted important catalysts for precipitating ethnic and religious conflicts. Ganguly correctly adduces the shortcomings of India's secular practices and their exploitation by the BJP (and its predecessors) to explain the origins and persistence of fratricidal Hindu-Muslim conflict. He also shows that periodic disregard for the norms of federalism and regional autonomy contributed to the rise of various secessionist movements from the states of the northeast, the Punjab, and Kashmir. Despite these very tangible failures, Ganguly holds that Indian democracy faces no imminent danger of collapse and that the recent strengthening of federalism and political participation enables them to shore up the democratic edifice in important ways.

Christophe Jaffrelot's thoughtful chapter on caste and politics concludes this section on politics. Jaffrelot shows that despite a formal constitutional ban on caste discrimination and the practice of untouchability, this primordial and atavistic institution continues to thrive. The persistence of caste and caste-based discrimination, he contends, had long undermined India's embrace of a formal democratic order. Fortunately, the steady political mobilization of lower castes over the last several decades is now changing the physiognomy of Indian politics; this is especially true in northern India, a region that for complex historical reasons was the final bastion of upper-caste privilege. Jaffrelot argues that a combination of affirmative-action programs and access to the ballot box have contributed to a virtual "silent revolution" in enfranchising the lower castes in India.

The book's second section begins with Subrata Mitra's important chapter on the structure and functions of Indian federalism. Mitra argues that India's federal system, despite myriad strains, not only has

managed to survive but has bolstered Indian democracy largely because of the perceived interest of the constituent units in staying within
a federation rather than attempting to survive on their own. Mitra cogently argues that the tenuous internal and external circumstances of
the state at the time of its emergence from the detritus of the British
colonial empire led its founders to constrain the scope of the federal
structure. Yet the democratic political process, also enshrined in the
constitution, has helped ensure that the federal structure accommodates
most demands for regional autonomy. Still, Mitra is hardly blind to the
important failures of Indian federalism, especially during much of Prime
Minister Indira Gandhi's tenure in office. Mitra concludes that India's
recent and fitful embrace of more market-oriented strategies of economic development is likely to strengthen federal arrangements as the
national government sheds a labyrinthine set of regulations.

Pratap Mehta finds a more mixed record of performance in his analysis of the Indian judiciary. His chapter focuses on the dramatic rise of
judicial activism and provides a more cautionary tale. Mehta is torn: He
sympathizes with many of the substantive results that activist judges
have produced, but cannot shake serious misgivings about the consequences that such judicial assertiveness must hold for the separation of
powers. He generally lauds the innovative process of public-interest
litigation, yet voices serious concerns about both the democratic legitimacy and the effectiveness of such expanding judicial reach. As he
correctly underscores, voters can throw out inept, corrupt, or otherwise
undesirable politicians, but judges are mostly shielded from such accountability. He concludes that judicial activism can be justified only
if it helps to create a political and constitutional culture that enshrines
certain fundamental values, which become legitimate constraints on
the behavior of governments and their citizens. Another way of putting
this might be to observe that democracy, in its full modern sense, means
liberal democracy (that is, a system of majority rule which nonetheless
scrupulously safeguards minority rights, including the rights of the individual). Courts, precisely because of their relative insulation from
majority sentiment, arguably bear a larger share of the immediate responsibility for preserving and defending the indispensable and
transmajoritarian liberal dimension of the democratic regime than do
the other branches of government. In this duty lies the best claim to
legitimacy that the courts can muster when they extend their writ in an
activist fashion.

Arvind Verma's chapter on the coercive apparatus of the Indian state
reminds us that not all institutions have fared as well as the edifices of
India's federalism and judicial system. Verma carefully documents that
much of colonialism's legal and repressive apparatus managed to survive, and indeed thrive, in the postindependence era. More disturbingly, he draws attention to the stunning and extraordinary array of

legislation that the postindependence state has passed with the ostensible purpose of maintaining law and order. A substantial portion of this legislation has placed important constraints on personal rights and civil liberties. Worse still, underpaid, overworked, corrupt, and callous police personnel frequently circumvent existing legal procedures in their attempts to curb criminal activity. The existence of an array of repressive laws dating from colonial times and after, plus the feckless behavior of those charged with guarding law and order, have corroded the quality of democracy. Accordingly, Verma argues that the government desperately needs to undertake a thorough review of these procedures and practices in order to restore the probity and efficacy of the coercive institutions that no state can do without and that a democratic state must watch with special care.

Civil Society and the Economy

The three previous chapters underscore the distinctly uneven performance of the key institutions of the Indian state. Fortunately, a robust civil society—which most theorists of democracy consider a vital component of the workings of a viable democracy—appears to be thriving in India. Niraja Jayal's contribution, the first chapter in the section on Indian society, underscores the vital contributions that civil society organizations have made to the functioning and well-being of India's democracy. Specifically, she identifies the important work of three distinct genres of civil society organizations: environmental movements; organizations focused on the rights of the dispossessed; and those seeking more responsive governance. She also draws attention to those groups that have sought to act as a counterweight to overweening state power. Finally, she discusses the growth of a plethora of nongovernmental organizations (NGOs) focused on promoting development.

Yet her assessment of the growth of civil society is far from uncritical. She correctly underscores that certain civil society organizations have distinctly "uncivil" features. Some of these organizations, affiliated with prominent political parties, possess illiberal characteristics and are hardly conducive to the growth of a pluralist democracy. Even those entities that are committed to the promotion of liberal-democratic values and practices suffer from serious limitations. She alerts us to the upper-class and urban bias of the leadership of many civil society organizations, their lack of support among the burgeoning middle classes, and the limited access of poor people to these organizations. But despite these important limitations, she argues that Indian democracy would be poorer in the absence of these entities. Warts and all, they have contributed to greater public accountability and responsiveness.

To a large degree, Rob Jenkins echoes Jayal's optimistic estimate of the prospects for India's democracy. His essay on today's burgeoning anticorruption movements argues that the proliferation of NGOs dedicated to exposing and battling corruption is the fruit of a yearning for deeper democracy on the part of an electorate that is growing more sophisticated with each passing year. The actions of the NGOs, along with the growing participation of hitherto quiescent groups, are gradually resulting in a political system that is more accountable to the citizenry. The growth of accountability is hardly linear or uniform but it is nevertheless underway. Although the anticorruption NGOs' record of success may be less than striking, they have nevertheless focused attention on myriad failures of governance and have sought their redress. In doing so, contends Jenkins, they have hit upon innovative methods to improve governmental accountability and state responsiveness to public needs.

Two such strategies are worthy of comment. The first is the creation of public forums in which official government records can be read aloud in the presence of local inhabitants with enough personal knowledge and experience to vet the records' veracity. Jenkins argues that this strategy, which has been adopted in many rural areas, performs the role of a useful "social-audit" mechanism. A second example of strategic innovation involves the decision by a middle-class group in New Delhi to expand its social base. Members of the group realized that this would boost their clout with officialdom dramatically. Thus, knowing how heavily the indigent must rely on the state for vital services, the middle-class activists reached out to slum-dwellers and formed an unlikely alliance that made local politicians more responsive to community needs.

No discussion of Indian democracy and society would be complete without some attention to the vital role of the free press. Praveen Swami's chapter carefully addresses this critical component of India's democracy. Swami provides a sweeping and succinct overview of the evolution of the Indian press and mass media from colonial times to the present day. He notes that during Indira Gandhi's brief flirtation with authoritarian rule, most of the press failed to maintain its independence, but argues that this subsequently contributed in an ironic fashion to a dramatic interest in and expansion of the mass media. He also emphasizes that journalists are now far more resistant to official sallies aimed at curbing their autonomy or encroaching on their privileges. These positive developments notwithstanding, Swami sounds the tocsin about the rise of the blatantly antisecular sentiments in certain segments of the press as well as its growing commercialization. These tendencies, if left unchecked, could prove deeply corrosive of democratic values and practices.

Two chapters on India's economic performance constitute the concluding section. Aseema Sinha's nuanced essay shows that India's fitful embrace of the market has had, on balance, positive consequences for the stability and perhaps also the quality of its democracy. To be sure, the rapid growth that the country has experienced since the onset of economic liberalization in the early 1990s has had mixed effects. The rising tide has not lifted every household, city, or state in India equally. Some have in fact suffered as old industries and patterns of livelihood have disappeared or drastically changed.

Yet while regional and socioeconomic disparities have increased and reform has created losers as well as winners, economic change has benefited democracy in important and unexpected ways. Sinha argues that those who have done well amid this new growth spurt have, thanks to their market-fueled prosperity, felt no need to seize or subvert state institutions to further their own parochial interests. Nor, for that matter, have the disadvantaged aimed their frustration at democratic institutions. On the contrary, they have directed their grievances into and not against peaceful party and electoral politics. Moreover, significant chunks of the emergent middle classes have been forging multiplying and ever more intense cultural, personal, and consumerist links with the West that make these Indians feel more committed than ever to democratic and liberal institutions. Finally, Sinha contends, national and regional governments are aware of the growing socioeconomic disparities that growth has fueled, and have already begun using public policy to address them.

The sadly uneven distribution of the fruits of India's recent economic success forms the topic of Sunila Kale's chapter. She addresses the issue of interstate and intrastate inequalities and their ramifications for Indian democracy. Her central focus is the role and significance of persistent spatial inequality. She cogently argues that such territorially defined inequality has generated demands which have covered the gamut from greater autonomy to outright secession. She examines these demands by looking at movements within two states with varying degrees of economic prosperity, Maharashtra and Andhra Pradesh. Both states have had to contend with the problem of persistent regional inequalities and have thereby faced important (and occasionally violent) movements for regional autonomy and even secession. Kale argues that the problem of gross economic inequalities within states could well worsen in an era of growing market-dominated economic-development strategies.

One way to deal with these inequalities would be to redraw the boundaries of some large and unwieldy states. In 1956, the government of India successfully redrew inherited internal colonial boundaries when confronted with demands for linguistically homogeneous states. The key question, in Kale's judgment, is whether or not India's federal structure will prove supple enough to accommodate a second set of demands for the reorganization of certain large states.

As India approaches its sixtieth year as an independent and democratic state, there is little question about the durability of its democratic institutions and practices. The relevant topics facing both scholars and activists touch instead on the quality of India's democracy. Will the country's leaders and citizens be able to improve the efficacy of key institutions, cope with the social challenges that rising inequality is generating, and sustain the secular ethos that undergirds the democratic order? Only the future can reveal the answers. Nevertheless, it is important to hazard a few responses, however tentative or incomplete.

Perhaps the most important single development has been the transformation of India's economy since policy makers fitfully steered away from statism and embraced the market in 1991. The flowering of a dynamic market-based economy holds considerable promise for the future of Indian democracy. At least four hopeful possibilities present themselves. First, the logic of economic liberalization is working in favor of a deeper and fuller federalism. As the enthusiasm for centralized economic interventionism continues to wane, the power of the national government in New Delhi shrinks and power over economic and fiscal policy shifts to the dozens of state capitals in a process that dovetails neatly with the regionalization of politics in the post-Congress era.

Second, sustained economic growth could open up new streams of public revenue that will allow national and state governments to ameliorate growing disparities by offering more and better schooling, helping to train people and placing them in true wealth-creating jobs, and underwriting programs meant to soften the market's harsher effects on job security and well-being. Such efforts could help to forestall the social unrest that widening gaps in wealth and income could otherwise generate.

Third, as growth and opportunities expand across India, civil society should benefit. Civil society actors are already pressing national and state governments to address public problems and grievances; an expanding economy should help them do even more to promote responsive and responsible governance.

Finally, sustained economic growth may be raising a grand support buttress for liberal democracy in the form of a new, more educated, and cosmopolitan middle class. Such a prospect is hardly chimerical. An expanding middle class is likely to be more secure, vocally self-confident, linked to a wider world of ideas, and concerned about India's honorable reputation as a free country well on its way toward becoming an open, plural, and tolerant society possessing considerable global influence directly connected to these traits as well as to its sheer size and wealth. Although such an outcome is hardly foreordained, it is at least one possible future for the world's largest democracy.

NOTES

The author would like to thank Jack Snyder for his comments on earlier drafts.

1. Seymour Martin Lipset, "Some Social and Economic Requisites for Democracy," *American Political Science Review* 53 (March 1959): 69–105.

2. Adam Przeworski and Fernando Limongi, "Modernization: Theories and Facts," *World Politics* 49 (January 1997): 155–83.

3. In nominal U.S. dollars, India's annual per-capita income was $720 in 2005. Yet in Purchasing Power Parity (PPP) dollars—a more realistic estimate of the real value of per-capita income in developing countries—India's estimated per-capita income was a much more impressive $3,700 in 2006, according to the *CIA World Factbook*. Adjusting for inflation, this puts India slightly above the threshold of the middle-income category (beginning at $2,000 in 1985 PPP dollars) that Adam Przeworski and his colleagues identified as having only a modest 3 percent chance of democratic breakdown in any given year. See Adam Przeworski et al., "What Makes Democracies Endure?" *Journal of Democracy* 7 (January 1996): 36–55.

4. For example, British colonial officials saw to it that much of the senior Congress party leadership spent the Second World War in detention even as the leaders of the Muslim League and the Indian Communist Party faced few restrictions. Neither of the latter two entities was known for internal democracy or commitment to liberal-democratic norms.

5. For an articulate exposition of this perspective see Rajeev Bhargava, "Democratic Vision of A New Republic," in Francine Frankel et al., eds., *Transforming India: Social and Political Dynamics of Democracy* (New Delhi: Oxford University Press, 2000).

6. Granville Austin, *The Indian Constitution: The Cornerstone of a Nation* (Oxford: Clarendon Press, 1966).

7. Consider, for example, the brilliant self-critique that Nehru penned as early as 1937 under a *nom de plume*. Chanakya [Jawaharlal Nehru], "The Rashtrapati," *Modern Review*, November 1937.

8. All children attending primary school in India are required to learn three languages: their mother tongue, Hindi (the dominant language of northern India), and English. See Jyotindra Das Gupta, "Language Policy and National Development in India," in Michael E. Brown and Sumit Ganguly, eds., *Fighting Words: Language Policies and Ethnic Relations in Asia* (Cambridge: MIT Press, 2003).

9. During the state of emergency declared by Indira Gandhi in 1975–77, there was widespread use of coercion to contain population growth. There is little question that the harshness of those policies contributed to her political ouster in the 1977 national elections. On the state of emergency, see Henry Hart, ed., *Indira Gandhi's India: A Political System Reappraised* (Boulder, Colo.: Westview, 1976).

10. For an ideologically charged and partisan critique, see Ayesha Jalal, *Democracy and Authoritarianism in South Asia: A Historical and Comparative Perspective* (Cambridge: Cambridge University Press, 1995).

11. Jyotindra Das Gupta, "A Season of Caesars: Emergency Regimes and Development Politics in Asia," *Asian Survey* 18 (April 1978): 315–49.

12. Sumit Ganguly, "The Crisis of Indian Secularism," *Journal of Democracy* 14 (October 2003): 11–25. See also Pratap Bhanu Mehta, "Hinduism and Self-Rule," *Journal of Democracy* 15 (July 2004): 108–21.

13. For a nuanced discussion of India's democratic political culture and its discontents, see Pratap Bhanu Mehta, *The Burden of Democracy* (New Delhi: Penguin, 2003).

14. Amelia Gentleman, "Killings in Delhi Slum Expose Unequal Justice for

India's Poor," *International Herald Tribune,* 6 January 2007.

15. On the question of deaths in police custody, see the National Human Rights Commission annual report for 2004–2005, available at *www.nhrc.nic.in.*

16. Devesh Kapur and Pratap Bhanu Mehta, *The Indian Parliament as an Institution of Accountability* (Geneva: UN Research Institute for Social Development, 2006).

17. Much of this section on secularism has been drawn from Sumit Ganguly, "South Asia Faces the Future: India's Multiple Revolutions," *Journal of Democracy* (January 2002): 38–51.

18. A formal commitment to secularism was added to the Indian Constitution of 1950 as late as the Forty-second Amendment, which dates from 1976.

19. The rise of the BJP is discussed at length in Christophe Jaffrelot, *The Hindu Nationalist Movement in India* (New York: Zed, 2002). For an astute analysis of the 2004 election results, see Steven Wilkinson, "Elections in India: Behind the Congress Comeback," *Journal of Democracy* 16 (January 2005): 153–67.

20. See Ganguly, "The Crisis of Indian Secularism."

21. Some of these concerns are dealt with in Jagdish Bhagwati, "Secularism in India: Why Is It Imperiled?" at *www.columbia.edu/jb38/Secularism%20in%20India. doc.*

22. On this point see the discussion in Fareed Zakaria, "The Rise of Illiberal Democracy," *Foreign Affairs* 76 (November–December 1997): 7.

I

Politics

1

PARTIES AND THE
PARTY SYSTEM, 1947–2006

M.V. Rajeev Gowda and E. Sridharan

M.V. Rajeev Gowda *is associate professor of economics and social sciences at the Indian Institute of Management, Bangalore. He is co-editor of* Judgments, Decisions, and Public Policy *(2002). He is also active in politics.* **E. Sridharan** *is academic director of the University of Pennsylvania Institute for the Advanced Study of India, based in New Delhi. He is coeditor of* India's Living Constitution *(2002, 2005) and* India's Political Parties *(2006).*

Since independence, India has enjoyed improbable democratic success. Lacking such democracy-enabling conditions as industrialization, urbanization, mass literacy, and a minimum standard of living, India has overcome such obstacles to democratization as religious, linguistic, and ethnic heterogeneity; inequality; and extreme poverty; and has developed into a vibrant democracy.

In this chapter, we explore the roles of political parties and the party system in deepening Indian democracy. We focus specifically on their role in the evolution of institutionalized mechanisms of power-sharing and the promotion of an inclusive and resilient state. Political power in India has shifted since 1996, as the grand encompassing parties which had once dominated have been replaced by diverse multiparty coalitions. Given this profound shift in the organization of political power, we conclude this chapter with an assessment of the quality of Indian democracy.

India adopted a detailed written constitution in 1950 after three years of debate in the Constituent Assembly, which at that time was dominated by veterans of the independence struggle. The constitution's key democratic features—fundamental rights and freedoms, and universal adult franchise—were postindependence introductions, and not colonial legacies. The constitution mandates a bicameral parliament in which the executive is responsible to a directly elected lower house known as the Lok Sabha (House of the People), an independent judiciary with the power of judicial review, and a federal system with legislative powers divided between the national and state legislatures.

India is currently organized into twenty-eight states and seven federally administered union territories. The states were reorganized on a linguistic basis after 1956 (except for Jammu and Kashmir, and the six northeastern rim states). The electoral system is a single-member district, simple-plurality system (a "first-past-the-post" system as in the United States). There have been fourteen national elections since 1952 (most recently in 2004) and at least one election has been held every five years at the state level.[1]

India's politicized social cleavages are those of religion, language, caste, tribe, rural versus urban residents, and class. Caste and class cleavages are related: The upper castes tend to constitute disproportionately the higher classes while the lower castes tend to constitute disproportionately the lowest classes.

Hindus, who are internally divided by language, caste, and sect, constitute about 80 percent of the population and are a majority in all states and union territories except Arunachal Pradesh, Jammu and Kashmir, Lakshadweep, Meghalaya, Mizoram, Nagaland, and Punjab. Within each state, the Hindu population is traditionally and unofficially layered into five overarching caste categories—the Brahmins (priests), Kshatriyas (warriors), Vaishyas (merchants), Shudras (farmers), and the Dalits (formerly the untouchables). Caste is not a racial division but an endogamous and therefore ethnic division based historically on the traditional division of labor.

The broad caste categories are subdivided into more than four thousand castes (jatis) but the number in each state is different. All states have broad caste clusters but not necessarily the same specific (endogamous) castes, making it difficult to mobilize castes politically across states. The broad caste clusters are the upper castes (the Brahmins, Kshatriyas, and Vaishyas), the intermediate castes (Shudras) and two constitutionally recognized groupings called Scheduled Castes (or ex-untouchables) and Scheduled Tribes (or aboriginal peoples). Since the Scheduled Castes and Scheduled Tribes have historically suffered discrimination, they are provided with quotas of 15 percent and 7.5 percent respectively in Parliament, as well as in college admissions and public-sector employment.

The numerically significant minority religious communities are Muslims (13.4 percent), Christians (2.3 percent), and Sikhs (1.9 percent). India also has small numbers of Buddhists (0.8 percent), Jains (0.4 percent), and Zoroastrians. Muslims are in a majority only in Jammu and Kashmir, as well as in three parliamentary constituencies in the states of Assam, Kerala, and West Bengal, and in one constituency in Lakshadweep. Only 10 percent of India's Muslims live in Muslim-majority areas.[2] Christians are in a majority only in Meghalaya, Mizoram, and

Nagaland, and live in significant numbers in a few constituencies in Kerala. The majority of the Christian population lives as a minority in other areas.

The Scheduled Castes (16.2 percent) are distributed as minorities throughout the country, including in constituencies reserved only for their candidates, making the non–Scheduled Caste vote decisive in such constituencies. The Scheduled Tribes (8.2 percent) are geographically much more concentrated, enjoying majorities or near-majorities in many of their reserved constituencies. They are not, however, the majority in any states except Arunachal Pradesh, Meghalaya, Mizoram, Nagaland, and the union territories of Lakshadweep, and Dadra and Nagar Haveli. The population in these states is less than 5 percent of the Scheduled Tribe population.[3]

There are twenty-two recognized languages in India. Hindi has the single largest share of speakers (40 percent of the population). It is the language of nine of the twenty-eight states, including the largest, Uttar Pradesh. Bengali is the language of two states. The other major languages are each the official language of one state. India is 28 percent urban and 72 percent rural, although the proportion of people primarily dependent on agriculture is about 57 percent. The proportion of the population below the official poverty line is currently 26 percent.

Theories of Party-System Evolution

Democracy's success depends on vibrant competition among political parties. Political parties evolve within party systems. There are, broadly speaking, two classes of explanations for how party systems evolve. The first—the social-cleavage theory—postulates that party systems are a reflection of the principal cleavages in a given society. For example, the cleavage between capital and labor in the more homogeneous industrialized societies causes the emergence of parties positioned on a left-right ideological spectrum.[4] In the Indian context, social-cleavage theory would predict that the numerous politically salient cleavages described earlier would manifest as political parties.

The second—the electoral-rules theory[5]—postulates that the rules of the political system, and in particular of the electoral system, create incentives for political forces to coalesce or to splinter. Such incentives affect the number, relative weight, and ideological position of political parties. The principal causal features are the size of electoral districts (number of representatives elected from each), the structure of the ballot (choosing a party list, an individual candidate, or a mix of the two), and the decision rule or electoral formula (proportional representation, first-past-the-post, or variants of each).

A leading electoral-rules theory, "Duverger's Law," might predict that India's single-member–district, first-past-the-post electoral system would generate a two-party system, at least at the constituency level. Maurice Duverger argues that a combination of "mechanical" (under-representation of parties below a certain varying threshold vote share) and "psychological" (voters gravitating to parties with a chance of winning so as not to "waste" their votes) effects tends to produce a two-party system.[6]

Pradeep Chhibber and Ken Kollman argue that the division of powers between levels of government—national, state or provincial, and local—affects the formation of parties at different levels.[7] All else being equal, the greater the political and economic powers of state governments in federal systems over decisions that most affect the lives of citizens, the greater a political prize the capture of power at the state level represents. Hence the greater incentive there is for political entrepreneurs to form state-level political parties and for voters to vote for them, producing a multiparty system. Conversely, the more centralized are powers over decisions that most affect citizens, the more incentive there is for political entrepreneurs to form nationwide political parties and for voters to vote for them at the expense of state-level parties. Such circumstances are more likely to produce a two-party system.

The Unlikely Survival of Indian Democracy

There are several theories about the success of India's democracy. Arend Lijphart credits the success to India's "consociational" political system that has institutionalized grand-coalition governments and has included all religious and linguistic groups; allowed cultural autonomy for these groups; provided proportionality in political representation; and granted a minority veto on issues vital to minority rights and autonomy.[8] He points to the "catchall" Indian National Congress which was internally a grand coalition; linguistic federalism; educational autonomy and separate personal laws for religious minorities; roughly proportional accommodation of linguistic and religious groups in cabinets; and reservations for Scheduled Castes and Scheduled Tribes. These features are all a legacy of the Congress, which carried forward its umbrella character that had developed during the freedom struggle. The Congress's electoral dominance ensured that politically salient cleavages did not translate into parties during the first two decades after independence. Atul Kohli supports Lijphart's power-sharing explanation for India's democratic success, stating that "moderate accommodation of group demands, especially demands based on ethnicity, and some decentralization of power strengthens a democracy."[9]

Two arguments that can be related to power-sharing, though they address other issues, are those of Lloyd and Susanne Rudolph; and Juan Linz, Alfred Stepan, and Yogendra Yadav. The Rudolphs argue that Indian politics is persistently centrist because of the marginality of class politics; the fragmentation of the confessional majority; cultural diversity and social pluralism; and the single-member plurality system; among other factors.[10] The Rudolphs' focus is on political economy, however, and not on democratic survival and consolidation, nor on the parties' role in these processes. Their argument nonetheless suggests that the political system's tendency to avoid political polarization—despite poverty and inequality—is conducive to democracy's survival.

Linz, Stepan, and Yadav conceive of India not as a nation-state or a multinational state but as a "state-nation"; in other words, a nation that is forged by state institutions and policies that respect and protect multiple and complementary identities, and that is not limited to ethnolinguistic federalism.[11] The argument, if applied to the question of India's democratic survival and consolidation, focuses on how such policies engender identification with the state by all groups in the nation. It is related to power-sharing in that it does not privilege any one identity. Linz, Stepan, and Yadav's focus, however, is not on parties and the party system.

Kanchan Chandra argues that the Indian political economy is conducive to the ethnification of parties, but that this enhances the stability of democracy. She argues that India is a patronage democracy, where most modern-sector jobs and services are in the public sector and public officials have discretion in the allocation of public jobs and services. "An ethnic party is likely to succeed in a patronage democracy when it provides elites from across the 'subdivisions' included in its target ethnic category or categories with greater opportunities for ascent within its party organization than the competition, and when voters from its target ethnic category or categories are numerous enough to take the party to a winning or influential position."[12] We can see that this incentivizes political mobilization, including party formation, on a caste basis for numerically large caste clusters at the state level or for regional-linguistic groups in India.

The political mobilization of intermediate castes and Scheduled Castes supports Chandra's argument. This caste mobilization first began under the leadership of Charan Singh in the 1970s, in the form of the umbrella Bharatiya Lok Dal (BLD) which spanned intermediate castes across different north Indian states. In the 1990s, similar parties arose at the state level, such as the Samajwadi Party (SP) in Uttar Pradesh and the Rashtriya Janata Dal in Bihar. The most salient caste-based party to emerge has been the Bahujan Samaj Party (BSP), which seeks a pan-Indian mobilization of Scheduled Castes. An example of the political mobilization of regional-linguistic groups would be the Federation for Progress of Dravidians (DMK) and its offshoots that have dominated Tamil Nadu since the 1960s.

Chandra argues, however, that if ethnic categories are "constructed" ones—as are India's Scheduled Castes, Scheduled Tribes, and the even more nebulous Other Backward Classes—the dangers of permanent majorities and minorities can be sidestepped, and the ethnification of parties can be redistributive and conducive to power-sharing in its operation without being exclusionary.[13] In India, even caste-based parties face the need to be accommodative of other communities, as no group constitutes a majority or significant plurality. Caste groupings tend to be circumscribed by language and region, and there is typically intra-group competition.

Even the poor have secured a stake in Indian democracy. As Ashutosh Varshney argues, pressure from below has ensured that parties promote interventions that mitigate poverty.[14] These policies tend to be politically rewarding but economically inefficient, as they are typically redistributive (through, for example, quotas and subsidies), rather than potentially more effective (market- and export-oriented structural reforms).

The Congress—especially under the leadership of Indira Gandhi with her populist "Garibi Hatao" (eliminate poverty) campaign in 1971—came to embody pro-poor policy and was perceived to be pitted against capitalist-landlord parties. Socialist, communist, and even regional parties were committed to poverty alleviation. Indeed, the Communist Party's stranglehold over West Bengal for the last three decades can be attributed to its ability to implement pro-poor policies and integrate the poor into the party apparatus.

Paul Brass critiques the consociational argument, asserting that "political accommodation in democratic societies is an art not a system . . . [and that] consociationalism is a device for freezing existing divisions and conflicts."[15] He emphasizes that "parties play independent roles in creating, shaping, and moderating ethnic group loyalties and antagonisms,"[16] thus hinting at the role of parties and implicitly the party system in structuring political competition. The eventual fragmentation of India's political system and the emergence of cleavage-based parties do point to the difficulty of practicing the art of political accommodation over time, especially on the part of the Congress party.

We focus on the role of political parties and the party system as power-sharing mechanisms in India's democracy. We begin by outlining the evolution of the party system from a one-party–dominant system to a highly fragmented one dominated by large, multiparty coalitions and minority governments, and provide competing explanations for these outcomes. Finally, we assess the impact of these changes on the quality of India's democracy.

Party-System Fragmentation

Indian National Congress hegemony, 1952–67. The first four Lok Sabha elections (1952, 1957, 1962, and 1967) coincided with elections to state assemblies.[17] In the first three, the Indian National Congress won more than two-thirds of the seats in the Lok Sabha on the basis of only a plurality of votes (45 percent in 1952, 48 percent in 1957, and 45 percent in 1962). Competing against fragmented oppositions which varied from state to state, it also won a majority of seats in the state assemblies on the basis of vote pluralities.

The multiple bipolarization of state party systems, 1967–89. The year 1967 marked the beginning of a decline in the Congress's strength at the national and state levels. In 1967, the Congress won only 283 seats with about 40 percent of the vote, and lost power in eight out of the then sixteen states. Politically mobilized cleavages emerged, including language-based parties such as the DMK in Tamil Nadu and intermediate caste-based parties in northern India. Intrastate alliances of non-Congress parties—the Samyukta Vidhayak Dals—emerged and pooled votes to oust the Congress. The lack of ideological coherence in these alliances, however, doomed them to instability and collapse.

In 1971, parliamentary and state-assembly elections were delinked. This coincided with the suspension of organizational elections within the Congress and the centralization of power at the top of the party apparatus. Riding Indira Gandhi's charisma and populist Garibi Hatao campaign in the 1971 election, the Congress won a two-thirds majority in the Lok Sabha with around 43 percent of votes, and swept the subsequent state elections in 1972. In response to Congress's dominance, anti-Congress alliances slowly emerged, representing a consolidation of the non-Congress space at the state level. The Index of Opposition Unity (IOU) rose in state after state from 1967 to 1989,[18] particularly if one considers opposition coalitions as a single party for the purposes of the IOU.

In the "exceptional" elections following the 1975–77 emergency (when Indira Gandhi suspended civil liberties and arrested opposition leaders), the Congress faced a temporarily united opposition in the form of the Janata Party. The Congress was trounced, plunging to its then-lowest vote and seat tally of around 34 percent and 154 seats. The Janata Party won a majority of seats on the basis of about 41 percent of the vote. Janata's victory in 1977 was similar to Congress victories in previous elections: A catchall party won a seat majority on the basis of a vote plurality. Janata did not, however, compete against a fragmented opposition. For the first time, it appeared as if Duverger's Law had held at the national level and India had arrived at a two-party democracy, without significant ideological differences between the two dominant parties.

In 1980, following the disintegration of the Janata Party, the Congress won a near two-thirds majority on the basis of a vote plurality of about 42 percent. In the 1984 elections, following the assassination of Indira Gandhi, the Congress won its highest-ever vote share (about 48 percent) and a three-fourths majority.

The 1989 elections marked another turning point. Competing against the National Front coalition, an opposition alliance supported by the

TABLE—PARTY SEAT AND VOTE SHARES, 1952–2004 (SEAT SHARE ON TOP, VOTE SHARE ON BOTTOM)

	1952	1957	1962	1967	1971	1977	1980	1984	1989	1991	1996	1998	1999	2004
Total Seats	489	494	494	520	518	542	529ᵃ	542	529ᵇ	521ᶜ	543	543	543	543
Indian National Congress	74.4% / 45.0%	75.0% / 47.8%	73.0% / 44.7%	54.4% / 40.8%	68.0% / 43.7%	28.4% / 34.5%	66.7% / 42.7%	76.6% / 48.1%	37.2% / 39.5%	45.0% / 36.5%	25.8% / 28.8%	26.0% / 25.9%	21.0% / 28.3%	26.7% / 26.4%
Bharatiya Janata Party, BJS until 1971	0.6% / 3.1%	0.8% / 5.9%	2.8% / 6.4%	6.7% / 9.4%	4.2% / 7.4%	— / —	— / —	4.0% / 7.4%	16.5% / 11.5%	23.0% / 20.1%	29.6% / 20.3%	33.0% / 25.5%	34.0% / 23.8%	25.4% / 22.2%
JP 1977–84, JD 1989–98, JDU from 1999	— / —	— / —	— / —	— / —	— / —	54.4% / 41.3%	5.9% / 19.0%	1.8% / 6.7%	27.0% / 17.7%	11.3% / 11.8%	8.5% / 8.1%	1.1% / 3.2%	3.8% / 3.1%	1.5% / 1.9%
Praja Socialist Party, KMPP in 1952	1.8% / 5.8%	3.8% / 10.4%	2.4% / 6.8%	2.5% / 3.1%	0.4% / 1.0%	— / —	— / —	— / —	— / —	— / —	— / —	— / —	— / —	— / —
Samyukta Socialist Party, SOC until 1962	2.5% / 10.6%	— / —	1.2% / 2.7%	4.4% / 4.9%	0.6% / 2.4%	— / —	— / —	— / —	— / —	— / —	— / —	— / —	— / —	— / —
Swatantra Party	— / —	— / —	3.6% / 7.9%	8.5% / 8.7%	1.5% / 3.1%	— / —	— / —	— / —	— / —	— / —	— / —	— / —	— / —	— / —
INCO	— / —	— / —	— / —	— / —	3.1% / 10.4%	— / —	— / —	— / —	— / —	— / —	— / —	— / —	— / —	— / —

TABLE—PARTY SEAT AND VOTE SHARES, 1952–2004 (SEAT SHARE ON TOP, VOTE SHARE ON BOTTOM) (CONT'D)

	1952	1957	1962	1967	1971	1977	1980	1984	1989	1991	1996	1998	1999	2004
JPS in 1980, Lok Dal in 1984, Samajwadi Party from 1991	—	—	—	—	—	—	7.7% 9.4%	0.6% 5.6%	—	1.0% 3.4%	3.1% 3.3%	3.7% 5.0%	4.8% 3.8%	6.6% 4.3%
Bahujan Samaj Party	—	—	—	—	—	—			—	—	2.0% 3.6%	0.9% 4.7%	2.6% 4.2%	3.5% 5.3%
Communist Party of India	3.3% 3.3%	5.5% 8.9%	5.9% 9.9%	4.4% 5.0%	4.4% 4.7%	1.3% 2.8%	1.8% 2.6%	1.1% 2.7%	2.3% 2.6%	2.7% 2.5%	2.2% 2.0%	1.6% 1.8%	0.7% 1.5%	1.6% 1.3%
Communist Party of India–Marxist		—	—	3.7% 4.4%	4.8% 5.1%	4.1% 4.3%	7.0% 6.1%	4.1% 5.7%	6.2% 6.5%	6.7% 6.2%	6.0% 6.1%	5.9% 5.2%	6.1% 5.4%	7.9% 5.7%
Others	9.6% 16.5%	6.3% 7.6%	6.9% 10.5%	8.6% 10.0%	10.2% 13.8%	10.2% 11.6%	9.1% 8.5%	14.6% 10.0%	8.9% 13.4%	11.0% 12.2%	21.2% 21.5%	26.0% 26.3%	26.3% 27.1%	25.8% 28.6%
Independents	7.6% 15.9%	8.5% 19.4%	4.0% 11.1%	6.7% 13.7%	2.7% 8.4%	1.7% 5.5%	1.7% 6.4%	0.9% 8.1%	2.3% 5.2%	0.2% 3.9%	1.7% 6.3%	1.1% 2.4%	1.1% 2.8%	0.9% 4.3%

[a] Elections were not held in 13 constituencies: 12 in Assam and 1 in Meghalaya.
[b] Elections were not held in Assam (14 seats).
[c] Elections were not held in Jammu and Kashmir (6 seats) and Punjab (13 seats); 3 countermanded seats results excluded.
BJS–Bharatiya Jan Sangh; JDU–Janata Dal (United); JPS–Janata Party Secular; INCO–Indian National Congress (Organization); JP–Janata Party; KMPP–Kisan Mazdoor Praja Party; SOC–Socialist Party.
Sources: Election Commission of India, Statistical Report on General Elections, vol. 1; National and State Abstracts for 1996, 1999, and 2004, and www.eci.gov.in.

Bharatiya Janata Party (BJP) and other left-wing parties, and composed of the Janata Dal and regional and minor parties, the Congress's share of the vote crashed to about 39 percent and their seat total dropped to 197 seats.

The National Front coalition of 1989–90 was novel in three senses. First, learning from the Janata Party experience, it did not try to unify disparate parties but instead built a coalition of distinct parties based on a common manifesto. Second, it brought in explicitly regional parties like the DMK, Telugu Desam, and Assam Gana Parishad, as well as the parties of the left. Third, the coalition was the first spatially compatible interstate alliance of parties (where parties do not compete on each other's turf). The spatially compatible loose alliance put together by the National Front–BJP–Left in 1989 and 1990, however, foundered on the rocks of ideological incompatibility. This indicated once again the unsustainability of a broad anti-Congress coalition which had not moderated or set aside ideological extremes.

National party-system fragmentation and the emergence of coalition and minority governments, 1989–2006. The 1989 election results signified a seismic shift in India's party system (rooted in shifts in party organizational strength and support bases at the state level), in India's political economy, and in patterns of social mobilization. They heralded the relative decline of the Congress and the rise of the BJP and regional parties.[19] While the Congress retained a vote plurality in all six elections from 1989 to 2004, it failed to gain a seat majority, winning fewer seats than the BJP in 1996, 1998, and 1999 (See Table on pp. 10–11).

Prior to 1989, the BJP and its predecessor the Bharatiya Jana Sangh (BJS)—the political arm of the Hindu-nationalist organization Rashtriya Swayamsevak Sangh (RSS)—had never exceeded 10 percent of the vote or 35 seats nationally (except in 1977 when as a member of the Janata Party coalition it won 99 of 295 seats won by the alliance). Since then it has experienced a steady rise in proportion of the vote and seat shares. It experienced a meteoric rise in seats from two in 1984 (despite about 7 percent of votes) to 86 (out of 226 contested, mostly in de facto alliance with the Janata Dal) in 1989 due to the combination of three effects: seat adjustments with the Janata Dal which resulted in one-on-one contests against the Congress in most of the seats that the BJP contested in northern and western India; a sizeable swing in its favor; and the regional concentration of this increase in votes. In 1990, the BJP formed state governments on its own for the first time.

In 1991, the BJP contested alone with a religiously polarizing platform. In the midst of upper-caste backlash against the reservation of government jobs for Other Backward Classes based on the Mandal Commission Report and the interreligious tension and violence that followed BJP leader L.K. Advani's pilgrimage to "liberate" the supposed birthplace of the Hindu god Rama from inside the Babri Mosque, the

BJP's vote share grew to around 20 percent, earning the party 120 seats and making it the second largest in the country.

In 1991, the Congress managed to form a minority government, attaining a majority by adding defectors halfway through its term. In 1996, its vote share declined to a then-historic low of about 29 percent. For the first time, the Congress was overtaken by the BJP as the largest party, winning only 141 seats compared to the BJP's 161. The Congress did, however, remain the largest party by vote share with about 29 percent compared to the BJP's 20 percent.

While the BJP rose to new strength thanks to its more regionally concentrated vote in 1996, it ran into the limits of contesting alone with a religiously polarizing agenda. As the largest party in the Lok Sabha it was able to form a government for only thirteen days. But it failed to win enough parliamentary support from other parties to form a minority or coalition government. This rejection of the BJP represented a significant ideological statement on the part of a range of secular parties.

The 1996 results can be seen as a delayed reflection of the realignment of political forces that occurred during elections to fifteen state assemblies between November 1993 and March 1995. These represented major gains for the BJP and several regional parties. The Congress was only able to retain power in a few strongholds.[20]

A United Front (UF) government was formed in June 1996. It was a thirteen-party coalition, with nine parties participating in the government, supported externally by the Congress. This was another clear case of a spatial alliance as well as a postelection coalition; however, it had a certain secular ideological mooring, ranged as it was against a hardline, perceivedly "antisystem" BJP. The Congress withdrew support from Prime Minister Deve Gowda in April 1997, but continued to support the UF government under his successor I.K. Gujral until November, leading to fresh elections in February 1998.

The BJP learned one basic lesson from the elections in 1996: In order to have a legitimate chance to take power, it had to expand both its appeal to nontraditional states (through alliances or otherwise) and its social base in its strongholds. It therefore changed strategy in the 1998, 1999, and 2004 elections. In particular, the BJP sought a wide range of alliances in its nonstronghold states and shelved the religiously divisive points on its agenda.[21]

From the 1998 elections on, the BJP set aside its Hindu-nationalist agenda, which helped it to strike explicit or tacit alliances with a range of state-based parties, many of which had earlier been part of the UF. After its victory, the BJP continued with this strategy, which was bolstered by two factors: the Congress's success at toppling the UF government, and the Congress's position as the UF's principal opponent in several major states in the east and south. This allowed the BJP to contest the 1998 elections with thirteen preelection allies, and with seat-sharing arrangements spread over nine states. The BJP won about 25 percent of votes and its allies won around 11 percent, giving the alliance about 37 percent and 258 seats in the Lok Sabha (182 seats for the BJP including 3 seats won in later-held elections and 76 for its allies). The BJP was thus catapulted to power as the largest party in the Lok Sabha (the Congress got only 141 seats) and the leader of largest preelection alliance. With the help of 24 postelection allies—including 22 defectors from seven pre- and postelection supporting parties, as well as two nominated members—the BJP-led alliance reached a total of 282 seats.[22]

In 1999, the same 24-party, BJP-led preelection coalition opposed the Congress-led coalition (though the latter was a loose coalition held together by state-by-state agreements, not a common national platform). The BJP-led coalition won a decisive victory, winning 299 of the 537 contested seats (6 seats were deferred). The BJP, as in 1998, won 182 seats. Counting postelection adherents, the alliance's seat total rose to 305. The Congress earned a lowest-ever 114 seats and its alliance won only 134 all told.

The two BJP-led coalitions which ruled from 1998 to 1999 and 1999 to 2004 were based on both spatial compatibility (between the BJP and regional parties in the south and east) and ideological compromises (the BJP set aside its Hindu-nationalist agenda and the other parties ignored its communal character).

In 2004, a newly formed Congress-led coalition defeated the incumbent BJP-led National Democratic Alliance (NDA). Unlike in 1998 and 1999, the Congress party made the conscious decision to adopt a coalition strategy.[23] The Congress-led coalition—named the United Progressive Alliance (UPA) after the election—consisted of nineteen parties and won 222 seats based on around 36 percent of votes (only slightly more votes than the NDA but 33 more seats). With the external support of the leftist parties (61 seats) it gained a majority in the Lok Sabha and formed a government. The UPA coalition was based on a variety of intrastate spatial alliances as well as ideological commonalities (anti-BJP) and ideological compromises (on economic policy between the Congress and the left).

Since the 1990s, alliances have been based overwhelmingly on spatial compatibility, at the expense of ideological compatibility. This was the case with the BJP's alliances of 1998, 1999, and 2004, as well as the Congress-led UPA of 2004, and even the United Front coalition of 1996. Such coalitions improved upon the Samyukta Vidhayak Dal and the Janata Party alliances which were neither programmatically nor spatially compatible. Since the 1960s, however, alliances have been driven by the desire to aggregate votes and not by ideology, program, or social cleavages (except for the differences between the Congress and the BJP on secularism).[24]

A process of bipolar consolidation at the state level was the key feature of and driving force behind the fragmentation of the national party system: *Multiple bipolarities* (for example, Congress-BJP, Congress-left, Congress–regional party) in state party systems empowered a large number of state parties at the national level, where they wielded significant power as partners in coalition governments. This indirectly contributed to the bipolar consolidation of Congress-led and BJP-led alliances at the national level that we are currently witnessing.

How can we explain the fragmentation and reconsolidation of the party system into these two broad alliances? Social-cleavage theory explains the formation of regional autonomist, caste- and religion-based parties. As the Congress centralized, many marginalized leaders and groups who had felt underrepresented in the Congress left to form rival parties. Thus, strong regional parties emerged in Andhra Pradesh, Assam, and Tamil Nadu; intermediate-caste parties were formed in north India; and a party deriving support from Sikh religionists emerged in Punjab. In the 1990s, Muslims in north India shifted support from the Congress to local parties perceived to be friendlier to their security and interests; the Scheduled Castes embraced the BSP; and the upper castes, in a backlash against lower-caste assertiveness, consolidated behind the BJP.

The Duvergerian multiple-bipolarization explanation along with the Chhibber-Kollman explanation based on state powers in a federal system explains the incentives for single-state–based party formation, leading to the multiple-bipolarization of state party systems and thus a highly fragmented national party system with very large and ideologically disparate coalitions.

It is too early to say whether the inexorable imperative to aggregate votes regardless of ideology will push the national party system to evolve toward a sustained loose bipolarity at the national level between two broad spatial alliances—one broadly left of center and the other broadly right of center.[25] What we would like to emphasize here is that the two alliances and their predominantly narrowly based parties represent the *full* range of politically mobilized groups *across* states, indicating power-sharing among groups through their participation in diverse coalitions rather than in an umbrella party.

The Decline of Ideology

India has a long history of political parties forming alliances without regard to ideological differences. In the 1960s, the socialist ideologue Ram Manohar Lohia promoted broad alliances, arguing that an anti-Congress stance was ideologically sufficient. Lohia's strategy was successful in 1967, when the Congress received a bare majority in Parliament and lost power in eight major states. In most of these states, anti-Congress coalitions called Samyukta Vidhayak Dals formed governments for at least some of the period between 1967 and 1974. Since no ideological, policy, or social glue held these alliances together, they were unstable and did not survive for very long.

In the 1970s, parties adhering to diverse ideologies came together to participate in the veteran socialist Jayaprakash Narayan's protest movement against the Congress government. After the 1975–77 emergency, these diverse parties ranging from the socialists to the Hindu-nationalist BJS merged to form the Janata Party. Janata split after three years partly on ideological grounds. Former socialists in Janata led a campaign against the former Jana Sanghis on the issue of their dual membership—in the Janata as well as in the RSS, their parent "cultural organization"—which, the ex-socialists argued, clashed with the Janata Party's secular agenda. When asked to forgo membership in the RSS, the erstwhile Jana Sanghis left Janata to form the BJP.

Initially, the BJP was politically untouchable because of its perceived Hindu-nationalist agenda. But this was conveniently ignored when non-Congress parties needed to forge an anti-Congress front. For example, the National Front led by the breakaway Congress leader Vishwanath Pratap Singh was supported from outside by the BJP, which withdrew support in the aftermath of the Mandal Commission and Babri Mosque crises of the early 1990s. In its wake, three broad ideological alliances emerged: the Congress-led alliance; the alliance led by secular parties and the left; and the right-wing BJP-led alliance.

Despite the willingness of many secular parties to ally with the BJP since 1998, secularism has remained an important ideological divide in Indian politics. In 1998 and 1999, for example, the BJP-led coalition governments adopted platforms in which the BJP's Hindutva ("Hinduness") agenda items were dropped. Thus the BJP had to pay the price of at least tactical and temporary moderation in order to sustain its governing alliance.

The other major ideological issue in the Indian polity—liberalization of the economy—has ceased to divide parties. This is exemplified by the current Congress-led United Progressive Alliance that relies on key support from left-wing parties. The processes of liberalization, privatization, and globalization initiated by the Congress in 1991 have acquired the status of a de facto consensus, with the reform agenda proceeding, albeit sometimes haltingly, through United Front and BJP-led governments. The former BJP minister for disinvestment (privatization), Arun Shourie, argues that reforms generate a process of self-propulsion: "One reform creates pressure that other reforms be put through."[26] This momentum enabled the BJP leadership to overcome strong internal opposition to economic reforms.[27] The left too has at least partially supported economic reforms. Communist chief minister Buddhadev Bhattacharjee of West Bengal, for instance, has embraced foreign investment. Thus, aside from some reservations on the left, economic-reform issues have ceased to be a major ideological issue dividing parties.

Finally, at the level of individual candidates, ideological labels have gradually lost their significance. Politicians change parties without concern for the ideological baggage that comes with their new associations. The only exceptions seem to be the minority of hard-core cadres who grew up politically within the left-wing parties or the BJP and RSS. Overall, this development may merely reflect an ideological consensus: the acceptance of liberal economic reforms "with a human face," and a somewhat diluted secularism.

The Rise of Dynastic Politics

Dynastic politics is now pervasive across parties. While it appears that the Nehru-Gandhi dynasty has dominated the Congress for generations, dynastic politics are actually a post-1970s phenomenon. The success of the Nehrus—Motilal and Jawaharlal—resulted from their own political contributions within the Congress, a party with substantial internal democratic practice. Jawaharlal Nehru became prime minister partly because he was seen as Mahatma Gandhi's chosen heir, and had on occasion taken over the party presidency. He contributed substantially, however, to the establishment of democratic norms in the party and the polity, ensuring healthy policy debates and widespread sharing of power in the party (leading also to the emergence of strong regional leaders who came to be known as the "Syndicate").[28] Nehru did not promote his daughter, Indira Gandhi, as a prime ministerial successor but only encouraged her ascendancy to the party presidency. She earned that position and her subsequent membership in the Shastri cabinet partly through her heritage and proximity to the country's leadership, but also as a representative of the younger generation of freedom fighters.

The personalization of political parties can be traced to Indira Gandhi's fight to establish authority as prime minister in the face of efforts by the Syndicate to constrain her freedom to act independently. In 1969, when she split the Congress and launched a separate Indian National Congress (the "New Congress"), the levers of the organization, including party funds, were in the hands of the Syndicate. Using her parliamentary majority, she abolished political contributions from industry.[29] This froze the flow of funds to other parties, including the "Old Congress" which was composed of the party leadership who had opposed her. The "New Congress" was able to channel resources (now typically unaccountable "black" money) garnered from industrialists favored under the so-called License Raj toward building the party politically.[30] Over time, as the Congress became more centralized, influential state leaders began to leave the party, choosing instead to create alternatives at the state level. Indira Gandhi was able to centralize control without opposition within the party because her charismatic leadership led to victory in the 1971 Lok Sabha elections and the subsequent 1972 state polls. Centralized control led to the institutionalization of top-down rule in the Congress, the decline of internal democracy, and the emergence of an inner circle of advisors who mediated information flows and managed political conflicts by encouraging multiple factions in state units, thus controlling the party through a "divide-and-rule" strategy.

Dynasticism in the Congress took root thereafter in the mid-1970s, when Indira Gandhi's younger son Sanjay showed an interest in politics. She encouraged him to lead the Youth Congress and to bring a new set of followers into the party. His untimely death led to his elder brother Rajiv's induction into the party leadership. Indira Gandhi's assassination and Rajiv's subsequent ascension to prime minister (there were no natural successors in the party) concretized dynastic succession. It was Rajiv Gandhi's success in leading the Congress to resounding victory in the 1984 polls and in rising to the challenges of the office, however, that lent legitimacy to dynastic succession. After Rajiv Gandhi's 1991 assassination, the Congress managed with leaders from outside the dynasty. But faced with a dramatic decline in its fortunes after 1996, it eventually turned to Rajiv Gandhi's Italian-born widow, Sonia, to lead the party. This move solved the leadership problem that plagues most political parties, and brought to center stage the dynasty's "brand appeal" as torchbearers of poverty alleviation and inheritors of the freedom movement's legacy. After a hesitant start, Sonia Gandhi has demonstrated significant political acumen, led the party back to power, and has become a towering Indian political leader. Her son Rahul has also entered politics and is now a member of parliament.

Taking a cue from the Congress, charismatic leaders of smaller regional parties, leaders who left the Congress like Sharad Pawar, and even leaders of caste-based parties such as BSP's Mayawati have chosen to run highly personalized parties. K.C. Suri explains the logic behind dynastic politics: Across parties, charismatic leaders maintain weak party organizations to prevent challengers from emerging.[31] These leaders, as viable contenders for power, attract political funding. When they look for trusted individuals to manage the unaccounted funds that are central to running political parties and campaigns, they inevitably turn toward family members, who are unlikely to oust them (Chandrababu Naidu is an exception; he ousted his father-in-law, N.T. Rama Rao, in Andhra Pradesh). When succession issues arise in the absence of significant political movements, the "brand appeal" of a well-known political family can lead to electoral rewards for dynastic successors: They inherit a network of political connections and do not have to go through the Herculean efforts required to construct a political base.

Given the extraordinary challenges involved in becoming a charismatic leader with mass appeal and the limitations inherent in being a leader of an identity-based or regional party, however, it is sometimes difficult for dynastic successors to emerge as leaders with broad appeal.[32] Further, successors may not be able to retain control over the parties that they inherit. Charan Singh's son Ajit Singh is an example: His intermediate-caste coalition broke down as various leaders in his party found it more profitable to establish their own regional parties.

Because dynastic politics stifles the emergence of grassroots leadership, some scholars are critical, and also blame it for the fragmentation of parties, the decline in democratic deliberation, and the decline of parties as mediating institutions. To counter these trends, they advocate a return to intraparty democracy, and transparent and open funding of political parties.[33]

A larger consequence of the decline of ideology and the rise of dynastic politics—characterized by parties controlled by families and dependent on unaccounted funds—is the reduction of party organizations to mere election-winning machines. Even the formidable BJP organization has not been able to penetrate very far beyond its RSS roots in urban centers.[34] This is partly because organization building and electoral opportunities have been delinked, as the BJP famously demonstrated in 2004, when it went overboard in nominating neophyte film stars or celebrities as candidates. This has its consequences for the quality of democracy even though it is a manifestation of the dispersal of political power to a wide range of regional political entrepreneurs and social groups.

The Impact on the Quality of Democracy

The fragmentation of the party system, the nature of coalition politics, and the internally top-down character of political parties have had mixed effects on the quality of India's democracy. In assessing quality, we follow Larry Diamond and Leonardo Morlino's eight dimensions of democratic quality.[35] Our broad conclusion is that on at least four criteria—freedom, participation, competition, and horizontal accountability—there have been positive effects, while on the criteria of rule of law, equality, vertical accountability and responsiveness, there have been mixed, sometimes polarized effects. On balance, the quality of democracy has improved, though there are state-specific variations because of the nature of parties and the type of party systems that prevail within them.

The decline of one-party dominance and the emergence of a large number of smaller or regional parties which ensure that state-level elections are vigorously contested have had positive effects on *competition*. We agree with Yogendra Yadav that these developments represent political empowerment of historically marginalized groups and reflect favorably on the vibrancy of political entrepreneurship.[36] This fragmentation has not led to significant instability because of the political system's ability to include these smaller parties in power-sharing arrangements.

The post-1990 period has also seen an increase in *participation* (as measured by voter turnout), especially by the lower castes and classes, as well as women and rural voters. Constitutionally mandated (since 1993) local-government institutions *(panchayati raj)* have increased participation by allowing people to run their own lives from top to bottom. These institutions also have a significant number of seats and elected positions reserved for historically marginalized groups, thereby ensuring access to power across the board. Elections to these local bodies have also given political parties an opportunity to develop a support base at the village level, even though some of these elections are ostensibly nonpartisan affairs.

The emergence of national multiparty coalitions has weakened the influence of the executive branch and hence the governing parties' ability to dominate other organs of *horizontal accountability* such as the Election Commission, the courts, and the legislative opposition. All these institutions of horizontal accountability have become notably more independent. The shift away from government ownership and monopoly on television has ensured that India now has diverse, competitive, and penetrative television media in addition to its vigorous print media. These developments have bolstered democratic *freedoms*.

On *equality,* the influence of the poor and rural; Scheduled Castes and Scheduled Tribes; and minorities and women has increased due to greater opportunities for electoral participation and these groups' greater importance to smaller parties. The rise of an explicitly anti-Muslim party like the BJP and of upper-caste backlash to the assertiveness of lower castes, on the other hand, has threatened not only the equality formally enjoyed by minorities, Scheduled Castes, and Scheduled Tribes, but often even the rule of law in states where such parties or movements are dominant. An example is the state of Gujarat, where perpetrators of large-scale violence against Muslims in 2002 have gone unpunished. Thus the rule of law has been both strengthened by greater party competition, voter participation, and the strengthening of some institutions, as well as weakened where forces opposed to minorities and lower castes are dominant. The rule of law has also been weakened by attempts of new lower-caste parties to use state power to further their social bases' interests in a manner that damages norms and institutions (such as in Bihar and Uttar Pradesh).

Another serious impact on the *rule of law* is the trend of parties across the political spectrum to appoint corrupt and criminal candidates because they have enough local clout to win their seats. The increasing criminalization of politics has led to a backlash from civil society. In response to public-interest litigation filed by the Association for Democratic Reforms, the Supreme Court in 2002 ruled in favor of citizens' right to know about candidates' credentials.[37] Parliament ultimately passed legislation mandating that candidates file affidavits along with their nomination papers containing information on their education, financial position (assets and liabilities), and criminal record, if any. This indicates that despite corruption and criminalization, there are systemic self-correction mechanisms at work.[38]

On *vertical accountability* and *responsiveness,* our verdict is again mixed. On the one hand, the high turnover of incumbent parties in office at both the central and state levels is an indicator of high vertical accountability. This turnover, however, is also the result of low responsiveness to voter demands in between elections or selective responsiveness to only some voters, which results in part from the top-down character and ethnification of parties. Corrupt fundraising has paved the way for the decay of democratic institutions, ensnared even the common citizen in the web of corruption, and resulted in a decline in the overall quality of governance. Anti-incumbent sentiment at election time is the inevitable result. Campaign-funding reforms may hold the key to turning around this disturbing trend.

The Consolidation of Democracy

While we do not go as far as Lijphart in characterizing India's political system as consociational, we do agree with Lijphart and Kohli that the system has been a power-sharing one, and that it has been situated within a constitutional framework and a conception of the nation that is civic, territorial, and inclusive, rather than ethnic, religious, or linguistic. Further, democracy and the constitution are not seen as imports or impositions but as indigenous products. And, importantly, the system's centrist tendencies and generation of pressures toward poverty-alleviation policies, as illustrated by the Rudolphs and Varshney, have limited class polarization and contributed to stability.

The evolution of the party system can be explained both by the first-past-the-post system's Duvergerian bipolarization dynamic as well as by the politicization of social cleavages along party lines. Taken together with the personalization and dynasticization of parties, this contributes to a very fragmented multiparty system at the center and hence, large, multiparty coalitions in which regional and religious or caste-identity–based parties are key players.

This fragmentation of the party system from Congress dominance to multiparty coalition governments in India's regionalized and "ethnicized" party system has not undermined the basic power-sharing character of the system, and has thus helped to consolidate democracy. Whereas in the pre-1967 heyday of Congress dominance, power-sharing took place within an internally democratic and federal Congress party, it now takes place through the politics of group presence in large multiparty coalitions in which regional and religious or caste-group–based parties share power. Paul Brass's "art" of political accommodation has now to be applied to coalitions as well as to intraparty politics. Additionally, the rise of personalized parties controlled by powerful mass leaders with a state base allows disaffected leaders and factions a share of power. The decline of ideology and the general acceptance of the economic-reform program across the spectrum in varying degrees are also conducive to the functioning of multiparty coalitions.

While the institutional mechanism through which power-sharing occurs has changed from a grand-coalitional party to diverse, multiparty coalitions, power-sharing in India's diverse polity continues, as does an inclusive conception of the state. Accommodative politics thus remains the norm. The Indian political system has been able to absorb the pressures for increased political participation that have grown since the 1990s.[39]

NOTES

1. Jammu and Kashmir is only required to hold state-assembly elections every six years.

2. See Lloyd Rudolph and Susanne Rudolph, *In Pursuit of Lakshmi: The Political Economy of the Indian State* (Chicago: University of Chicago Press, 1987), 196, Table 16, for constituency estimates.

3. See Ashish Bose, *India's Basic Demographic Statistics* (New Delhi: BR Publishing Corporation, 1996) for the state (not electoral district) percentages of Muslims, Christians, and Scheduled Tribes.

4. See Seymour Martin Lipset and Stein Rokkan, *Party Systems and Voter Alignments* (New York: Free Press, 1967) for the classic statement of social-cleavage theory of party systems, and Stefano Bartolini and Peter Mair, *Identity, Competition and Electoral Availability: The Stabilisation of European Electorates, 1885–1985* (Cambridge: Cambridge University Press, 1990) for a modified version which argues that social cleavages do not translate automatically into party systems but offer easy mobilization opportunities. Much the same is argued by Rajni Kothari in his "Caste and Modern Politics" in Sudipta Kaviraj, ed., *Politics in India* (Delhi: Oxford University Press, 1997), 58, when he says: "Those who complain of 'casteism in politics' are really looking for a sort of politics which has no basis in society. . . . Politics is a competitive enterprise . . . and its process is one of identifying and manipulating existing and emerging allegiances in order to mobilise and consolidate positions."

5. For recent works within the electoral-rules theory of party systems, see Arend Lijphart, *Electoral Systems and Party Systems* (New York: Oxford University Press, 1994); Rein Taagepera and Matthew Soberg Shugart, *Seats and Votes* (New Haven: Yale University Press, 1989); Bernard Grofman and Arend Lijphart, *Electoral Laws and Their Political Consequences* (New York: Agathon Press, 1986); and older classics, Maurice Duverger, *Political Parties: Their Organization and Activity in the Modern State* (New York: Wiley, 1963); and Douglas Rae, *The Political Consequences of Electoral Laws* (New Haven: Yale University Press, 1967).

6. See Riker's discussion of Duverger's Law in William Riker, "The Two-Party System and Duverger's Law," *American Political Science Review* 76 (December 1982): 753–66. Duverger's result holds well at the constituency level; see Pradeep K. Chhibber and Ken Kollman, *The Formation of National Party Systems: Federalism and Party Competition in Canada, Great Britain, India, and the United States* (Princeton: Princeton University Press, 2004), 40–43.

7. Pradeep K. Chhibber and Ken Kollman, "Party Aggregation and the Number of Parties in India and the United States," *American Political Science Review* 92 (June 1998): 329–42, and Chhibber and Kollman, *The Formation of National Party Systems.*

8. Arend Lijphart, "The Puzzle of Indian Democracy," *American Political Science Review* 90 (June 1996): 258–68.

9. Atul Kohli, ed., *The Success of India's Democracy* (Cambridge: Cambridge University Press, 2001), 19.

10. Lloyd Rudolph and Susanne Rudolph, *In Pursuit of Lakshmi: The Political Economy of the Indian State* (Chicago: University of Chicago Press, 1987), particularly 19–59.

11. Juan Linz, Alfred Stepan, and Yogendra Yadav, "'Nation State' or 'State Nation': India in Comparative Perspective," in K. Shankar Bajpai, ed., *Democracy and Diversity: India and the American Experience* (New Delhi: Oxford University Press, 2007), 50–106.

12. Kanchan Chandra, *Why Ethnic Parties Succeed: Patronage and Ethnic Head Counts in India* (Cambridge: Cambridge University Press, 2004), 13–14.

13. Chandra, *Why Ethnic Parties Succeed,* 287–88.

14. Ashutosh Varshney, "Why Haven't Poor Democracies Eliminated Poverty?" in Ashutosh Varshney, ed., *India and the Politics of Developing Countries* (New Delhi: Sage, 2004), 205–26.

15. Paul Brass, *Ethnicity and Nationalism: Theory and Comparison* (New Delhi: Sage, 1991), 342.

16. Brass, *Ethnicity and Nationalism,* 344.

17. In this section we draw on E. Sridharan, "The Fragmentation of the Indian Party System, 1952–1999: Seven Competing Explanations," in Zoya Hasan, ed., *Parties and Party Politics in India* (New Delhi: Oxford University Press, 2002), 475–503.

18. A measure of the fragmentation of the opposition space is represented by the percentage share of the largest non-Congress (in today's terms, nonruling party) vote in the total opposition vote. The higher the IOU, the less fragmented the opposition space.

19. "Regional party" is something of a misnomer as it implies a party strong in two or more states in a region. All the regional parties, however, are single-state–based parties except the Janata Dal (JD, United), strong in Bihar and previously in Karnataka, and the Communist Party of India–Marxist (CPI-M) strong in West Bengal, Tripura, and Kerala. These sets of states, however, do not constitute recognizable regions. The JD(U) and the CPI-M are really national parties with a limited geographical spread, the former being a rump of the once much larger Janata Dal.

20. Yogendra Yadav, "Reconfiguration in Indian Politics: State Assembly Elec-

tions 1993–1995," *Economic and Political Weekly* (Mumbai), 13–20 January 1996, 95–104.

21. For the BJP's use of coalitions as a strategy to expand its base across states, see E. Sridharan, "Coalition Strategies and the BJP's Expansion, 1989–2004," *Commonwealth and Comparative Politics* 43 (July 2005): 194–221.

22. For details of the alliances, pre- and postelection in 1998, see Balveer Arora, "Negotiating Differences: Federal Coalitions and National Cohesion," in Francine Frankel et al., eds., *Transforming India: Social and Political Dynamics of Democracy* (Delhi: Oxford University Press, 2000), 184–85, 190, 194.

23. The Congress has historically resisted participating in coalitions. When it has allied with regional parties, it has witnessed a decline in the party's strength at the state level. For example, in Tamil Nadu, after it worked out a bargain whereby the regional ally got the bulk of assembly seats in exchange for giving the Congress the bulk of parliament seats, it has never been a contender for power based on its own strength.

24. For a detailed overview of state-level coalition politics in India, see E. Sridharan, "Principles, Power and Coalition Politics in India: Lessons from Theory, Comparison, and Recent History," in D.D. Khanna and Gert W. Kueck, eds., *Principles, Power and Politics* (Delhi: Macmillan, 1999). For a detailed state-wise analysis of the BJP's coalition strategies since 1989, see E. Sridharan, "Coalition Strategies and the BJP's Expansion, 1989–2004." For a detailed analysis of the Congress's coalition strategies and their importance in the 2004 elections, see E. Sridharan, "Electoral Coalitions in 2004 General Elections: Theory and Evidence," *Economic and Political Weekly,* 18 December 2004, 5418–25.

25. Peter Ordeshook and Olga Shvetsova, "Ethnic Heterogeneity, District Magnitude and the Number of Parties," *American Journal of Political Science* 38 (February 1994), 100–23, argue that Duverger's law will work even under conditions of social (ethnic, religious, linguistic, and the like) heterogeneity, while Taagepera and Shugart tend to argue that the effective number of parties will increase with the increase in social heterogeneity. See Taagepera and Shugart, *Seats and Votes.*

26. Arun Shourie, "When Spirit Is Willing, Flesh Has a Way," *Indian Express* (Mumbai), 4 February 2004.

27. Rob Jenkins, "The NDA and the Politics of Economic Reform," in Katharine Adeney and Lawrence Saez, eds., *Coalition Politics and Hindu Nationalism* (New York: Routledge, 2005): 173–92.

28. James Warner Bjorkman, "India: Party, Personality and Dynasty," in Alan Ware, ed., *Political Parties: Electoral Change and Structural Response* (London: Basil Blackwell, 1987), 51–71.

29. For an account of election and party funding and its relationship with party control, see E. Sridharan, "Toward State Funding of Elections in India? A Comparative Perspective on Possible Options," *Journal of Policy Reform* 3 (November 1999): 229–54, especially 234–38.

30. The License Raj refers to the system of elaborate permits that were required to set up a business in India between 1947 and 1990.

31. K.C. Suri, *Parties under Pressure: Political Parties in India since Independence* (New Delhi: Centre for the Study of Developing Societies, 2006).

32. Pratap Bhanu Mehta, "The End of Charisma?" *Seminar* 539 (July 2004): 16–19.

33. For example, Pratap Bhanu Mehta, "Reform Political Parties First," *Seminar* 479 (January 2001): 38–41.

34. James Manor, "In Part, A Myth: The BJP's Organisational Strength," in Adeney and Saez, eds., *Coalition Politics and Hindu Nationalism,* 55–74.

35. Larry Diamond and Leonardo Morlino, "The Quality of Democracy: An Overview," *Journal of Democracy* 15 (October 2004): 20–31.

36. Yogendra Yadav, "Electoral Politics in the Time of Change: India's Third Electoral System, 1989–99," *Economic and Political Weekly,* 21–28 August 1999, 2393–99.

37. Trilochan Sastry, "Electoral Reforms and Citizens' Initiatives," *Economic and Political Weekly,* 27 March–2 April 2004, 1391–97.

38. Sanjay Kumar, "Reforming Indian Electoral Process," *Economic and Political Weekly,* 24–30 August 2002, 3489–91.

39. For rising turnout and other indicators of political awareness and participation, particularly by the poor and less educated since the 1990s, see Yogendra Yadav, "Understanding the Second Democratic Upsurge: Trends of Bahujan Participation in Electoral Politics in the 1990s," in Frankel et al, eds., *Transforming India,* 120–45.

2

READING THE ELECTION RESULTS

Steven I. Wilkinson

Steven I. Wilkinson *is associate professor of political science at the University of Chicago. He is the author of* Votes and Violence: Electoral Competition and Ethnic Riots in India *(2004), and the editor with Herbert Kitschelt of* Patrons and Policies *(2007), which examines patronage politics in India and elsewhere. A version of this article originally appeared in the January 2005 issue of the* Journal of Democracy.

Many people in India, including the leaders of the opposition Indian National Congress (INC), were convinced that the incumbent Bharatiya Janata Party–led National Democratic Alliance (BJP-NDA) would handily win the April–May 2004 Indian parliamentary elections. In the days before the election results were announced, BJP leaders were already jostling for plum ministerial posts in the expected postelection reshuffle, while Congress party leaders were on television trying to reduce expectations before what many anticipated would be yet another dismal performance.

The BJP had reason to be confident. The country was enjoying near-record economic-growth rates, there was progress on negotiations with Pakistan over the troubled state of Kashmir, and Indians consistently told pollsters that BJP prime minister Atal Bihari Vajpayee was the person they most wanted to lead the country. Moreover, the BJP had done very well in several state elections in late 2003, prompting its leaders to call an early national election rather than wait until the end of their five-year term in November. Opinion polls suggested that this was the right move. Although they showed a narrowing of the gap between the BJP-NDA and the Congress-led United Progressive Alliance (INC-UPA) in the run-up to the elections, most surveys continued to predict a solid BJP-NDA majority.

And then, to everyone's surprise, Congress won. It was of course far from the kind of overwhelming victory that the party used to get in its glory years from the early 1950s to the late 1980s (see Figure 1), when it often won two-thirds to three-quarters of the seats in the Lok Sabha (House of the People). This time Congress itself captured only 145 (27 percent) of the 543 seats in Parliament outright, just ahead of the BJP, which won 138 (25 percent). But the INC-UPA as a whole won 219 seats (40 percent), compared to 185 (34 percent) for the BJP-NDA, putting it close to a stable majority in Parliament. After a few days of negotiations with the regional, state, and left-of-center parties, Congress cobbled together a coalition that the Communist Party of India–Marxist (CPI-M) agreed to support from the outside.

Congress's Italian-born leader Sonia Gandhi was wise enough to understand that to become prime minister herself, though constitutionally permissible, would be a political millstone around the coalition's neck. The BJP had previously campaigned against her using the Hindi slogan *swadeshi ya videshi*[1]—"self-reliance or the foreigner"—and seemed bent on using her foreign origin as a wedge issue to break up the Congress-led coalition. So Sonia stood aside and let the widely respected former finance minister Manmohan Singh—the architect of India's successful economic reforms in the 1990s—assume office as the first prime minister from the country's 2 percent Sikh minority.

Despite predictions that the coalition would fail, it has held together quite well and looks likely for several reasons to complete its full five-year term. First, the Congress, like the last few Indian coalition governments, has taken care to form an "oversized coalition" with more MPs than it needs for a bare majority, giving Congress a much stronger bargaining position when its coalition partners or individual MPs threaten to defect. Second, given that the Congress's allies gain a lot from incumbency and that the only alternative seems to be a BJP-led coalition, the Congress's allies do not want the government to fail. We can see this for instance in the CPI-M's failure to follow through on its threats when India sided with the United States on voting in the International Atomic Energy Agency in September 2005 to refer the Iran nuclear case to the UN Security Council, despite earlier dire warnings from the Communists that doing so would endanger their support for the coalition.[2] It would take a serious disagreement over an issue that affects a large portion of these parties' vote base—such as a dispute over subsidies for farmers, or new exit policies for industry—to upset this balance. Third, the opposition BJP has, since its defeat, been consumed by internecine warfare over the leadership succession, as younger leaders such as Arun Jaitley and Uma Bharati challenge the older generation and each other for power. This has given Congress a temporarily weakened opposition that seems incapable of taking advantage of divisions within the coalition, even on topics such as foreign policy, where Congress is pressing ahead over the objections of its allies on the left.

To begin with, why did the BJP lose an election in 2004 that everyone thought it would win? Once the outcome of the elections became clear, three initial theories were put forward to explain the BJP-NDA defeat. First, those on the Indian left claimed that the Congress-UPA victory represented the Indian people's rejection of economic liberal-

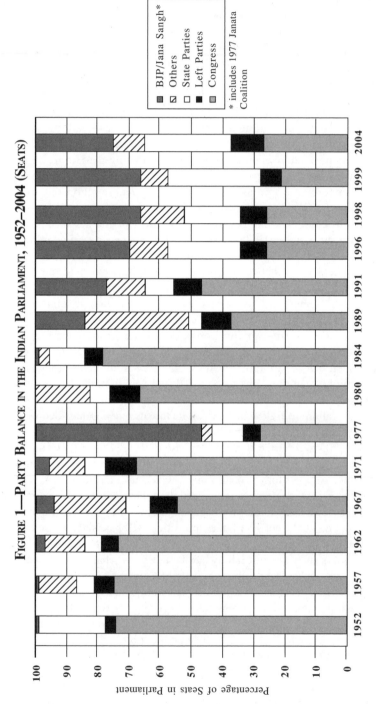

FIGURE 1—PARTY BALANCE IN THE INDIAN PARLIAMENT, 1952–2004 (SEATS)

ization; a call for government to focus on helping poor and rural Indians rather than the software engineers, exporters, call-center employees, and other assorted yuppies in such boomtowns as Bangalore, Hyderabad, Pune, and Chennai (Madras). One postelection newspaper cartoon showed defeated Andhra Pradesh chief minister Chandrababu Naidu, often called the "laptop minister" for his high-technology and economic-modernization initiatives, being beaten over a peasant's knee with the caption "The Laptop."[3]

Second, supporters of secularism claimed that the election results represented a clear rebuke to the BJP's Hindu-nationalist ideology, and the polarizing politics that led to the massive anti-Muslim pogrom in the BJP-ruled state of Gujarat in 2002. A third explanation saw the elections as part of a now-familiar pattern of anti-incumbency in India: State and national governments generally perform so badly that India is perhaps the only country where it is statistically better to be a challenger than an incumbent.[4]

None of these three explanations made much sense. First, it is hard to see the elections as a reaction of the poor against liberalization when the results show that many of the booming metropolitan areas such as Hyderabad and Chennai (Madras) voted heavily against the BJP-NDA, while several of the poorest states in the country, such as Orissa and Chhattisgarh, voted strongly for the coalition. Second, the view that the Congress victory was a firm vote in favor of secularism and against the BJP's divisive Hindu-nationalist politics is hard to square with several strong BJP performances in state elections in 2002 and 2003, which took place after the Hindu-Muslim violence in February and March 2002. Moreover, opinion polls have consistently shown that most Indians, most of the time, place communal violence and secularism far down the list of issues that determine their vote—well beneath such issues as employment and inflation. Lastly, though the anti-incumbency theory holds true in some states, it fails in many more: Incumbent parties performed well in such states as West Bengal, Bihar, Rajasthan, and Madhya Pradesh.

So what did happen? To begin with, it should be made clear that in 2004, as in all elections except possibly the 1977 poll that threw Indira Gandhi out of power, no single factor determined the elections in all 28 states. Different issues mattered in different states—drought and farmer suicides in Andhra Pradesh, growing Hindu-Christian polarization in Goa, and the autocratic rule of Chief Minister Selvi Jayalalitha in Tamil Nadu.[5] Even allowing for the numerous local swings against the BJP-NDA, however, the emerging consensus in India is that the coalition could still have won—had it made the right alliances.[6] Many Indian constituencies have three, four, or even more credible parties putting up candidates, often leading to a situation where the opposition vote is split several ways and the winning candidate obtains only 30 to 35 percent of the vote. To avoid this, parties try to negotiate seat adjustments: Party A makes a deal with Party B so that B's candidates step down in some seats, and urge their supporters in these seats to vote for Party A, while A returns the favor to B's candidates in other constituencies.

The New Era of Coalition Politics

The importance of such electoral alliances has become increasingly clear over the past fifteen years, a period in which (see Figure 2) the rise of "Other" regional and caste parties has meant that no Indian party has been able to win an outright majority in Parliament. The relative electoral success of Congress and the BJP is now determined by how well they work out their alliances and seat-adjustment deals with: 1) the many state-level parties, which now provide almost 30 percent of the MPs, up from 5 percent in the late 1980s; 2) the CPI-M, which has won 7 to 10 percent of seats in Parliament in recent elections; and 3) regional parties that are too small to be officially considered state parties but which nonetheless win 8 to 10 percent of the seats. Collectively, these three groups of parties now occupy almost half the seats in the Lok Sabha.

Congress generally has a greater range of choice than the BJP when it comes to selecting alliance partners. This is because the CPI-M consistently refuses to ally itself with the communalist BJP, as do several smaller parties that also rely heavily on Muslim votes. So the BJP has to select its allies from the remaining state parties, calculating how well it would do in each state in various alliance scenarios. In the 2004 election, the BJP played this alliance game very badly, choosing to ally in some states with unpopular parties that controlled the state government, and failing to make any tie-ups at all in others. The Congress, on the other hand, having tasted bitter defeat under its old policy of minimizing alliances to avoid undercutting its own candidates, changed tactics in time for the 2004 election. In early January 2004, the Congress leadership decided to go all out for strategic alliances, and began holding daily meetings to plan alliances and seat adjustments in each of the states. Throughout January and February 2004, Sonia Gandhi made an effort to maximize Congress's coalition possibilities by paying courtesy calls to the leaders of the most important state and regional parties. She also sent Manmohan Singh to Tamil Nadu to lay the groundwork for a successful multiparty coalition against the state's ruling party, the BJP ally All India Anna Dravida Munnetra Kazhigam (AIADMK).[7] Most impressively, Sonia made peace with Sharad Pawar, the leader of an important INC splinter faction, the Nationalist Congress Party (NCP), even though Pawar had earlier split with Congress over the issue of Sonia's foreign origin and allegedly poor leadership abilities. As a result of these efforts, Congress soon began to push through—sometimes in the face of bitter opposition from its own party members—various seat-adjustment deals with state and regional parties.

These newly formed alliances proved crucial in the May 2004 elections. Even though the BJP-NDA actually received a slightly larger share of the national vote than the INC-UPA (35.91 percent to 35.82 percent), the latter's web of alliances meant that it secured more seats in the Lok Sabha.[8] In Maharashtra state, for instance, the INC's decision to team up with Pawar's NCP meant considerably more seats for Congress even though the party's overall vote share declined against the BJP-NDA. In Kerala and Karnataka, the BJP vote share also increased but a lack of alliances prevented seat gains. In Tamil Nadu, the Congress-aligned multiparty Democratic Progressive Alliance won 57 percent of the vote and all 39 seats, crushing the BJP, which dominates the state government. And in Haryana, the BJP's failure to ally with the leading state party, the Indian National Lok Dal (INLD) meant that there were numerous races where the vote split three ways—nearly all of which Congress won.

Nowhere was the BJP failure to get its alliances right greater than in India's most populous state, Uttar Pradesh, which has 166 million people and 80 seats in Parliament. Prior to the election, BJP leaders were forecasting that the party would win 40 or more seats in the state: As it turned out, despite getting 23 percent of the vote, they won only 11 seats, well behind the Samajwadi Party, which won 35 (27 percent of the vote) and the Bahujan Samaj Party (BSP), which got 25 percent of the vote and 19 seats. Many seats were lost in three- or four-way fights, in which the BJP fell just a few percentage points short. If the BJP had been able to make an alliance with the BSP, however, as seemed possible in February, the outcome would have been drastically different. Even making the conservative assumption that only 50 percent of the BSP votes would have transferred to the BJP (given the suspicion of the BJP among many of the BSP's lower-caste and Muslim voters), such an alliance would still have won enough seats to make the BJP the largest single party in Parliament, and almost enough to push the BJP-NDA ahead of the INC-UPA. If it had forged a similar alliance in one other medium-sized state, the BJP-NDA would have won the election.

India has a generally effective and impartial electoral system, especially so when we compare it to its neighbors, but also for that matter, if we compare it to the politicization of boundary demarcation and the proliferation of different ballot and registration systems that have made recent elections in the United States so controversial. India's constituencies are drawn by a Delimitation Commission that answers to Parliament, and the national and state elections themselves are overseen by an independent Election Commission of India (ECI), which ensures the integrity of the process and the safety of voters, drafting in central forces if necessary.[9] The Commission has in recent years taken steps to im-

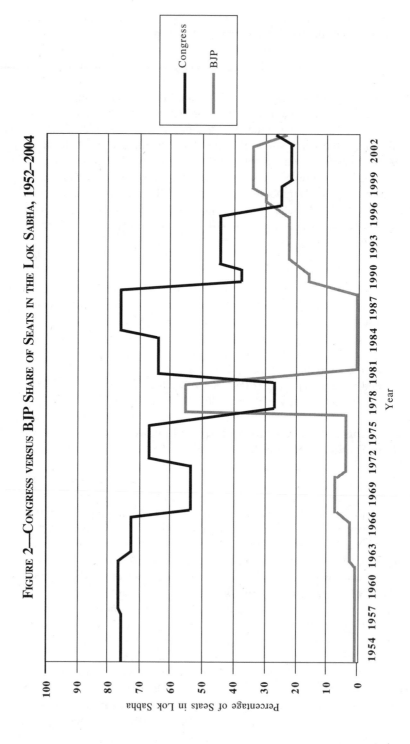

FIGURE 2—CONGRESS VERSUS BJP SHARE OF SEATS IN THE LOK SABHA, 1952–2004

prove the electoral process, issuing national photo-identity cards for voters, as well as trying to speed up the counting process and prevent ballot stuffing by moving to an all-electronic voting system. India's 2004 election was the world's first fully electronic election (employing more than a million indigenously manufactured and simple-to-operate voting machines), conducted in a vast country whose 28 states contain roughly four times as many voters as the United States. Despite numerous predictions that the voting machines would malfunction or that they would be vulnerable to fraud, balloting went smoothly and by popular consensus the machines were a huge success.

All this is not to say that things are perfect, and in particular there are complaints by opposition parties in some states as well as by the Scheduled Castes (SCs) and Muslims that the boundary-drawing process is biased against them. Scheduled Castes have reserved constituencies, in which only SCs can stand for election, but they have long complained that because many of these reserved constituencies do not have a majority of SC voters, the representatives who are elected are not "authentic" representatives of the community. Many of the reserved SC constituencies in fact have substantial proportions of Muslims, and Muslim community leaders in turn complain that they are not able to elect a greater number of Muslim MPs because Muslims are being packed into SC constituencies. The Prime Minister's High-Level Committee on the Status of Muslims (the Sachar Committee) analyzed constituency data in several states and largely substantiated both complaints in its November 2006 report into the Social, Economic, and Educational Status of the Muslim community, finding that Muslims were indeed being disproportionately packed into seats reserved for Scheduled Castes.[10] In addition to these general complaints, there have also been more specific complaints about voter registration, boundary demarcation, and ballot stuffing in West Bengal, where the Communists have held power since 1977. Some of this is sour grapes, but West Bengal's inexplicably high turnout rates *since* the CPI-M came to power (10 to 20 percent higher than the Indian norm, and pre-1977 rates) and the fact that the CPI-M allegedly drafted much of the state-assembly demarcation for the 2006 elections gives credence to the complaints.[11]

Having pointed to these problems, we should not exaggerate their effect on the overall integrity of the process at the national level and in most states. India and Pakistan both inherited an electoral system at independence that was elite-dominated (only 14 percent of the population could vote) and highly communalized, with separate electorates for the major religious minorities that structured political competition along religious lines. But India has done much better than Pakistan at turning this colonial structure into a genuinely representative, secular, and legitimate system with institutions that work. India has now held fourteen national elections since universal franchise was established in 1950, and Indian voters' commitment to this system is shown in many ways: by generally high turnout rates of 55 to 65 percent (twice the recent turnout in Pakistani elections), especially among India's poor and lower castes; by opinion polls that consistently demonstrate great faith in the democratic process and in key institutions such as the court system and Election Commission; and by the massive wave of opposition to Indira Gandhi's 1975–77 emergency, the one time when a prime minister has tried seriously to interfere with the integrity of the system. And as Alistair McMillan has pointed out, even the few determined attempts to rig the elections through the delimitation process that do go on tend to be undercut by India's very high degree of electoral competition and electoral volatility, which makes gerrymandering highly unpredictable.[12]

There is one important problem, however, that the Indian political system has not been able to solve: the growing criminalization of politics and the widespread corruption of individual politicians. It is widely acknowledged that many politicians have criminal links, and also that many politicians who possess few assets at the beginning of their political career mysteriously emerge from the Lok Sabha and the state assemblies with great wealth, often including extensive land holdings. Because the spoils of office are so great, politicians and their underworld allies are prepared, especially in some states, to go to almost any lengths to win elections and intimidate their opponents. Data I collected show that the number of MLAs and MPs murdered in India averaged two per decade in the 1960s and 1970s, but has been averaging ten times this rate (23 a decade) in the 1980s and 1990s. And the death toll among these senior-level politicians clearly understates the overall magnitude of the country's problem with politically motivated violence, because MPs and MLAs tend to be relatively well protected. In Bihar for instance, while five MPs and MLAs were murdered in the 1990s, the state police estimated that as many as 371 other political workers had also been killed.[13] Several institutions have tried to shine a light on the problem, which was first explicitly tackled in the (unpublished) appendices to a 1993 report to the Government of India by former home secretary N.N. Vohra, who wrote of a "politician-criminal-bureaucratic nexus." In 1997, the Election Commission released a widely discussed report that highlighted the level of criminality in politics, and showed that 40 out of the 543 MPs and 700 of the 4,072 members of the various state assemblies had criminal records.[14] In the 2004 parliamentary election, the Indian press reported that close to 20 percent of all the MPs elected had criminal records: 26 from the BJP, 15 from Congress, 5 from the CPI-M, and 54 from other regional and state parties.[15]

And there have periodically been media exposés of political corruption, most recently in December 2005, when 10 MPs were expelled from the Lok Sabha for taking cash to ask parliamentary questions. But the suspicion remains that corruption and criminality are widespread, and that politicians' control over the police gives them virtual immunity from prosecution unless their political rivals want to get rid of them or, as in the case of the ten MPs in December 2005, they are unlucky enough to be caught on camera.

A Brighter Future for Communal Relations

For the past 25 years, India has had to deal with major secessionist movements by linguistic and religious minorities in Assam, Jammu and Kashmir, Punjab, and a host of smaller states in India's troubled northeast. Outbreaks of secessionist strife have cost tens of thousands of lives, and have at times tied down half of the Indian army as well as hundreds of thousands of paramilitary troops. The country has also seen periodic politically motivated violence against members of its 13 percent Muslim minority and 2 percent Christian minority. In Gujarat in early 2002, the murder of 58 Hindu nationalists in their train carriage sparked massive anti-Muslim pogroms, which fortunately did not spread to other states. There is clear evidence that Gujarat's BJP-run state government and several Hindu-nationalist organizations were instrumental in causing this violence.

Amid this gloomy scene, reasons for optimism may seem few and far between. But the 2004 elections have already led to a drop in communal and secessionist violence that looks set to continue. The secessionist movements in Assam, Kashmir, and Punjab became violent largely when these states' federal autonomy and legitimate constitutional means of protest were closed off—for example, when the central government interfered with democratically elected state governments by rigging elections or by imposing emergency "president's rule." (President's rule has in the past been used—many would say misused—by majority-party governments at the center to remove irksome state governments.)[16] In recent years, the center's ability and will to interfere in state politics have dropped significantly. Recent presidents, bolstered by a 1994 Supreme Court ruling, have been increasingly unwilling to approve central-government attempts to impose emergency rule on states. More importantly, the character of the central government has itself changed. In contrast to the years in which Congress controlled the Lok Sabha and the presidency, and used its control to advance its own electoral fortunes throughout India's states, the central government now includes many state and regional parties that have every reason to be cautious about central meddling in state politics. In September 1998, for example, when former president K.R. Narayanan refused to approve the BJP-led central government's request to impose president's rule on Bihar, the main regional-party leaders in the Lok Sabha promptly praised him for his independence and staunchness in defense of the constitution.

For many of the same reasons that violent secessionist campaigns will probably recede in the next few decades, so in all likelihood will Hindu-Muslim conflict. That is not to deny that there will be many attempts by those on the Hindu right to foment it. Through my own research I have found that, in preelection periods, Hindu-Muslim violence has frequently been used as an electoral tactic, with the aim of rallying the Hindu electorate around the party with the strongest anti-Muslim and pro-Hindu profile.[17] For instance, in the run-up to the 2002 state elections in Gujarat, anti-Muslim riots were most likely in those constituencies where electoral competition between the BJP and Congress was most intense—even controlling for previous violence and the socioeconomic profile of each constituency. And the riots were effective. They completely turned around the BJP's poor electoral showing in the state over the previous three years. Constituencies that had been directly affected by riots saw the largest swings to the BJP.[18]

The good news, however, is that the state and central governments now have much stronger incentives to prevent such violence. Given the increasing intensity of political competition in Indian states over the past decade, few parties want to alienate Muslims, whose geographical concentration in certain states makes their votes pivotal to a large number of parliamentary seats. States have chosen to protect Muslims from attack either where there is a strong secular government in power, as in communist-ruled West Bengal, or more often, where Muslims are an important voting bloc for the party in power. Higher levels of electoral competition create a greater demand for minority swing votes, which in turn motivates Hindu-led governments to protect their local minorities.[19] State governments in Maharashtra and Uttar Pradesh, for instance, were quick to prevent Islamist terrorist attacks from sparking off wider communal conflagrations in the sensitive towns of Varanasi and Malegaon in March and September 2006, in part because they recognized the electoral damage that communal violence could cause in terms of alienating Muslim voters and fragmented support among Hindus.[20]

The 2004 elections have also, at least for the term of this government, changed the political incentives for state governments to act to prevent violence. India's central governments have generally been loath to impose president's rule for a state government's failure to prevent communal violence.[21] This has been especially true, of course, when the center's own party has been in power in a state. The five cases from 1950 to 1996 in which the center dismissed state governments for allowing communal violence to take place were *all* cases where the government in the state was opposed to the party or coalition in power at the center. In 2002, most recently, the BJP-led central government refused to impose president's rule on the BJP-run Gujarat state government when it allowed (many would say encouraged) communal riots in the state.

The new Congress-led central government has, however, tried to change the incentive structure for state governments, and has signaled to them that they will face severe consequences if they allow violence to take place. First, the Congress is overtly secular, and also supported by the Communists, who have India's best record on preventing anti-Muslim violence. Second, Congress and its major coalition allies—the Rashtriya Janata Dal (RJD), the Dravida Munnetra Kazhagam (DMK), and the CPI-M—rely heavily on Muslim votes. So Congress has both an ideological and a pragmatic reason to intervene if BJP-run state governments foment or allow communal violence. Prime Minister Manmohan Singh, whose own Sikh community was victimized by 1984 riots in Delhi, is especially sensitive to this issue. Soon after being appointed, he announced that "painful incidents like [that of 1984] and the Gujarat riots should never happen again," and that "an atmosphere should be created wherein such incidents do not take place."[22] The fact that state governments now believe the center is serious is shown by the actions of the BJP government in Gujarat when communal riots broke out in the city of Vadodara in May 2006. This time, in contrast to its inaction and partiality in 2002, the Narendra Modi government called in the army almost immediately to quash the riots, having been warned that the center was only too willing to impose president's rule on the state if it failed to do so.[23]

In addition to these steps to prevent communal violence, Congress has also made efforts to undo what many saw as a creeping Hinduization of curricula in India's educational system. Under the former BJP government, the Human Resources and Development Ministry (HRD) had cleansed primary and high-school textbooks of facts that clashed with the Hindu-nationalist interpretation of history—such as evidence that early Aryans ate beef or that Muslim rulers relied on Hindu soldiers and administrators—and had promoted a view of Indian history in which Hinduism and India were seen as virtually synonymous, portraying Muslims as bigoted "foreigners."[24] The ministry also infringed on the autonomy of institutions devoted to higher learning by packing research bodies with Hindu nationalists and blocking cooperation with foreign institutions, especially in Muslim countries. One of the first actions of the new Congress HRD minister was to appoint a committee to review the textbook changes carried out during the BJP regime. And in August 2004, the HRD withdrew a year-old requirement that it had to approve all cooperative agreements between higher-education institutions in India and their counterparts abroad.

What's Next for Economic Reforms?

In the month leading up to the election, the BJP tried to capitalize on India's robust 8 percent annual growth rate with feel-good media advertisements showing a diverse collection of happy and prosperous citizens around the slogan "India Shining." But many Indians feel removed from this touched-up image of their country, as they remain mired in poverty and illiteracy—especially in such northern states as Bihar, Chhattisgarh, Jharkhand, and Uttar Pradesh. The economic gap separating these regions from booming states like Gujarat and Punjab in the west and Karnataka and Tamil Nadu in the south is wide and expanding. Even within the boom states, rural areas have been hard hit by drought and rising prices of food and such agricultural inputs as fuel and electricity.

Even though opposition to economic liberalization was not the deciding factor in the elections, many Indians nonetheless continue to feel apprehensive about proposals to dismantle the inefficient government enterprises and subsidy regimes which have been built up over the past fifty years. A postelection poll conducted by a Delhi think-tank found that only 29 percent of voters supported a reduction of the number of state employees and that only 22 percent were in favor of privatizing public-sector enterprises.[25] This unease is not surprising, given that there is no way of knowing where the gains of such economic liberalization might flow. Most voters seem to prefer a predictable albeit very low payout today—subsidized food and electricity, and access to government jobs, medical care, and other social services—to the prospect of a more vibrant economy in which they might receive nothing, despite overall high growth rates. Opinion polls consistently show that around two-thirds of Indians expect further economic reforms to benefit the wealthy and the middle class rather than the bulk of the Indian population.[26]

Those who are uneasy about further liberalization or structural reforms seem to be in luck, because the 2004 election produced a coalition that will make it difficult to carry out dramatic reforms during its five-year mandate. Subsequent state election victories in 2006 by the left in Kerala and West Bengal add to the political support for a "go slow" policy. The center can push forward on some areas, such as airport privatization, but has had in 2005 and 2006 to pull back on others, such as plans to sell some of its shares in a few successful public-sector companies such as Bharat Heavy Electricals Limited (BHEL).[27] The coalition's budgets have reflected the government's need to balance its various constituencies. In the first budget in 2004, for instance, Finance Minister P. Chidambaram kept the reformers happy by announcing the further relaxation of restrictions on foreign ownership in the civil aviation, insurance, and telecom industries. To please the left, he provided the equivalent of US$3.8 billion to keep the many troubled public enterprises and their employees afloat, and reduced the number of public-sector units to be privatized in 2004–2005. And to show the population that the Congress-led coalition is indeed "with the common man," as the party had claimed during the election campaign, he announced a plan to fund eight years of schooling for all Indians, a massive new employment program, and debt relief, as well as US$610 million for new irrigation projects to help farmers in drought-prone regions.

Despite these plans, however, real progress seems unlikely. First of all, despite the rising tax revenues by India's recent economic growth, there is simply not enough money in the central government's coffers to fulfill all the budget's development and anti-poverty promises and deal with widening income inequality. Moreover, several of the new anti-poverty schemes announced in the budget seem to be little more than ways to disguise the transfer of pots of central money to the Congress's key allies—such as the RJD in Bihar and NCP leader Sharad Pawar in Maharashtra. In the budget debate, an upper-house opposition MP from Orissa, a state that supported the BJP-NDA in the 2004 elections, complained that even though his state was in absolute terms just as badly off as Bihar, the latter had received a special allotment of about US$652 million in government antipoverty programs while his state received nothing.[28]

On past evidence, the implementation of many of the new agricultural loan and employment programs will be similarly inefficient and politicized, with loans and jobs going disproportionately to the politically connected, to core groups of INC-UPA supporters, and to those who can afford to pay off the officials in charge of the programs. One recent study has estimated that no more than a fourth of the billions of dollars allocated each year through the centrally sponsored employment programs ever reaches the intended beneficiaries.[29] It has often been pointed out that it would be much more efficient simply to send each family a check representing its share of the national and state antipoverty budgets (currently such a check would total about US$174) than to filter it through inefficient schemes.[30]

Moreover, despite the budget commitment to cut back debt, the Congress and its allies will not be able to do much about the ballooning deficits that most state governments as well as the central government are now running, and which now hover at 10 percent of GDP. The previous government increased the country's deficit by providing its allies with massive loans and direct subsidies, in order to keep the government coalition together. The former chief minister of Andhra Pradesh, Chandrababu Naidu, was the acknowledged master of extracting funds from the central government by threatening to withdraw his party's electoral support if the money was not forthcoming. In 2001, for instance, Naidu extracted hundreds of millions of dollars in emergency drought relief and price-support grants. Congress, given its dependence on regional coalition partners, has to pay off its allies in just the same way.

But this does not mean that the reforms will suddenly grind to a halt. Transfers from the center and antipoverty programs that retain the support of the rural and urban poor are in fact what allow the reforms to continue. Many politically influential industries stand to gain from further economic liberalization; states want more jobs; and consumers recognize that the quality, supply, and price of such goods as telephones, cars, and consumer products have significantly improved as these sectors have been opened up to competition. No one wants to go back to the days when a phone took years to obtain and continuing payoffs to the lineman were required to keep it working, or when buying a car involved a wait of a year or more for an expensive Hindustan Motors Ambassador based on 1950s technology.

Therefore, we can expect to see continued progress in the consumer-product sectors, the capital markets, and other areas that will bring in large numbers of manufacturing or service jobs. Even the Communists, generally thought to be opposed to reform, have created several special economic zones in their citadel of West Bengal, with the aim of attracting more high-paying service and manufacturing jobs to the state. The West Bengal chief minister Buddhadev Bhattacharjee frankly acknowledged in April 2006 that

> What we are practicing here is capitalism. Socialism cannot be created in the given situation even if we preach it. I am a realist and not a fool. . . . I know Marxism teaches us that the contradiction between labor and capital is irreconcilable . . . [but] we are no more in the opposition and our responsibility to govern makes it imperative that we cooperate with captains of industry to maintain the momentum of the flow of investment into Bengal.[31]

Despite this political support for loosening the conditions attached to new investments, more fundamental reforms—which would reduce the massive spending on subsidies for food and farming inputs or reduce the headcount in the public-sector enterprises that continue to drain capital from more productive segments of the economy—remain unlikely because of their high political cost.

One economic issue that has already caused massive conflict is the Congress-led coalition's commitment greatly to extend affirmative-action programs—called "reservations" in India—to the private sector and to the most prestigious higher-educational institutions, such as the six Indian Institutes of Management, the seven Indian Institutes of Technology, and various other medical, scientific, engineering, and advanced-research institutions that have so far largely been outside the system of reservations.

The extension of reservations to the private sector has been a key demand of several lower-caste parties for years, and came to national attention in 2004 when the government of the state of Maharashtra passed a bill, not yet implemented, that mandated reservations for lower castes in enterprises regulated by the government, which could theoretically include all private firms. Lower-caste politicians have claimed that, without such explicit quotas, the liberalization and expansion of India's private sector—still largely dominated by the upper castes—

will undo the advances that lower castes have made since independence through reservations in the civil service and public-sector enterprises. Private industry, not surprisingly, generally opposes such measures, but until 2004 kept quiet on the issue because nothing seemed likely to happen. That silence was broken after the election, with several leading Indian industrialists and both of the major business organizations, the CII and FICCI, voicing their opposition to private-sector reservations in late August and September. Business leaders highlighted the need for government to increase the supply of highly educated and well-trained lower-caste workers before talking about employment quotas, and FICCI president Y.K. Modi expressed his support for U.S.-style programs whereby the government would favor minority contractors or provide tax breaks as preferable to more formal requirements that private industry employ set percentages of lower-caste workers. Lower-caste activists see such stances as a recipe for doing nothing, and point, with some justification, to the entrenched bias against lower castes in Indian society. The intense social discrimination against ex-untouchables, in particular, means that even if the supply of educated lower-caste youths increases sharply, it is not clear that private industry will employ them unless there is some legal requirement to do so.

Despite the private-sector opposition to reservations, the introduction of some form of private-sector quotas is likely for two reasons. First, there seems to be broad public support in favor of reservations at least for Dalits (ex-untouchables) and so-called Backward Castes, with 61 percent of those who were asked in a summer 2004 poll in favor, or roughly the percentage of Dalits and Backward Castes in the population.[32] Only 22 percent of the population, or roughly the percentage of "upper castes," opposes reservations. Second, reflecting this political reality, the government committee appointed in August 2004 to examine the issue is composed mainly of middle- and lower-caste leaders known to be supporters of private-sector reservations, such as Laloo Prasad Yadav and Ram Vilas Paswan. Whatever this committee proposes—probably some form of reservation in companies in which the government owns a stake and voluntary programs in other companies—will no doubt be toned down after consultation with business bodies, but the longer-term trend toward the expansion of reservations to more and more sectors of the economy seems likely to continue.

This was sharply demonstrated in May 2006 when HRD Minister Arjun Singh announced that the government would implement the Mandal Commission's recommendations and create a 27 percent reservation for Other Backward Classes (OBCs) in the most prestigious government higher-educational institutions. The upper-caste students who dominate these institutions saw this as a government attack on their job prospects and on the last bastion of merit in India's educational institutions, and they launched what came to be termed "Mandal II," a series of mass protests, hunger strikes, and sit-ins in and around the country's elite educational institutions. Much of the press and many senior policy voices supported their stance, and in May 2006 two prominent academics on the government's Knowledge Commission, Pratap Mehta and André Beteille, resigned in protest. At the time of writing, it appears as if the reservations will go through (on 14 December 2006 there was a voice vote in the Lok Sabha approving a 27 percent reservation) but with one important modification: the expansion of the overall number of places in the higher-educational institutions so that the absolute number of "merit" places remains the same.

The political turnaround that India saw in its April–May 2004 parliamentary election will bring surprisingly little real change. The Congress-UPA government will most probably continue BJP policies on many domestic issues, especially on economic reforms, and it will seek to maintain a basic stability and greater engagement with the United States (while not sacrificing India's autonomy) in foreign affairs. On many issues, the new government simply wants to go in the same direction as its predecessor, though the composition of its coalition means that progress will require a lot more effort. Only in the area of communal relations is there significant change, as the Congress-UPA's staunch secularism and its Muslim and lower-caste support base have led to a welcome reduction in Hindu-Muslim violence.

The election was in no sense a repudiation of the BJP, despite what that party's opponents would like to believe. In fact, the election paradoxically confirms the fundamental weakness of the Congress party, because Congress could only form a government by giving up on its own prospects in many states and constituencies, and entering into coalitions of convenience with a diverse collection of regional and state parties. Because Congress is dependent on so many coalition partners, no one, including the current prime minister and other senior party leaders, really seems to know what the party stands for apart from its commitment to secularism. Neither has the current leadership made an effort to rejuvenate the party at the state and local level, where it remains only a shadow of the potent grassroots organization that it was in the 1950s and 1960s. Today, Congress is not so much an ideology or an organization as a national focal point for the many regional, state, and left-of-center parties who seek to ally against the BJP. But no doubt the BJP, once it gets over its own internal struggles, will learn from its mistakes and improve its alliances—and thereby its performance—next time around.

NOTES

I thank Devesh Kapur for his valuable comments on an earlier article, published in the January 2005 issue of the *Journal of Democracy*.

1. The word *swadeshi* refers to a movement for national independence in India

boycotting foreign goods and encouraging the use of domestic products.

2. CPI-M general-secretary Prakash Karat had warned that "[t]he Left shall not spare the government if it votes against Iran." See "Bow-wow in Delhi," *The Week* (Kochi), 19 February 2006, 12–14.

3. *The Hindu* (New Delhi), 12 May 2004.

4. One estimate is that incumbents are 14 percent less likely to win an election than similar challengers. Leigh Linden, "Are Incumbents Really Advantaged? The Preference for Non-Incumbents in Indian National Elections," MIT Department of Economics, 25 November 2003. Available at *http://econ-www.mit.edu/graduate/candidates/download_res.php?id=89.*

5. For an excellent state-by-state review of the election results that demolishes much of the conventional wisdom on the reasons for the BJP's defeat, see "How India Voted," an eight-page supplement to *The Hindu* (New Delhi), 20 May 2004. Available at *www.hindu.com/elections2004/verdict2004/index.htm.*

6. "How India Voted."

7. Purnima S. Tripathi, "Joining Forces," *Frontline,* supplement to *The Hindu,* 31 January–13 February 2004.

8. For a full breakdown of results, see "How India Voted."

9. The best guide to the system is Alistair McMillan, *Standing at the Margins: Representation and Electoral Reservation in India* (New Delhi: Oxford University Press, 2006).

10. The November 2006 Sachar Committee Report is available at *http://indianmuslim.gov.in/pmhlc_report.pdf.*

11. "Vote Catchers," *The Week,* 12 March 2006, 29–30; and Bibhuti Bhusan Nandy, "Farce or Fraud: Inadequacies and Bias of Delimitation Commission Exposed," *The Statesman Weekly* (Calcutta and Delhi), 22 October 2005, 11.

12. McMillan, *Standing at the Margins.*

13. Steven I. Wilkinson, "Cleansing Political Institutions," *Seminar* 506, October 2001.

14. "Discussion Document" of the National Commission to Review the Workings of the Constitution, September 2000, 17. India's election law bars *convicted* criminals from standing for election, but the wheels of the Indian legal system grind slowly, allowing some decidedly shady politicians to contest election after election on the grounds that they have not (yet) been convicted of anything.

15. "Criminals Sap Parliamentary Democracy," *Deccan Herald* (New Delhi), 23 June 2004.

16. President's rule refers to the constitutional process through which the government, subject to approval by Parliament and the president (and, in some cases since 1978, review by the courts), can impose central rule on a state for six months or more if the state is judged to be politically or financially unstable, or the state government is judged to be governing in an unconstitutional manner. President's rule has been imposed more than a hundred times since independence, often for primarily partisan political reasons.

17. Steven I. Wilkinson, *Votes and Violence: Electoral Competition and Ethnic*

Riots in India (New York: Cambridge University Press, 2004).

18. See Steven I. Wilkinson, "Ethnic Violence as Campaign Expenditure: Riots, Competition and Turnout in Gujarat 2002," unpubl. ms., Duke University, September 2004.

19. For data to support this argument see Wilkinson, *Votes and Violence.*

20. On the Varanasi attacks, see *Communalism Combat,* January–March 2006, 9–11.

21. Steven I. Wilkinson, "Political Competition and Communal Violence in India," unpubl. ms., December 2006.

22. "Create Atmosphere Wherein Painful Incidents Don't Happen: PM," *www.outlookindia.com,* 12 June 2004.

23. "Army Deployed in Vadodara," *The Statesman Weekly,* 6 May 2006.

24. See Indian History Congress, *History in the New NCERT Textbooks: A Report and an Index of Errors* (Kolkata: Indian History Congress, 2003).

25. K.C. Suri, "Reform: The Elites Want It, the Masses Don't," *The Hindu,* 20 May 2004, AE-7.

26. "Mood of the Nation," *India Today* International Edition (New Delhi), 30 August 2004, 16–23.

27. "Challenging Liberalism," *Frontline,* 30 June 2006, 4–7.

28. Uncorrected proceedings of parliamentary debates (Council of States) on the 2004 budget for 20 July 2004. Available at *http://rajyasabha.nic.in/rsdebate/deb_ndx/202/20072004/3to4.htm.*

29. Radhika Nayak, N.C. Saxena Nayak, and John Farrington, "Reaching the Poor: The Influence of Policy and Administrative Processes on the Implementation of Government Poverty Schemes in India," ODI Working Paper 175, September 2002, 6. Available at *www.odi.org.uk/publications/working_papers/wp175.pdf.*

30. "Union Budget 2004," *India Today* International Edition, 19 July 2004, 11–13.

31. *The Statesman Weekly,* 15 April 2006.

32. A poll of 17,885 voters conducted between 26 July and 5 August 2004. "Mood of the Nation–Poll," *India Today* International Edition, 30 August 2004, 16–23.

3

DEMOCRACY AND ETHNIC CONFLICT

Rajat Ganguly

Rajat Ganguly *is senior lecturer in politics and international studies at the School of Social Sciences and Humanities and fellow at the Asia Research Centre at Murdoch University, Western Australia. He is author of* Kin State Intervention in Ethnic Conflicts: Lessons from South Asia *(1998), coauthor of* Understanding Ethnic Conflict: The International Dimension *(2006, 2002, 1998) and* Ethnicity and Nation-Building in South Asia *(2001), and coeditor of* Ethnic Conflict and Secessionism in South and Southeast Asia: Causes, Dynamics, Solutions *(2003). He also serves as editor-in-chief of the* Journal of South Asian Development.

Over the past two decades, India has made significant progress in fostering high levels of economic and industrial development, reducing poverty, and promoting the general well-being of the population. During the same period, however, democracy, human rights, and the rule of law have been undermined or significantly eroded in several parts of the country. Ethnoreligious violence has flared up in many corners and the tentacles of transnational terrorism have spread rapidly. Rapid economic progress seems to have unleashed violent class warfare in some areas. Ethnic conflicts in various forms have thus become an enduring feature of the Indian political landscape. Why is India prone to ethnic conflicts? What implications do these conflicts and the Indian state's response to them have for the state of Indian democracy? These are the main questions that this chapter attempts to answer.

India's diversity is remarkable. Hinduism and Islam are the two main religions of the country although Sikhism, Buddhism, Jainism, and Christianity also flourish. Of the total population of approximately 1.1 billion, around 80 percent are Hindus, about 11 percent are Muslims, and Sikhs, Buddhists, Jains, Christians, Parsees, and Jews together make up around 7 percent. More than a dozen major languages (belonging to either Dravidian South India or Indo-European or Aryan North India) and hundreds of village or regional dialects and tribal languages are spoken in India.[1] The Hindus, while sharing a common religious tradition, are not a homogeneous community. They are divided into myriad sects, castes, and *jatis* or subcastes that are traditionally ranked hierarchically and vary according to region. The Hindus also speak different languages and have different regional identities with distinct cultural traditions. The Muslims too are not ethnically homogeneous. They are scattered throughout India with the largest concentrations in Uttar Pradesh, Bihar, and West Bengal. Fairly large numbers of Muslims can also be found in Assam, Gujarat, Maharashtra, Tamil Nadu, and Kerala. Muslims constitute a majority of the population in only one state, Jammu and Kashmir, and in one union territory, Lakshadweep. The Muslims also speak different languages: While Urdu is popular among north Indian Muslims, other Muslim communities speak Bengali, Assamese, Gujarati, Tamil, and Malayalam depending upon their location. The Muslims are further divided along sectarian lines: Most Muslims belong to the Sunni sect, but Shia, Aga Khani Khoja, and Bohra sects can be found as well.[2]

Managing India's Ethnic Diversity

During the time of India's freedom struggle, the leaders of the Indian National Congress, including Mohandas Gandhi and Jawaharlal Nehru, argued that India's immense ethnic, religious, and linguistic diversity could only be effectively managed through the creation of a secular and democratic state. The Congress view of a secular and democratic India was challenged by Mohammad Ali Jinnah and his Muslim League. Fearing that Muslims would forever be an entrapped minority at the mercy of an overwhelming Hindu majority (Muslims were outnumbered four to one by the Hindus in undivided British India), Jinnah and the Muslim League argued that British India was made up of "two nations," Hindus and Muslims, without much interaction or common ground between them; therefore, British India should be partitioned to create a state for Hindus (India) and a state for Muslims (Pakistan). Jinnah further argued that only in an Islamic state of Pakistan—created by merging the Muslim-majority areas of British India—could Muslims find protection and fully develop themselves. The partition of British India in 1947 was accompanied by large-scale population movements and major incidents of communal violence.

After independence, the Indian political elites' most important challenge was to create an overarching Indian identity while also accepting and accommodating ethnic and regional identities. The architects of Indian democracy tried to achieve this dual objective through several means. The Indian constitution, which was promulgated on 26 January 1950, laid down a set of fundamental rights and specific provisions to safeguard the interests of minorities. The fundamental rights included freedom of religion, cultural and educational rights, the right not to be exploited, and the right to constitutional remedies. Article 14 guaranteed the equality of all persons before the law. Under Article 15, any discrimination between citizens on the grounds of religion, race, caste, sex, or place of birth was strictly prohibited. The constitution abolished the practice of "untouchability" with Article 17. Under Article 20, all minorities were given the right to preserve and promote their language, script, and culture. Under Article 25, all persons were entitled to freedom of conscience and to freely practice and propagate their religions. For reasons of social justice and to create socioeconomic opportunities, the constitution also advocated affirmative-action policies (through reservations or quotas) for the Scheduled Castes and Scheduled Tribes in college and university admissions as well as government employment (Article 335). The constitution also allotted seats in the Lok Sabha (the lower house of the national Parliament) and in the state legislative assemblies for Scheduled Castes and Scheduled Tribes in proportion to their numbers.[3]

The administrative reorganization of the Indian state that was carried out in the 1950s further strengthened ethnolinguistic and regional identities by accepting the demand for provinces based on broad ethnolinguistic criteria. Such demands had been voiced before independence but were never acted on by the British for fear of strengthening nationalist sentiments. In the traumatic initial postpartition years, the Congress government also was hesitant to endorse the idea of linguistic provinces out of fear that this could lead to the further balkanization of the country.[4] In 1953, however, the States Reorganization Commission was established, which eventually led to the States Reorganization Act of 1956. Under this act, fourteen states and five union territories were created. Subsequent reorganizations and the creation of additional states essentially followed the basic principle that major ethnolinguistic groups ought to have their separate states within the Indian union.

Even as Indian political elites accepted ethnic plurality and worked to promote and strengthen such diversity, they agreed that national integration and development required the creation of a secular and federal polity. Elite consensus on the need for a secular state had existed prior to independence. The debate after independence therefore focused on the specifics: what kind of secularism to promote and how to obtain the right balance between the preferences of the majority and the interests of the minorities. In this context, as constitutional provisions and practices indicate, Indian secularism does not mean the strict separation between church and state but rather the recognition and promotion of all religious communities by the state.[5] The idea of a federal polity also had historical roots and "was envisaged as a project to ensure reasonable national agreement across regions and communities to support and develop durable political order."[6] At the same time, Indian leaders were mindful of the dangers of ethnic secession and balkanization of the state. Hence, as Bhimrao Ramji Ambedkar, the chief architect of the constitution, told the Constituent Assembly, "though India was to be a federation, the federation was not the result of an agreement by the states to join in a federation, and that the federation not being the result of an agreement, no state has the right to secede from it."[7] Indian federation was therefore to be a "division for convenience of administration while the country continued to be one integrated whole."[8] The main benefit of India's federal design then is that it allows the state to accommodate ethnic plurality and encourages cultural distinctiveness without allowing any one ethnic group to dominate at the national or federal level. Cultural conflicts within each state seldom spill over into other states. The center can thus compartmentalize and more effectively manage center-state frictions and contain conflicts within states.[9]

Along with constitutional provisions, the political-party system that evolved in postindependence India further helped leaders to manage ethnic differences and conflict. During the freedom struggle, the main political organization was the Indian National Congress. The Congress party was a large democratic "umbrella" organization that included the groups, interests, and opinions of various regions. Broadly, it espoused a social-democratic ideology and populist welfare policies. As the vanguard of the nationalist movement, the Congress party naturally emerged as the dominant political party after independence. Although India adopted a multiparty system, the Congress party's hold over Indian politics for the first two decades after independence was almost total. After the mid-1960s, however, India gradually witnessed the growth of regional parties; some of which challenged the Congress party in state elections by tapping into ethnolinguistic, religious, and regional sentiments.

Under Indira Gandhi, the Congress party increasingly resorted to undemocratic, illegal, and draconian measures to retain its monopoly over political power at the center and in several states. This creeping authoritarianism—which criminalized the Indian polity, politicized the bureaucracy and security agencies, and rode roughshod over opponents of the Congress party—eventually resulted in a suspension of democracy in 1975 with the declaration of a state of emergency. Forced by popular pressure to withdraw the emergency and to hold national elections in 1977, the Congress party lost power for the first time against an opposition consisting of a coalition of smaller national and regional parties. Over the next three decades, the phenomenal rise of regional parties and leaders, the gradual weakening of the Congress party both politically and organizationally, the emergence of the right-wing Bharatiya Janata Party (BJP), and the formation of weak coalition governments at the center contributed to the outbreak and spread of ethnic conflict and violence in India.

India's choice of development model also contributed to the effective management of ethnic problems and conflicts in the first three decades after independence. The model was based "upon a system of indicative plans within a mixed economic structure in which both private capital and a state-owned public sector" played a major role.[10] The major objective of the model was to "promote rapid and balanced economic growth with equity and justice."[11] This commitment to social welfare gave the center a significant role in the socioeconomic development of ethnic communities and allowed it to regulate both politics and the economy in India. In practice, however, the development of different ethnic groups and regions was hardly balanced, leading to feelings of relative deprivation across communities and provinces.

Ethnic Conflicts

In spite of the best efforts of Indian leaders to create institutions, structures, and processes to deal effectively and fairly with ethnic political mobilization and demands, ethnic conflicts have occurred with regular frequency. It would be futile to search for causal uniformity across cases, however, since social phenomena like ethnic conflict exhibit complex causation; it is more useful to identify convergent causal conjunctures—how different causes combine in different ways to produce the same result.[12] When it comes to ethnic conflict in India, four sets of causal conditions have usually combined in different ways in different areas to produce conflict and violence.

First, the fear of assimilation or cultural dilution and unfulfilled national aspirations have often played key roles in ethnic political mobilizations and conflicts. Second, the process of modernization—by inducing large-scale migrations and by raising standards of literacy and aspirations—has not only forced ethnic groups to live closely together and to compete for rewards and resources, but has also sharpened their sociopolitical awareness and increased their capacity to mobilize for collective action. Such ethnopolitical mobilization tends to occur where there is a lack of civil society linkages that could foster mutual understanding, respect, and trust among ethnic groups and help defuse crises before they flare up into violent conflicts. Third, unequal development, poverty, exploitation, lack of opportunity, and threats to existing group privileges have often engendered strong feelings of relative deprivation among ethnic groups and sparked ethnic political mobilization and conflict. Finally, political factors such as endemic bad governance; the growth of antisecular forces; institutional decay and political chicanery; and vote-bank politics (maintaining a loyal bloc of voters through divisive policies) on the part of unscrupulous political parties and politicians have greatly contributed to the outbreak of ethnic conflict. In essence, four different types of ethnic conflicts occur in India.

Statehood agitations. The states reorganization of the 1950s did not put a stop to demands for the creation of new states. For example, in 1960, mainly due to the agitations of Marathi- and Gujarati-speaking populations of the state of Bombay, the Bombay Reorganization Act created the linguistic states of Maharashtra and Gujarat. Similarly, in 1966, the Hindi-speaking state of Haryana was created by dividing the Punjab. In the northeast, the Indian government tried to bring the Naga insurgency to a close by accepting the Nagas' demand for a separate state; hence, in 1962, three districts of Assam were detached to create the new state of Nagaland. In the early 1970s, three more new states— Meghalaya, Manipur, and Tripura—were created in the northeast. The demands for new states, however, did not stop there. In West Bengal, the Gorkhas of Darjeeling and the Rajbonshis of Cooch Behar have long agitated for the creation of a separate Gorkhaland and Kamtapur. In Assam, the Bodos have made a similar demand. The Telengana agitation in Andhra Pradesh, the movement to create Vidharbha in Maharashtra, and the demand for a separate state of Jammu are all cases with relatively long histories of political agitation. In recent years, under the National Democratic Alliance (NDA) government, three new states were created by breaking up existing states—Jharkhand by breaking up Bihar, Uttaranchal by breaking up Uttar Pradesh, and Chattisgarh by breaking up Madha Pradesh; further breakups look inevitable.

Why has there been a spurt in the demand for statehood by ethnic groups in India? Although states in postindependence India were reorganized on the basis of ethnolinguistic criteria, the policy failed to eradicate the problem of "entrapped ethnic groups"—peripheral ethnic groups that were politically and economically subordinate to the majority ethnolinguistic communities that wielded power in the states.[13] Many of these entrapped ethnic groups expected the States Reorganization Commission to consider their cases with sympathy. When that did not happen, they felt frustrated and aggrieved. In the years following the states reorganization, these ethnic groups came to resent their endemic poverty and underdeveloped status and became convinced that they were being deprived (deliberately or otherwise) by the dominant communities that controlled the state governments. Such perceptions often convinced them that the state government either had done very little to solve the socioeconomic ills confronting the group or had been responsible for creating and preserving their marginalized status. Their only option, it seemed to them, was to create their own state and to enter into a direct relationship with the Indian central government for assistance and guidance; for instance, Gorkha leaders in Darjeeling who demanded the creation of a separate "Gorkhaland" usually gave the example of Sikkim, which has one-third of Darjeeling's population but receives almost ten times more aid.[14]

Regional assertiveness. The reorganization of states on a linguistic basis reinforced regional identity which often led to demands for greater state or regional autonomy. The creation of linguistic states greatly expanded political participation and allowed people to access state and local governments more effectively; however, the process did too often reflect "the parochialism of language and region."[15] In many states outside the Hindi heartland of central India, parochial sentiments gave rise to "militant nativist movements" that demanded preferential policies for the "sons of the soil" (especially in the areas of education and employment) and aimed to rid the state of ethnic outsiders. Regional political parties found it convenient to stoke the fires of parochialism in order to capture power in the state; once in office, these parties had little option but to promote and protect the interests of the dominant community.

One of the most militant regional political organizations is the Shiv Sena in Maharashtra. Founded in 1966 by Bal Thackeray, the Shiv Sena's ideology is based on the concept of the *bhumiputra* ("son of the soil") and Hindutva ("Hindu-ness"). Taking advantage of the socioeconomic grievances and frustrations of the Hindu Maharashtrian community, the Shiv Sena rose to political prominence in Maharashtra under the banner of "Maharashtra for Maharashtrians" and by launching "verbal and physical attacks at South Indian immigrants and Muslims."[16] Such conflicts were not, however, confined to Maharashtra. In the Indian northeast, a number of states witnessed the steady growth of parochial sentiments and the formation of regional political parties that championed the cause of the sons of the soil. In Assam, the All Assam Students Union (AASU) and the United Liberation Front of Assam (ULFA) steadfastly promoted the interests of the ethnic Assamese and launched attacks against Bengalis, Biharis, and other outsiders. In Mizoram, too, violence broke out between the majority Mizos and members of minority tribes after the Mizoram government headed by the Mizo National Front (MNF) started adopting policies blatantly favouring the Mizo community.[17] In Tamil Nadu, the Dravida Munnetra Kazhagam (DMK) party emerged in the 1950s and 1960s "as the harbinger of Tamil ethnicity and nationhood."[18] The DMK clashed with the Indian government over the imposition of Hindi as the sole official language. By portraying the center's language policy as the cultural imperialism of the north, the DMK cultivated enough anti-Hindi agitation to force the Indian government to back down and allow major regional languages to coexist with Hindi and English as national languages.[19]

Secessionist conflicts. The most serious challenges to the national integration and political stability of India have come from secessionist ethnic conflicts, most notably in Assam, Punjab, and Kashmir. In the initial postindependence period, the Indian government had to deal with the Naga and Mizo insurgencies in the northeast, both of which maintained secessionist aspirations. The Dravidian movement in the Madras

Presidency (province) and in Tamil Nadu, headed by the Dravida Kazhagam (DK), also had a strong secessionist tone. The center also had to respond to demands for independence from Jammu and Kashmir, Hyderabad, and Junagadh (three of the 565 princely states that India had inherited from the British) and Goa (a Portuguese enclave on the western coast of India). The Naga and Mizo insurgencies were suppressed with a combination of force and political negotiation that led to the signing of ceasefire agreements and peace accords. The secessionist sentiments within the Dravidian movement also gradually faded after the DMK entered the electoral process and the center withdrew the policy of Hindi as the sole official language of India. The princely states of Hyderabad and Junagadh, which were located deep inside India, were annexed by force. Goa was also "liberated" by the Indian military in 1961 and politically incorporated within the Indian state as a union territory.

Jammu and Kashmir presented a different problem as the state was contiguous to both India and Pakistan and claimed by both states; while Pakistan's claim was based on religion (a majority of the population of Jammu and Kashmir is Muslim), India's claim was based on popular political sentiments (the state had a popular democratic and secular political movement led by Sheikh Mohammad Abdullah and the National Conference (NC) party which favored accession to India over Pakistan).[20] With the Hindu ruler of Kashmir undecided, the issue was ultimately resolved by the first Indo-Pakistan war in 1947. As a result of the war, Kashmir was bifurcated with about one-third of its original territory going to Pakistan and the remaining two-thirds—including the famous Vale or Valley—remaining with India. India's claim over Kashmir was further legitimized when the ruler of Kashmir (Maharaja Hari Singh), facing an invading force from Pakistan, formally acceded to India, a move that had the blessings of Sheikh Abdullah and the National Conference party. In return, Indian prime minister Jawaharlal Nehru promised that once Pakistani troops had been withdrawn from Kashmir and normalcy had returned to the entire state, India would hold a plebiscite under the supervision of the United Nations to ascertain the views of the people of Kashmir on the question of accession.[21]

Under the treaty of accession signed by Maharaja Hari Singh in 1947, India was responsible for defense, foreign affairs, and communication in Kashmir. In other matters, Kashmir was autonomous. The treaty of accession was incorporated in the Indian constitution (which came into force on 26 January 1950) under Article 370, which bestowed a "special status" on Kashmir. Over the next thirty years, Kashmir's special status was systematically whittled away. Although this created substantial resentment among Kashmiri Muslims, such sentiments did not lead to a major insurgency for two reasons. First, although it encouraged and condoned the political machinations in Kashmir, New Delhi did not directly interfere with the state's democratic process—elections were held regularly and voting fraud was generally absent. Second, because of Kashmir's economic backwardness and their own peripheral position, political consciousness among Kashmiri Muslims was quite low and, consequently, people often could not see through the shenanigans of local and national politicians and parties.

By the late 1980s, growing public frustration and anger had led to a full-blown secessionist insurgency against the Indian state. As a result of demographic changes and the spread of modernization and communications, a younger, more educated, and more politically conscious generation had emerged in the Valley. Economic development and employment opportunities had not expanded commensurately, however, leading to a rise in the number of the educated unemployed.[22] The lack of adequate economic development and employment opportunities—in contrast to the large amounts of development aid that the central government had given to the state over the past three decades—raised people's suspicions of corruption within the state government and the National Conference party.

After the death of Sheikh Abdullah in 1982, there was a power struggle within the National Conference party between his son, Farooq Abdullah, and his son-in-law, G.M. Shah. The central government under Prime Minister Indira Gandhi wanted to take advantage of this factional infighting to further promote the interests of the Indian National Congress–Indira (Congress [I]) party in Kashmir. This led the central government to do what it had not done before—directly intervene to manipulate the democratic political process in Kashmir. To this end, the center encouraged the governor of Kashmir, Shri Jag Mohan, to engineer a split within the NC. This was achieved in May 1984 when an NC faction decided to expel Farook Abdullah and to install his sister, Khalida Shah (the wife of G.M. Shah) as the party president. On July 2, twelve NC Members of the Legislative Assembly (MLA) along with an independent member broke with Farooq Abdullah and gave their support to G.M. Shah; they were joined by 26 MLAs belonging to the Congress (I) party. This gave the rebels a slender majority in the Legislative Assembly. Governor Jag Mohan lost no time in dismissing Farooq Abdullah and inviting G.M. Shah to form a new government. Anticipating trouble from this blatant manipulation of the state's democratic institutions and process, Jag Mohan ordered the deployment of security forces in the Valley. Nonetheless, violent clashes throughout Kashmir continued to rise as people viewed the G.M. Shah government as a "puppet of New Delhi ruling through the governor."[23] The Congress (I) MLAs finally withdrew their support from the G.M. Shah government on 6 March 1986, using the deteriorating security situation in the state as their excuse. G.M. Shah resigned the next day and the state was put under the governor's rule. Six months later, Kashmir was placed under direct rule by the center.

In November 1986, the suspension of the Kashmir Legislative Assembly was lifted and direct rule by the center brought to an end after a rapprochement between Farooq Abdullah's NC and the Congress (I) state unit in Kashmir led by Mufti Mohammed Sayeed. As part of the deal—which had the blessings of the Congress (I) chief and prime minister, Rajiv Gandhi—Farooq Abdullah was brought back as the head of a NC–Congress (I) coalition government in Kashmir. Fresh state elections were scheduled for March 1987. In this election, considered by most critics to be thoroughly rigged by the NC–Congress (I) combine, the NC won 38 seats (mostly in the Valley), the Congress (I) won 24 seats (mostly in the Jammu area), and 2 seats went to the Hindu-nationalist Bharatiya Janata Party (BJP). On 27 March 1987, Farooq Abdullah was sworn in as chief minister of a NC–Congress (I) coalition government. Ominously, however, the coalition government was not supported by all the NC MLAs.[24] This blatant electoral abuse that was encouraged by the Congress party and Farooq Abdullah's "betrayal" led to widespread resentment among Kashmiri Muslims toward the central government as well as the NC and its key leaders. The Kashmiri insurgency began with student demonstrations in 1987 after angry and frustrated students turned to violence against the Indian state and the Kashmir government. Faced with a challenge to its authority, New Delhi, on the advice of the governor of Kashmir and the state government, resorted to harsh measures to crush the agitation by force. Instead of cooling down, over the next two years or so, the upward spiral of violence in Kashmir led to the almost total alienation of the local population from the Indian state and the onset of a full-blown secessionist insurgency.

Although the crisis in Kashmir dominated the headlines from the mid-1980s onwards, two other secessionist ethnic conflicts had emerged in the early 1980s. The first of these was in the far-northeastern state of Assam, where the steady in-migration of ethnic "outsiders" in the 1950s, 1960s, and more prominently in the 1970s eventually led to a backlash from the *bhumiputras*.[25] Historically, the economic backwardness of the Assamese along with the absence of an indigenous educated middle class had led to the migration of outsiders (mostly Bengalis) into Assam to perform administrative tasks and to run the plantation industries. Over the years, a relationship where outsiders dominated the subordinate sons of the soil developed: Bengalis controlled important sectors of Assam's economy and bureaucracy, while the local Assamese worked on farms and plantations. The pressure on land in Assam, therefore, had always been high. After India became independent, Assam's economic situation did not greatly improve although some development did take place with the growth of the oil industry.

The economic situation took a turn for the worse in the 1970s when Bengali-speaking Muslims from the newly created country of Bangladesh started pouring (illegally) into Assam, initially to flee the secessionist war of 1971 but later to escape the severe economic conditions in Bangladesh. These new Bengali immigrants were mostly poor farmers, which brought them into direct competition with the local Assamese and further increased the pressure on land. The influx also occurred at a time when the issue of Bengali dominance of the state bureaucracy was at the center of Assamese grievances against the Indian government, as few educated Assamese youth obtained jobs in the local bureaucracy.[26] Furthermore, the Bengali influx roused Assamese fears of cultural erosion and the serious political and economic consequences that would accompany it.[27] The Assamese also suspected that the Congress (I) party (in power until 1978)—driven by the exigencies of electoral competition and vote-bank politics—was deliberately turning a blind eye to the problem of illegal immigration from Bangladesh. Faced with these pressures, the Assamese resorted to political agitation.

The AASU and the ULFA led the agitation to prevent the further influx of Bengali Muslim immigrants from Bangladesh; to repatriate those non-Assamese settlers who had entered the state illegally; and to bring about rapid socioeconomic development in order to create more opportunities for educated Assamese youth. The AASU and the ULFA therefore called on the state and central governments to implement tighter border controls (including border fencing) to stop the influx of illegal immigrants and to repatriate those who had already settled. They also demanded a raise in the state's oil royalty so that more revenue could then be used for development purposes. Finally, the groups demanded the development of more petrochemicals and other industries so that Assam's annual crude oil production could be refined within the state while providing employment to Assamese youth.[28] Although the AASU and the ULFA both directed violence against the Indian state and ethnic "outsiders" in Assam, their ultimate political objectives differed. The AASU saw its ultimate political objective as access to political power in Assam within the framework of the Indian state (achieved with the formation and election victory of the Assam People's Council [AGP] in 1985). They could then use their power to redress the grievances of the Assamese people. The ULFA, on the other hand, believed that outright secession from the Indian union and the creation of an independent country to be called Assam was the only way that the problems faced by the Assamese could be successfully redressed.[29]

The 1980s also witnessed the outbreak of a secessionist Sikh insurgency in Punjab. The Sikhs in India are a small ethnoreligious group that has achieved tremendous economic success because of the agricultural revolution that occurred in Punjab (the Sikhs' ethnic homeland) in the late sixties and seventies. The Green Revolution, which brought immense prosperity to Punjab, also produced certain adverse side effects that led to the political mobilization of the Sikhs. First, it "increased landlessness among segments of the Sikh peasantry as small tracts of

land were consolidated to promote modern, large-scale, mechanized agriculture."[30] Those who were dispossessed of their land flocked to urban
centers where, lacking any special skills, they often performed menial
jobs. Thus, the benefits of Punjab's growing prosperity mostly went to
big farmers and gave rise to social tensions between the rich and poor.[3]
Second, the economic prosperity of Punjab attracted agricultural laborers and other economic migrants from nearby states, further worsening
the plight of the small Sikh farmers who were dispossessed of land and
had to compete with these "outsiders" for menial jobs in urban centers.
Third, the Green Revolution also created, by the early eighties, high
unemployment among the educated Sikh youth. Through Punjab's development, the educational levels of the Sikh youth rose considerably
and they (like the Jat Sikhs) became reluctant to perform agricultural
tasks, instead seeking employment in the industrial and service sectors.
But while the Green Revolution had ushered in the era of mechanized
agriculture, the reluctance of the Indian government to set up heavy
industries because of Punjab's status as a high-risk border state with
Pakistan kept nonagricultural employment opportunities limited.[32] Feelings of discrimination on the part of the educated and unemployed Sikh
youth further intensified when it became known that the overall proportion of Sikhs in the armed forces—their traditional avenue of employment—had declined.[33]

The economic prosperity of Punjab also raised fears of "cultural dilution" in the minds of Sikh religious elites. Since Sikhism is an offshoot
of Hinduism, a major concern of the Sikh religious leadership has been
the preservation of the Sikhs' unique sociocultural and religious identity and the development of communal boundaries with the Hindu community.[34] These two tasks became increasingly difficult in the 1970s.
Unwilling to work in the agricultural sector, many literate and wealthy
Sikhs emigrated from Punjab. At the same time, the economic prosperity of Punjab attracted a vast number of lower-caste agricultural laborers from other states. Furthermore, the Sikh religious leadership feared
that the influence of modernization and development would lead younger
Sikhs to abandon their distinctive religious and cultural practices.[35]
Militant Sikh religious leaders such as Jarnail Singh Bhindranwale advocated the creation of an independent Sikh state—Khalistan—to be
achieved through a secessionist insurgency. Once created, a "pure" Sikh
state would help to safeguard Sikhism by preventing Sikhs (especially
the affluent younger generation) from discarding the symbols of their
faith. Bhindranwale also advocated a terrorist campaign in Punjab with
the intention "to trigger an exodus of Hindus from the province. If such
violence would prompt reprisals against Sikhs outside the Punjab, this
in turn would only lead to Sikh immigration into the Punjab from other
parts of India. By this process, Punjab would become a Sikh majority
state."[36] Some of these grievances and demands could be presented po-

litically in a nonsectarian way so that all the major ethnoreligious groups in the state (such as Punjabis, Sikhs, and Hindus) could support them. But the main Sikh political party, the Akali Dal, "set these issues in the context of various demands for the protection of Sikh religious interests that excluded Hindus and to which the central government, affirming its commitment to secularism, would not yield."[37] The Akali Dal chose to play the ethnoreligious card for the exigencies of electoral politics— to ensure that most of the Sikh votes would go to the Akali Dal, ensuring electoral success and access to political power in the state.[38] But the center's refusal to accede to these demands convinced the militants that the Sikh religion could only be protected in a theocratic Sikh state.[39]

Communal violence. Although India is a constitutional secular democracy, violent conflicts between majority Hindus and minority Muslims have flared on a regular basis. Part of the problem has been the way secularism has been defined and the level of commitment that Indian leaders have had toward religion. As noted earlier, secularism in the Indian constitution was not understood to mean a wall of separation between church and state but rather the state's tolerance, promotion, and equal treatment of all religions. But the early stewards of Indian democracy, notably India's first prime minister Jawaharlal Nehru, for ideological reasons and also perhaps with the trauma of partition and its communal riots fresh in mind, preferred "to deny religiosity in any arena of Indian public life."[40] This stance greatly upset the majority Hindu community and played into the hands of fundamentalist Hindu political parties such as the Jana Sangh, the predecessor of the BJP. Referring to issues such as the assignment of "special status" to Kashmir, the Jana Sangh argued that the Congress government was pandering to the Muslims and ignoring the legitimate interests and grievances of the Hindus.

The trauma of the partition and the communal bloodbath that accompanied it, along with the massive population migration and human hardship that it generated, also contributed in large measure to feelings of mistrust and hatred between members of the Hindu and Muslim communities. Religious fundamentalists, Indian nationalists, and so-called secularists all tried to take advantage of this situation. Under pressure from Muslim religious elites, the Nehru administration allowed Muslim personal law to be retained and applied in matters of marriage, divorce, and inheritance. At the same time, other Indians were brought under a uniform civil code. Hindu fundamentalists and nationalists immediately saw this as evidence of Congress's "pseudosecularism" and pandering to minorities at the expense of the majority community. There was some truth to these accusations, not so much during Nehru's time but more so under Indira Gandhi and her son Rajiv. By the time Indira Gandhi took over the leadership of the Congress party, the era of complete Congress dominance of Indian politics had started to fade and the party began to face serious electoral competition from the Hindu nationalists and fundamentalists, regionalists, communists, and a group of mainly ex-Congressmen who professed a socialist and welfarist ideology. To ensure Congress's survival and electoral success, Indira Gandhi made overtures to both Muslims and Hindus. For instance, to win state-assembly elections in Kerala, the Congress made electoral alliances with a number of political parties including the blatantly communal Indian Union Muslim League (IUML). In Punjab, however, Indira Gandhi refused to negotiate with any of the Sikh parties or groups for fear of upsetting the Hindu voters whom her party was trying to woo.

Rajiv Gandhi continued this tradition of making "concessions" to minority communities in order to win support and votes. This was dramatically displayed during the Shah Bano affair in 1985. Shah Bano, a 73-year-old Muslim woman, was divorced by her husband after forty-three years of marriage. Under Muslim personal law, her husband was not required to pay any alimony to her. When Shah Bano challenged this in the Supreme Court, the court ruled in her favor and ordered her husband to pay a monthly maintenance allowance. Muslim clerics and fundamentalists denounced the judgement and suggested that Islam was under attack in India. Coming under pressure from Muslim religious groups and his own party, which feared a loss of Muslim votes in future elections, Prime Minister Rajiv Gandhi, though initially in favor of the Supreme Court judgement, threw his support behind the Muslim Women (Protection of Rights on Divorce) Bill that scuttled the Supreme Court's decision. To Hindu nationalists, this act was a glaring appeasement of minorities by the Congress (I) for political purposes which once again exposed the party's pseudosecular credentials.

Throughout the 1980s, as Muslim-fundamentalist voices grew louder and communal tensions simmered, Hindu-nationalist parties such as the BJP gained popularity especially in the Hindi-speaking states of central, northern, and western India.[41] The ideology that the Hindu political parties promoted was known as Hindutva—which may be broadly translated as "Hindu-ness" or even "Indian-ness." Behind the notion of Hindutva is a particular vision of the Hindu or Indian "nation," and it is a matter of debate whether Muslims and other religious minorities have a place within it. But to Hindu organizations such as the Rashtriya Swayamsevak Sangh (RSS), the Vishwa Hindu Parishad (VHP), and the BJP, Hindutva "embodies the notion that all Indians—including Muslims—are part of a Hindu nation and that Ram and the gods and heroes of Hindu mythology are part of their patrimony."[42]

As the 1990s unfolded, Indian national politics seemed to be entering an era of turmoil and weak central governments. The BJP and its allies chose to play the religion card as a way of capturing political power by tapping into the "Hindu vote." On 6 December 1992, in violation of Supreme Court orders and government warnings, cadres belonging to the RSS, the VHP, the Shiv Sena, and the Bajrang Dal descended

on a sixteenth-century mosque (the Babri Masjid) in the north-Indian
city of Ayodhya, Uttar Pradesh, and completely destroyed the structure.
The Babri Mosque had been a source of friction between Hindus and
Muslims for a very long time. The BJP and its allies claimed that the
mosque had been constructed by the Mughal Emperor Babar after the
destruction of a Hindu temple that had venerated the birthplace of Lord
Ram, a revered icon in Hindu mythology. Irrespective of the merits or
demerits of the case made by the BJP and its allies, the audacious destruction of the mosque and the complete failure of the Indian government to prevent it sparked Hindu-Muslim rioting across the country
leaving several thousand dead or injured. To avenge the destruction of
the Babri Mosque, Muslim criminal gangs in Mumbai with help from
allies in foreign states set off a series of bomb blasts in India's major
commercial city in January 1993. In retaliation, Hindu mobs, organized
by the ruling Shiv Sena and other Hindu-nationalist parties and report-
edly receiving support from segments of the state-security forces, carried out a nine-day massacre of Muslims. Even though Indian society
reeled from the shock and destruction of these terrible communal conflicts, the political strategy paid off. After winning just two seats in the
1984 national elections, the BJP emerged as the single largest party in
the 1996 balloting, a feat that the party repeated in 1998 and 1999.
Although the coalition governments it headed in 1996 and 1998 did
not last for more than 13 days and one year respectively, the coalition
government that the BJP led in 1999 survived a full term.

As the new millennium dawned, trust between Hindus and Muslims
seemed to have hit rock bottom and communal tensions once again
showed signs of intensifying. The VHP periodically threatened to begin
the construction of a Hindu temple on the site of the demolished Babri
mosque and set 15 March 2002 as the deadline to bring thousands of
stone pillars to the site. For this purpose, hundreds of workers were
being brought in by train to Ayodhya from faraway places such as
Gujarat, where a BJP government led by Narendra Modi was in power.
On 27 February 2002, several compartments of a train (the Sabarmati
Express) that contained Hindu workers and pilgrims who were returning
to Gujarat from Ayodhya caught fire just as it pulled out of Godhra
station, killing 58 workers and pilgrims. Rumours quickly spread that
the train had been attacked by Muslim mobs (Godhra station was located in a predominantly Muslim area of the town) although no conclu-
sive evidence of how the fire started or whether it was a planned attack
has so far emerged. The Godhra incident sparked some of the worst anti-
Muslim violence in Indian history. The BJP-led Gujarat state government headed by Chief Minister Narendra Modi and the state's police
and security forces were thoroughly implicated in the campaign of terror and death.[43] On 7 March 2006—even before the fallout from the
Gujarat riots and the subsequent investigations had settled—twin bomb

attacks were carried out by terrorists in the Hindu holy city of Varanasi (Benares), Uttar Pradesh. The first bomb exploded in the complex of the Sankat Mochan temple, killing 21 people; the second blast occurred in Varanasi Cantonment railway station, killing 2 more people. More than 100 people were injured in the blasts.[44] Although the incidents were clearly designed to set off another Hindu-Muslim riot, such a calamity was averted when leaders of both communities publicly condemned the blasts and appealed to their respective members not to fall into the trap set by the terrorists.

How can one account for the outbreak of violence in communal relations? For some critics, such as Paul Brass, Hindu and Muslim identities in the Indian subcontinent are too distinct to be properly reconciled; hence, the possibility of communal violence is ever present. The role of the state is of critical importance in this equation—the state can instigate or prevent the outbreak of communal violence if it so wishes.[45] From this point of view then, the communal riots in Mumbai in 1993 and Gujarat in 2002 had at least the tacit blessings of the main political parties which formed the state governments (Shiv Sena in Maharashtra and the BJP in Gujarat).

Other critics, such as Ashutosh Varshney, emphasize the role of civil society in the outbreak or absence of communal riots. Arguing that most communal riots tend to be localized, Varshney suggests that if civic engagement (both associational and in everyday forms) between the Hindu and Muslim communities in a particular area or town is strong, such areas or towns are more likely to prevent the outbreak of communal conflicts; and if somehow conflict does start, it will prove relatively easy to stop. Conversely, if civic engagement between the two communities is either absent or weak, the propensity for communal violence will be high. Varshney also disagrees with Brass that the state can prevent a communal riot if it so chooses. Varshney argues insteadthat the effectiveness of the state's response is at least partly a function of the degree of civic engagement between members of the two communities. Using this framework, Varshney explains persuasively why, during the 2002 Gujarat riots, towns such as Ahmedabad and Vadodara witnessed shocking violence while nearby Surat saw very little.[46] Philippa Williams has taken Varshney's ideas further by adding human agency to the importance of civic engagement. In trying to explain the "non-riot" in Varanasi in 2006, Williams shows that even though the civic engagement between Hindus and Muslims in Varanasi is particularly strong, much of the credit for diffusing the postblast tensions must be given to the mohant (head priest) of the Shankat Mochan temple, Veer Bhadra Mishra, and to the mufti (Islamic scholar) of Varanasi, Maulana Abdul Batin.[47]

A third view, put forward by Steven I. Wilkinson, posits that there exists a strong correlation between communal riots and exigency of electoral politics. Wilkinson argues that if a party in power depends on the Muslim vote to win elections, then it is unlikely that riots will take place. This suggests that riots are often deliberately instigated by parties in power to polarize the electorate and scare voters into voting as part of a community vote bank. Indeed, Wilkinson's analysis suggests that the BJP in Gujarat had much to gain from the communal riots in the state elections that took place shortly thereafter; the riots ensured the complete polarization of Hindus and Muslims, with the Hindu vote going almost entirely to the BJP thereby ensuring its victory in the polls.[48]

A fourth explanation for Hindu-Muslim conflicts focuses more on the socioeconomic factors that have set these two communities on different trajectories of development and reinforced their stereotypical perceptions of each other. Some critics have argued that the *ulama* (in effect, the Muslim clergy) and the mainstream political parties have used Muslims, for different reasons, as a vote bank and therefore benefit from the low socioeconomic status of the Muslim community. The *ulama* have thus raised the banner of "Islam in danger" to thwart efforts to modernize the community; political parties went along with this so long as the Muslim religious elite could deliver the Muslim vote.[49] But in many parts of India, low social status combined with a lack of formal education and inadequate employment opportunities leads to a disproportionately high number of Muslims being involved in the criminal sector. The frustration and anger that this generates often expresses itself as collective violence against the state and the majority community, which is perceived to be the major beneficiary of development. Muslims' low socioeconomic status and links to the criminal underworld, however, reinforce their stereotypical image in the minds of the Hindus—that Muslims as a community are socially inferior, nonprogressive, and criminally violent. In a recent report, the Rajinder Sachar Committee endorsed the view that Muslims in India are a severely deprived community; the Sachar report pointed out that although Muslims constitute around 11 percent of the total population, their social, economic, and educational status puts them on a par with Scheduled Castes, Scheduled Tribes, and Other Backward Classes. The report went on to recommend education and government employment quotas for Muslims.[50]

Coping with Ethnic Conflict

To deal with the outbreak of various ethnic conflicts, New Delhi has tended to rely on force and repression. In June 1984, Prime Minister Indira Gandhi ordered the Indian army to enter the Golden Temple in Amritsar, Punjab, to flush out militant Sikh leaders (most notably Sant Jarnail Singh Bhindranwale) who had taken up shelter there. Known as Operation Blue Star, the Indian army's incursion into the Golden Temple—including the massacre of Sikh leaders holed up there and the infliction of severe damage to a key Sikh religious shrine—alienated most Sikhs from the Indian government. Seeking revenge, two Sikh body-guards assassinated Prime Minister Gandhi in October 1984. In May 1988, as part of Operation Black Thunder, Indian paramilitary forces again laid siege to the Golden Temple to flush out militants who had moved back in to the complex and were using it "as a sanctuary and as a nerve center for planning and coordination."[51] With the installation of a new Congress government in Punjab after the 1992 state elections, the responsibility for counterinsurgency operations fell on the state police force. Between 1992 and 1995, the Punjab police carried out harsh coun-terinsurgency operations. As a result, Sikh militancy in the state was considerably weakened and normalcy gradually returned.

This "success" in Punjab prompted the Indian government to go forward with a similar approach in Kashmir. Confronted with a violent separatist insurgency by Kashmiri Muslims in 1989, New Delhi autho-rized the deployment of forces from the Central Police Organizations (CPOs) and the Indian army in the Valley. Together with the Jammu and Kashmir Police (JKP), the CPOs and the army were responsible for carry-ing out counterinsurgency operations that had two main objectives: 1) the "direct liquidation of the insurgents and their support base *within* Kashmir and [2)] the elimination of support of all kinds, but especially of the influx of armed insurgents, from sources *outside* the state."[52] The first objective led to "the creation and maintenance of *secure zones,* the mounting of *combing* (cordon and search) *operations,* and the adminis-tration of both *judicial and extrajudicial punishments.*"[53] The second objective required border-sealing and counterinfiltration operations.[54] The Indian security forces also raised, trained, and armed a small anti-insurgency force composed of former insurgents.

In the far-northeast as well, the Indian government responded to eth-nic insurgencies mainly through force. For instance, in November 1990, the Indian army launched a massive counterinsurgency strike called Operation Bajrang against the ULFA. This was followed in 1991 with Operation Rhino. Similar operations were mounted against the Bodo, Naga, Tripuri, Gorkha, Mizo, and Manipuri insurgents. At best, the op-erations in Kashmir and the Indian northeast have temporarily weak-ened the insurgents and allowed the government to keep violence within an acceptable level.[55]

In order to strengthen the capacity of the Indian military and security forces and the states' politico-administrative-judicial machinery to deal with the rise in ethnic and religious violence, the Indian government also introduced several pieces of legislation which were termed "draco-nian" by human rights groups and lawyers. The most famous of these was the Terrorist and Disruptive Activities (Prevention) Act or TADA, which was in force between 1985 and 1995. In 2002, the Indian govern-ment led by the National Democratic Alliance (NDA)—a coalition of right-wing parties including the BJP—introduced the Prevention of Terrorist Activities Act or POTA. The POTA was subsequently repealed by the Congress-led United Progressive Alliance (UPA) government in 2004. In addition to antiterrorist legislation, the Indian government also sanctioned the modernization of the police forces, especially in insurgency-affected parts of the country. This involved the creation of special units within the police forces, advanced training in counterinsurgency operations, and upgrades of weapons and equipment.

A third strategy adopted by the Indian government involved "peace accords" (such as the Punjab Accord and the Assam Accord) that contained specific provisions for resolving the insurgencies and rehabilitating the insurgents. In some cases, the accords contained provisions for the protection of local ethnic identities and ethnic minorities. In other cases, the accords devolved certain political and economic powers, such as the creation of local councils and the levying of local taxes and fees, to local areas. The myriad political accords, however, mostly failed (in part because they were seldom implemented fully or properly) to resolve the root causes that have alienated large areas of the country from the Indian state and strengthened separatist sentiments.[56]

The outbreak of ethnoreligious conflicts and the way they have been handled has raised serious questions regarding India's claim to be a secular democratic country. As I have shown, so-called secular parties in India have always paid lip service to secularism but behaved differently, thereby politicizing ethnoreligious identities and sparking communal violence. The net beneficiaries of this have been the fundamentalists and militants within the various communities who profit from a sharp deterioration in communal relations. The rampant politicization of governmental institutions—a trend that became prominent in the 1970s—has further weakened the capacity of these institutions to deal effectively and fairly with ethnic political mobilization, thereby causing widespread alienation of large segments of the population. This is particularly applicable in the case of the national and state criminal-justice systems' ability to deliver justice to victims of ethnic and communal violence and to arrest and punish those who are guilty of committing mass murder and crimes against humanity. Furthermore, harsh counterinsurgency operations and the indiscriminate use of TADA and POTA have resulted in allegations by leading NGOs and international human rights bodies of severe human rights abuses by security forces and state agencies. All of these developments have given Indian democracy a bad name.

Does this mean that democracy is failing in India? The answer is no, not yet. In spite of its imperfections and problems, India is still a firmly established constitutional democracy where people and groups can go about their business without much interference from the state. Over the years, the state has also built up a relatively decent track record of accepting ethnic diversity and broadening political participation. The growth of regionalism and the era of weak coalition governments at the center may also suggest the advent of "genuine federalism" in India. In terms of national and human development, too, the past sixty years have seen India taking major strides forward, gradually providing more opportunities for individuals and groups and slowly raising the general level of well-being for many. India's global standing has also never been higher than it is today. Hence, as John Keay notes, in spite of various stresses and strains, the democratic integrity of the Indian republic cannot be doubted.[57]

NOTES

1. Robert L. Hardgrave, Jr., "India: The Dilemmas of Diversity," *Journal of Democracy* 4 (October 1993): 54–68.

2. Omar Khalidi, *Indian Muslims since Independence* (New Delhi: Vikas Publishing, 1995).

3. Hardgrave, "India: The Dilemmas of Diversity."

4. Y.D. Phadke, *Politics and Language* (Bombay: Himalaya Publishing House, 1974); Paul Brass, *The Politics of India Since Independence* (Cambridge: Cambridge University Press, 1994).

5. Hardgrave, "India: The Dilemmas of Diversity."

6. Jyotirindra Dasgupta, "India's Federal Design and Multicultural National Construction," in Atul Kohli, ed., *The Success of India's Democracy* (Cambridge: Cambridge University Press, 2001), 54.

7. Dasgupta, "India's Federal Design and Multicultural National Construction," 56.

8. Dasgupta, "India's Federal Design and Multicultural National Construction," 56.

9. Hardgrave, "India: Dilemmas of Diversity."

10. Bob Currie, "Governance, Democracy and Economic Adjustment in India: Conceptual and Empirical Problems," *Third World Quarterly* 17 (December 1996): 793.

11. Currie, "Governance, Democracy and Economic Adjustment in India," 793.

12. Charles C. Ragin, *The Comparative Method: Moving Beyond Qualitative and Quantitative Strategies* (Berkeley: University of California Press, 1987), 133–49.

13. Robert L. Hardgrave, Jr., and Stanley A. Kochanek, *India: Government and Politics in a Developing Nation,* 4th edition (New York: Harcourt Brace Jovanovich, 1990), 123–44.

14. Rajat Ganguly, "Poverty, Malgovernance, and Ethnopolitical Mobilization: Gorkha Nationalism and the Gorkhaland Agitation in India," *Nationalism & Ethnic Politics* 11 (Winter 2005): 467–502.

15. Hardgrave, "India: Dilemmas of Diversity," 59.

16. Hardgrave, "India: Dilemmas of Diversity," 59.

17. Hemendra S. Bartwal, "Fear of Militants, Mizo Reprisal Keep Reangs Away From Mizoram," *Hindustan Times* (New Delhi), 27 May 1998.

18. Urmila Phadnis and Rajat Ganguly, *Ethnicity and Nation-building in South Asia*, Revised Edition (New Delhi:: Sage Publications, 2001), 223.

19. Phadnis and Ganguly, *Ethnicity and Nation-building in South Asia*, 218–232.

20. Josef Korbel, *Danger in Kashmir* (Princeton, N.J.: Princeton University Press, 1966), 18.

21. Michael Brecher, *The Struggle for Kashmir* (New York: Oxford University Press, 1953); Korbel, *Danger in Kashmir*; Alastair Lamb, *The Kashmir Problem: A Historical Survey* (New York: Frederick A. Praeger, 1966).

22. Sumit Ganguly, "Ethno-religious Conflict in South Asia," *Survival* 35 (Summer 1993), 92.

23. Alastair Lamb, *Kashmir: A Disputed Legacy 1846–1990* (Karachi: Oxford University Press, 1993), 330.

24. Lamb, *Kashmir,* 331.

25. Rehman Sobhan, "Regional Disparities and the National Question: An Asian Perspective," *Journal of Contemporary Asia* 13 (January 1983): 91–108.

26. Sandy Gordon, "Resources and Instability in South Asia," *Survival* 35 (Summer 1993): 73.

27. Ganguly, "Ethno-religious Conflict in South Asia," 98; Myron Weiner, *Sons of the Soil: Migration and Ethnic Conflict in India* (Princeton: Princeton University Press, 1978).

28. Subir Bhaumik and James Clad, "Lawless Localism," *Far Eastern Economic Review* (Hong Kong), 8 November 1990, 34.

29. Sushanta Talukdar, "ULFA Issues Fresh Threat," *The Hindu* (New Delhi), 19 January 2007.

30. Ganguly, "Ethno-religious Conflict in South Asia," 93.

31. Pravin J. Patel, "Violent Protest in India: The Punjab Movement," *Journal of International Affairs* 40 (Winter–Spring 1987), 279.

32. Gordon, "Resources and Instability in South Asia," 69–75.

33. Rajiv A. Kapur, "'Khalistan': India's Punjab Problem," *Third World Quarterly* 9 (October 1987): 1214.

34. Patel, "Violent Protest in India"; Kapur, "'Khalistan.'"

35. Ganguly, "Ethno-religious Conflict in South Asia," 93; Patel, "Violent Protest in India," 279.

36. Kapur, "'Khalistan,'" 1216.

37. Hardgrave, "India: The Dilemmas of Diversity," 54–68.

38. Patel, "Violent Protest in India," 278.

39. Hardgrave, "India: The Dilemmas of Diversity," 54–68.

40. Ganguly, "Ethno-religious Conflict in South Asia," 102.

41. For a detailed account of Hindu nationalism and the rise of the BJP, see Christophe Jaffrelot, *The Hindu Nationalist Movement in India* (New York: Columbia University Press, 1996).

42. Hardgrave, "India: The Dilemmas of Diversity," 54–68.

43. See the Report of the National Human Rights Commission of India on the Gujarat riots, 31 May 2002. Available at *http://nhrc.nic.in/guj_finalorder.htm*.

44. "Indian Temple City Hit by Blasts," *BBC News* (Online), 7 March 2006. Available at *http://news.bbc.co.uk/1/hi/world/south_asia/4782618.stm*.

45. Paul Brass, *Theft of an Idol: Text and Context in the Representation of Collective Violence* (Princeton: Princeton University Press, 1997), and Paul Brass, *The Production of Hindu-Muslim Violence in Contemporary India* (New Delhi: Oxford University Press, 2003).

46. Ashutosh Varshney, *Ethnic Conflict and Civil Life: Hindus and Muslims in India* (New Haven: Yale University Press, 2002).

47. Philippa Williams, "Hindu-Muslim Brotherhood: Exploring the Dynamics of Communal Relations in Varanasi, North India," *Journal of South Asian Development* 2 (October 2007).

48. Steven Wilkinson, *Votes and Violence: Electoral Competition and Ethnic Riots in India* (Cambridge: Cambridge University Press, 2006).

49. Mushirul Hasan, "Indian Muslims since Independence: In Search of Integration and Identity" *Third World Quarterly* 10 (April 1988): 818–42.

50. "Sachar Recommends Quota for Muslims," *Times of India* (Online), 30 November 2006.

51. Maya Chadda, *Ethnicity, Security and Separatism in India* (New York: Columbia University Press, 1997), 139.

52. Robert G. Wirsing, *India, Pakistan, and the Kashmir Dispute: On Regional Conflict and its Resolution* (New York: St. Martin's, 1994): 147.

53. Wirsing, *India, Pakistan, and the Kashmir Dispute*, 154.

54. Wirsing, *India, Pakistan, and the Kashmir Dispute*, 147–54.

55. Kanti Bajpai, "Diversity, Democracy, and Devolution in India," in Michael E. Brown and Sumit Ganguly, eds., *Government Policies and Ethnic Relations in Asia and the Pacific* (Cambridge: MIT Press, 1997): 75–76.

56. P.S. Datta, *Ethnic Peace Accords in India* (New Delhi: Vikas, 1995); Bajpai, "Diversity, Democracy, and Devolution in India," 76.

57. John Keay, *India: A History* (London: HarperCollins, 2000).

4

CASTE AND THE RISE OF MARGINALIZED GROUPS

Christophe Jaffrelot

Christophe Jaffrelot is a research director at France's National Center for Scientific Research (CNRS) and the director of the Center for International Studies and Research at the Institute for Political Studies (Sciences Po) in Paris, where he also lectures on South Asian politics.

For decades, Indian politics was ruled by traditional elites. The Indian National Congress (Congress party) dominated the political life of early postindependence India, and this "Congress system" of rule relied on the collaboration of elite groups.[1] Resorting to Marxist categories, Pranab Bardhan calls them the "proprietary classes"[2] because they exerted strong control over land as well as over industrial and business activities. Yet in addition to class, there was a strong element of caste behind the influence that these elites commanded.

The Congress leaders came mostly from the intelligentsia—many of them were lawyers by profession—whose caste backgrounds drew generally from the litterati castes, which includes Kayasths and, more importantly, Brahmins (Jawaharlal Nehru offers the best example of this milieu). These politicians had established close working relationships with traders and industrialists even before independence, as these businessmen began to finance the Congress party at that time because of their admiration for Mohandas K. Gandhi and because of their economic nationalism. Thus these groups were allies against the British and remained allies after 1947, when the Congress party realized that it needed the money of the *pujivadi* (capitalists) to compete in elections. Similarly, Congress politicians initiated some collaboration with the landlords—the former *zamindars, jagirdars, malguzars,* and *maharajahs*—when they understood that they needed the landlords in order to win elections. These landlords still exerted a strong influence over the peasants, not only because they were their bosses, but also because they lent them money on a regular basis. The authority of these elite groups derived from their socioeconomic domination and from their social status: They were all of the upper castes and therefore commanded symbolic power. The landlords were often either Kshatriyas or members of the dominant castes, and the capitalists generally came from the third *varna*, the Vaishyas.

Thus the Congress system worked with the social hierarchy in a clientelistic way, since the local notables who supported the party could call upon their "vote banks" at the time of elections. In this framework, the government depended upon these notables to a large extent. As a result, the socialist discourse of Nehru could not be taken to its logical conclusion. Land reform, for instance, was never really enforced in order not to alienate the rural big men who supported the Congress party. Even if the prime minister had tried to pass reforms in Parliament, he might have faced difficulties given the overrepresentation of these people among the Members of Parliament (MPs). Matters were even worse at the state level, where the Congress notables were well entrenched: The discourse was leftist but its implementation remained weak.[3]

This conservative brand of democracy was more in evidence in northern India than in the rest of the country. In the south and in the west, leaders from the lower castes—such as Jotirao Phule and Bhimrao Ramji Ambedkar in Maharashtra state,[4] and Periyar E.V. Ramasami in Tamil Nadu state—had initiated consciousness-raising movements which had exerted a strong political influence. Some of them even resulted in parties such as the Justice Party, which won the 1920 elections in Madras and introduced affirmative-action programs in favor of the Non-Brahmins, a new governmental administrative category. These policies prepared the ground for the rise to power of Non-Brahmin dominant castes such as the Marathas in Maharashtra, the Lingayats and the Vokkaligas in Karnataka, and the Reddys and Kammas in Andhra Pradesh. In most cases, the Congress party accommodated these upwardly mobile groups.

Nothing of that kind happened in the north, where the subalterns suffered from three handicaps. First, the upper castes were much more numerous in the north than in the south and the west; they made up about one-fifth of society, of which 10 percent were Brahmins. Second, the land-ownership pattern, the *zamindari* system that had been introduced by the British, gave the landlords many prerogatives ranging from the collection of taxes to powers of policing. Even though the landlords lost these rights after independence, they retained their prestige and authority. Last but not least, the Congress party did not implement any inclusive strategy vis-à-vis the lower castes, in contrast to what it did elsewhere.[5] Party leaders contented themselves with giving concessions to the Dalits and the Muslims in order to win their votes. This strategy, which turned out to be a success, resulted in what Paul Brass calls "coalitions of extremes"[6]—a phrase which may be misleading as it suggests that the groups involved are on par as coalition partners, though in actuality they are socially poles apart and the upper-caste leaders were the ones who were using the Dalit and Muslim party workers.

The social profile of the political personnel reflected this *modus operandi*. During the Congress-system period in the 1950s and 1960s, the party nominated many local notables from the upper castes who were easily elected to the Lok Sabha (Parliament's lower house). In the 1950s and 1960s, more than 55 percent of the north-Indian MPs belonged to the upper castes. Interestingly, Brahmins, Kshatriyas (mostly Rajputs), and Vaishyas formed the most important groups among these MPs. The radical, populist overtone of former prime minister Indira Gandhi in the early 1970s did not make any difference so far as the social representativeness of her Congress party was concerned. In fact, the ruling Congress had not been so Brahmanical since 1952.

The Rise of the Lower Castes

Things started to change when the Congress party lost power in 1977. For the first time, the share of the Hindi-belt (northern Indian states) MPs fell below 50 percent and the proportion of MPs from the intermediate castes and the Other Backward Classes (OBCs) rose to almost 20 percent—compared to 5.5 percent in 1952. This evolution reflected two different but parallel dynamics.

The rise of the intermediate castes began with the Jats. Jats can be considered "intermediate" because they are not part of the twice-borns, but they are still a dominant caste and therefore they have not been considered to be OBCs in most of the states where they are in large numbers, including Punjab, Haryana, Uttar Pradesh, and Rajasthan; they are not well educated, but their socioeconomic status is higher than that of most peasant groups.[7] In the 1960s, the Jats of Punjab, Haryana, Delhi, western Uttar Pradesh (UP), and northern Rajasthan were among the first beneficiaries of the Green Revolution. They began to invest in irrigation systems and fertilizers and came to a position where they could commercialize some of their surplus. Yet the state still decided the cost of the electricity used for the pumps, the level of fertilizer subsidies, and the price at which agricultural products could be sold. Jat leaders thus emerged to defend their interests.

The most famous was a Congress politician from western UP, Charan Singh, who was minister in the state government but who was never given his due by the party's high command of the province because of his peasant background. He broke from the Congress party in the 1967 elections, joined with other opposition parties, and eventually formed the government. This experiment was bound to be short-lived given the heterogeneity of the coalition, but the political force created by Charan Singh was to play a major role in Uttar Pradesh's politics for two de-

INDIA'S CASTE SYSTEM

The caste system has been an aspect of life on the subcontinent for thousands of years. It can first be divided into four ranked *varnas,* or classes:

Brahmin: priests, scholars
Kshatriya: rulers, warriors, landowners
Vaishya: traders, merchants
Shudra: laborers, artisans, agriculturalists

A fifth group, at first outside the caste system, has become part of the framework of the caste system in the course of time. This group is variously known as the "untouchables," Harijans ("children of God," the term Gandhi made popular), or Dalits ("oppressed," the term adopted by most of the people within this group). Officially they are known as the Scheduled Castes. The government has also created the category of Other Backward Classes, which includes the Shudra castes that have not been successful socioeconomically nor in education. The groups that are regarded as "intermediate castes" are mostly composed of Shudras from the dominant castes, who are peasants who own some land or cattle.

Within each *varna* there are *jatis,* or castes, which altogether number in the thousands. People are born into their caste. At the community level, caste may determine the way in which a person conducts certain aspects of his or her life, such as occupation, marriage, and diet. Not only Hindus but Muslims, Sikhs, and Christians follow the caste system. *Jatis* are endogamous. Marriages between members of two different *jatis* are still very rare today, especially in the countryside, and those between members of two different *varnas* are exceptional, even in the cities.

The system's exact origins are unknown, though its roots may be traced back to the last hymns of the *Rig Veda* (an ancient Hindu holy text). These hymns tell of the sacrifice of a cosmic being, Purusha, from whom the world and the *varnas* were born. Each *varna* is said to correspond to a different part of Purusha's body: Brahmins with the mouth, Kshatriya with the arms, Vaishya with the thighs, and Shudra with the feet. The caste system is a hierarchical structure of status and purity, with Brahmins being considered the most pure, followed by the Kshatriya, Vaishya, and finally Shudra, while the "untouchables" are even more evidently ostracized because of their perceived impurity.

The postcolonial government has made efforts to assist those of the lower castes and those outside the caste system. India's constitution, adopted in 1950, outlawed caste discrimination and "untouchability," but the caste system persists to this day, particularly in rural areas. Parliamentary seats, government jobs, and spots in schools are reserved for the lower castes and classes. Governmental reform efforts have met resistance from the upper castes, but economic development, urbanization, and education have been helping to break down the old social structures.

cades, though under different names. Charan Singh became more than a Jat leader: He became a peasant leader. He was the spokesperson of the *kisans,* the peasants who own and till their land, who needed better prices and lower costs. He mobilized cultivators who were accustomed to voting for their landlord or any other upper-caste notable and convinced them to emancipate themselves from this loyalty; thus cultivators started to vote for their own people, and primarily for the candidates of Charan Singh's party.

The rise of a new *kisan* constituency partly explains the rise of OBC MPs in 1977, as many *kisans* were OBCs. But in their case there is another, more significant, explanation.[8] The OBCs are not primarily defined by class criteria as the *kisans* are, but by castes.[9] This category emerged during the 1946 Constituent Assembly debates after Nehru, in his Objectives Resolution, mentioned that the state of postindependence India would have to cater to the needs of the Other Backward Classes— that is, the groups other than the Dalits and the tribals who were suffering from socioeconomic backwardness. Indeed, Article 340 of the Constitution of India reads:

> The President [of the Republic] may by order appoint a Commission consisting of such persons as he thinks fit to investigate the conditions of socially and educationally backward classes within the territory of India and the difficulties under which they labour and to make recommendations as to the steps that should be taken by the Union or any State to remove such difficulties and to improve their condition and as to the grants that should be made for the purpose by the Union or any State and the conditions subject to which such grants should be made, and the order appointing such Commission shall define the procedure to be followed by the Commission.

Soon after the constitution was promulgated, President Rajendra Prasad appointed a commission in order to identify the Other Backward Classes and their needs. The report of this commission, named after its president, Kaka Kalelkar, found that 1) the OBCs represented 32 percent of society which, in fact, were best defined on the basis of caste criteria (they were all lower Shudras), and that 2) they needed positive-discrimination programs. The government rejected these conclusions, arguing that caste was bound to disappear with the ongoing modernization process and that affirmative-action programs designed on the basis of caste would strengthen this archaic institution. The lower castes in turn resented the government's decision, attributing it to the fear of the upper-caste–dominated establishment vis-à-vis measures that might have prompted lower-caste empowerment.

The demand for positive-discrimination programs—and more precisely for quotas in the bureaucracy—became the rallying cry of OBC movements all over India. This was especially so in the northern states

TABLE 1—SOCIAL BACKGROUND OF THE MPs ELECTED IN THE HINDI BELT, 1952–2004 (IN PERCENTAGES)

Castes & Communities	1952	1957	1962	1967	1971	1977	1980	1984	1989	1991	1996	1998	1999	2004
Upper castes	64.00	58.60	54.90	55.50	53.90	48.20	40.88	46.90	38.20	37.11	35.30	34.67	35.40	33.00
Intermediate castes	1.00	1.43	1.88	2.75	4.11	6.64	5.33	5.31	8.00	5.43	7.53	8.89	7.90	7.10
OBCs	4.45	5.24	7.98	9.64	10.10	13.30	13.74	11.10	20.87	22.60	24.80	23.56	24.00	25.30
SC	15.76	18.10	19.72	18.35	18.26	17.70	17.78	17.26	17.78	18.10	18.14	18.22	18.60	17.80
ST	5.42	6.90	7.04	7.80	7.31	7.08	7.56	7.52	7.56	8.14	7.52	7.56	7.50	8.40
Muslim	5.42	4.76	4.23	3.67	4.57	5.75	11.56	9.73	5.78	4.52	3.54	5.33	5.00	7.10
Other minorities	1.48	0.96	0.94	0.46	0.46	0.44	0.89	0.44	0.44	0.90	0.89	0.89	0.90	0.80
Sadhu	—	—	0.47	0.46	0.46	—	0.44	—	—	0.90	—	—	0.90	0.40
Unidentified	2.96	4.76	2.82	1.38	1.40	0.89	0.89	2.21	0.89	1.36	2.21	0.89	—	—
Total	100	100	100	100	100	100	100	100	100	100	100	100	100	100
	n=203	n=210	n=213	n=218	n=219	n=226	n=225	n=226	n=225	n=221	n=226	n=225	n=221	n=225

Source: Database compiled by Christophe Jaffrelot on the basis of interviews conducted between 1988 and 2004 at the headquarters of the main Indian parties in Delhi and capitals of the Hindi belt states, with the help of the "Who's Who" published by the secretariat of the Lok Sabha after each general election. The Hindi belt is composed of Bihar, Chandigarh, Chhattisgarh, Delhi, Haryana, Himachal Pradesh, Jharkhand, Madhya Pradesh, Rajasthan, Uttar Pradesh, Uttaranchal, and the Hindi-speaking districts of Punjab before 1966.

where the Congress party had opted for a complete status quo, versus in the south and in the west, where quotas had been introduced or enlarged by the state governments. In Bihar, where caste divides were dramatic, the socialists were especially successful in mobilizing OBC voters at the time of elections by promising quotas of 60 percent for the different subaltern groups and by nominating many low-caste candidates. This strategy, initiated in the late 1950s by Ram Manohar Lohia, brought rich dividends in the 1960s and 1970s.

In 1977, the rise of the MPs from the intermediate castes and the OBCs stemmed from the electoral success of the Janata Party, an anti-Congress coalition in which the socialists and Charan Singh played a significant role. The Janata Party formed the government in March 1977 but was not able to retain power because of inner divisions. In 1984, the Congress party won an overwhelming victory in the wake of Indira Gandhi's assassination, and this comeback of the Congress resulted in the rise of the upper-caste MPs and the decline of the OBC MPs. Yet another "Janata" party, the Janata Dal, dislodged the Congress from power once again in 1989, and this second alternation of power resulted once again in a significant erosion of the share of the upper-caste MPs (who fell below 40 percent for the first time) and in a significant rise of the OBC MPs: Their share almost doubled, jumping from 11 to 21 percent. Intermediate castes registered a less marked increase, from 5.3 to 8 percent. These data prefigured the scenario that was about to unfold.

Certainly, the legacy of Charan Singh, who had died in 1987, was tied to that of the Janata Dal, but the leader of the Janata Dal, V.P. Singh, was less interested in promoting the cause of the *kisans* than in advocating that of the OBCs in a socialist vein. Even before the Janata Dal came to power, V.P. Singh had promised to reserve 60 percent of posts within the party to OBCs, an old socialist idea. He considered positive discrimination the most relevant technique, as it provided for long-term uplift.[10] In August 1990, V.P. Singh announced the implementation of the report submitted by the 1978 Second Backward Classes Commission or Mandal Commission (named after B.P. Mandal, its president), and more especially of the report's recommendation that 27 percent of the public sector's posts be reserved for the OBCs—a category which encompassed lower castes representing 52 percent of society, according to the Mandal Commission.

Retrospectively, V.P. Singh's decision to implement the Mandal Commission's report—which may be explained as much by his efforts to carve an electoral niche for himself as by his social concerns—was a turning point. Upper-caste Hindus immediately opposed what they perceived to be a threat to their large share of public-sector posts. Students demonstrated in Delhi and other northern Indian cities; more than 60 of them protested by publicly immolating themselves. As a result, the Supreme Court formulated a stay order. In reaction, OBC leaders gave reasons for supporting V.P. Singh's decision before orchestrating countermobilizations in the Hindi belt. The OBCs were no longer simply an administrative category. They had risen to the challenge of organizing themselves politically. In northern India they started to concentrate their vote on parties representing their interests, for instance the Janata Dal or its breakaway faction in Uttar Pradesh, the Samajwadi Janata Dal. In this context, the OBCs were joined by the Scheduled Castes who feared that the antireservationist campaign of the upper castes might affect their own quotas. The Dalit-led Bahujan Samaj Party (BSP), which also aspired to attract OBC voters, made an alliance with the Samajwadi Janata Dal in 1993.[11]

The Mandal affair helped the OBCs to transform themselves into an interest group. They organized outside the vertical clientelistic pattern typical of the Congress system. OBCs started to vote in large numbers for candidates from *their* milieu, instead of supporting the traditional, Congress notables. After the 1989 elections for the Lok Sabha, the proportion of upper-caste MPs fell for the first time below 40 percent, while the share of OBCs rose from 11.1 percent to 20.9 percent because of the electoral success of the Janata Dal. More importantly, the share of OBCs among MPs grew after the 1991 Lok Sabha elections, even with the return to power of the Congress party and again after the 1996 elections, despite the Bharatiya Janata Party (another upper-caste–dominated party) becoming the largest party in the Lok Sabha. This trend has remained the same in election after election since 1989.

After the 2004 general elections, the upper-caste MPs reached their lowest point: The Hindi-belt MPs won only 33 percent of the seats, whereas the OBCs won 25 percent. In twenty years, the gap between these two groups, which was as wide as 35.8 percent in 1984, has been reduced to 7.7 percent. Something changed over the 1990s that made all parties, irrespective of ideology, distribute an increasing number of tickets to OBC candidates—and not only in constituencies where they had little hope of winning, which had been a common practice earlier. The changing character of the main parties is a central element in what V.P. Singh termed the "silent revolution," a long-term transformation under which more and more people from the politically marginalized sections of society have been given access to power.

This transfer of power is even more significant at the state level. OBC chief ministers have become the rule. In 2006, OBC leaders governed Uttar Pradesh, Bihar, Madhya Pradesh, and Rajasthan. Interestingly, none of them is from the same caste: Vasundharaje Scindia in Jaipur, though a Maratha princess, may be considered to be a Jat because she married another prince from this caste which has been included in the 2000 list of the OBCs in Rajasthan; Shivraj Singh Chauhan in Bhopal is a Kirar (a cultivating caste); Nitish Kumar in Patna is a Kurmi (another cultivating caste); and Mulayam Singh Yadav in Lucknow is a Yadav (a caste of cow herders). These variations suggest that one needs to scrutinize the situation at the state level to understand the balance of power and the evolution of caste equations.

Caste Power in Uttar Pradesh

The case of Uttar Pradesh (UP) is especially interesting not only because it played a pioneering role in the silent revolution—ongoing since the time of Lohia and Charan Singh—but also because it is the largest state in India (with 166 million inhabitants, according to the 2001 census, it is more populous than Japan or Russia) and it is the province that set the tempo for the whole country for decades after independence. Also, in Uttar Pradesh the upper castes have represented a larger proportion of the population than in any other northern Indian state. According to the 1931 census, the last census to ask detailed questions about caste identification, the upper castes represented 20 percent of the population. The Brahmins made up 9.2 percent (the highest percentage of Brahmins in any Indian state) and the Rajputs (the largest Kshatriya caste of northern India) 7.2 percent. Among the intermediate castes, the Jats formed the most significant group. Jats represented only 1.6 percent of the state population in 1931, but were concentrated in western Uttar Pradesh, where they were a mainstay of the farming community and competed with the Rajputs for the status of dominant caste. The lower castes were either associated with service occupations, such as barbers (the Nais caste), toddy tappers (Telis), cultivators (Kurmis, Lodhis, Koeris, Gujjars), cow herders (Ahirs or Yadavs), and sheep herders (Gadaryas). The Yadavs alone accounted for 8.7 percent of Uttar Pradesh's population in 1931.

The largest caste of Uttar Pradesh was to be found among the Scheduled Castes, which represented 21 percent of the state's population according to the 1991 census,[12] and among whom a single *jati* represented 11 percent of the state's population (that of the Chamars or Jatavs, the shoemakers).[13] Chamars were politicized and adopted the name "Jatavs" long before many other Scheduled Castes, partly as a result of the work of Ambedkar, India's foremost Dalit leader during the British Raj and thereafter for many years. Not surprisingly, the Republican Party of India (RPI), the party that Ambedkar had founded shortly before his death in 1956, established pockets of influence in Uttar Pradesh as early as 1962.

Uttar Pradesh was the primary battleground for two conflicting mobilizational strategies. While the Lohia-ite socialists promoted affirmative-action programs, Charan Singh evolved a different approach by focusing on the defense of the *kisans*. Although he was a Vaishya and had been influenced by Marxism, Lohia looked at the eradication of

TABLE 2—CASTES AND COMMUNITIES IN THE UTTAR PRADESH
ASSEMBLY, 1952–74 (IN PERCENTAGES)

CASTES & COMMUNITIES	1952	1957	1962	1967	1969	1974
Upper castes	58	55	58	45.3*	43.9*	45.8*
Intermediate castes	3	3	2	—	—	—
OBCs	9	12	13	29.2	26.8	28.4
Scheduled castes	20	21	22	—	20.9	16.3
Muslims	10	9	7	5.6	8.2	9.6
Total	100	100	100	100	100	100

* includes Bhumihar, Tyagi, Jat, Vaishya, Kayasth, and Khatri
Source: Richard Meyer, *The Political Elite in an Under-Developed Society: The Case of Uttar Pradesh in India* (Ph.D. diss., University of Pennsylvania, 1969), 89.

caste as the primary objective of any socialist program because for him caste was "the most overwhelming factor in Indian life."[14] He did not regard affirmative action in the education system as desirable,[15] but emphasized the need for quotas in the administration and for the election of candidates for public office. In 1959, the third national conference of the Socialist Party expressed the wish that at least 60 percent of the posts in the administration be reserved for Other Backward Classes. These reservations were intended to give a share of power to the lower castes; it was an empowerment scheme. To show the way, the Samyukta Socialist Party nominated a large number of candidates from nonelite groups, and the socialists had more OBC members of legislative assemblies (MLAs) elected than any other political party in Uttar Pradesh or Bihar—the two states where the socialists achieved their best results.

The state of Uttar Pradesh also experienced the development of peasant movements under the aegis of Charan Singh. The Chaudhury (to use the Jat title under which he was known) did not emphasize caste as Lohia did; instead, he projected himself as the true advocate of the *kisans*.[16] Singh wanted to emancipate the peasants from the domination of the landlords as well as the state, which he accused, among other things, of not providing the cultivators with regular or fairly priced electricity and of offering unremunerative agricultural prices. His political parties took root in Uttar Pradesh more successfully than anywhere else.[17] In April 1969, Charan Singh became president of the Bhartiya Kranti Dal (BKD) but instead of being "bharatiya"—that is, a pan-Indian party—it appeared to be a regional party. This evolution was confirmed during the 1968–69 elections, in which it won 21.3 percent of the votes in Uttar Pradesh, versus winning 1.5 percent in Haryana, 2.1 percent in Bihar, and 1.7 percent in Punjab. In Uttar Pradesh, the core of the party's support was from the western region, and particularly among Charan Singh's Jat caste-fellows.[18]

Charan Singh was concerned with reaching out to members of the lower castes, who formed the bulk of the cultivating castes. In the mid-term elections of 1969, the BKD fielded 115 candidates from the backward and the intermediate castes, compared to just 23 on the Congress side.[19] This strategy certainly helped the BKD to become the second-largest party in the state assembly with 98 seats, compared to 211 for the Congress party. In 1974, the BKD seat total increased to 106.

Soon after, the BKD and the breakaway fraction of the Lohia-ite socialists led by Raj Narain merged into a new party, the Bharatiya Lok Dal (BLD). As a result, Uttar Pradesh became the birthplace of a political tradition representing the interests of the "rural workers," defined as people who were either from the lower castes or were *kisans*. Charan Singh's movement was indisputably non-OBC, both because it was spearheaded by a non-OBC caste and because its arguments did not rely on caste as the basis for political mobilization. Yet it sowed the seeds for the OBC movement that would be unleashed by the implementation of the Mandal Commission's report more than fifteen years later.

The caste backgrounds of the MLAs and ministers of Uttar Pradesh underwent a significant evolution during the 1960s and 1970s, when Charan Singh was making his strongest impact on the state polity. In 1967, for the first time the percentage of upper-caste MLAs dropped below 50 percent (and it remained at that level), whereas the share of the OBCs jumped from 13 percent to between 27 and 29 percent.

The trend initiated in the 1960s and 1970s became more pronounced in the 1990s, following a long plateau in the 1980s: The share of upper-caste MLAs fell below 40 percent in 1993 (and has not returned to that level since), whereas the proportion of the OBCs had already crossed the symbolic 25 percent line in 1991 (and since that time has fallen below this threshold only once, in 1996). Among the declining upper castes, the Brahmins have been the most affected. This group, which had cornered one-fifth of legislative-assembly seats in 1980, was left with only a tenth of them in 2006. In Uttar Pradesh, the Brahmin Raj is no more. In contrast, the Rajputs have displayed an impressive resilience. This caste is better represented than any other in the sitting 2006 assembly, its members holding almost 17 percent of the assembly seats. But this should not conceal the major phenomenon that is the rise of the lower castes, which has come at the expense of the former ruling groups.

The rise to power of the subalterns needs to be qualified from two points of view. First, their power has depended on which party has been in office. Second, all castes have not benefited from this phenomenon in the same way.

The "party" variable—that is, which party came into power or was in a majority in the assembly—played an important role from the 1960s through the 1980s. It continued to exert some influence in the post-Mandal context, but to a lesser extent. Indeed, since 1990 every party that has come to power has maintained a high level of OBC MLAs. This

TABLE 3—CASTES AND COMMUNITIES IN THE UTTAR PRADESH
ASSEMBLY, 1980–2002 (IN PERCENTAGES)

CASTES & COMMUNITIES	1980	1985	1989	1991	1993	1996	2002
Upper castes	42.40	39.45	39.24	41.77	33.42	37.67	35.38
Brahmin	19.61	17.62	14.18	12.91	9.23	10.34	9.83
Rajput	16.91	16.87	18.73	21.01	18.20	19.10	16.95
Others*	5.88	4.96	6.33	7.85	5.99	8.23	8.60
Intermediate castes	2.21	3.23	2.28	2.78	2.74	3.18	4.67
Jat	1.96	3.23	2.28	2.78	2.74	3.18	4.67
Vishnoi	0.25	—	—	—	—	—	—
OBCs	16.91	20.84	24.56	26.58	32.67	24.40	27.52
Yadav	4.41	8.19	9.11	8.86	11.72	10.08	9.09
Kurmi	1.96	2.98	3.54	3.80	6.73	5.84	6.88
Others†	10.54	9.67	11.91	13.92	14.22	8.48	11.55
Scheduled castes	22.06	22.33	21.77	22.28	22.19	23.61	21.87
Jatav	NA	NA	NA	NA	NA	NA	12.29
Passi	NA	NA	NA	NA	NA	NA	4.42
Others‡	NA	NA	NA	NA	NA	NA	5.16
Muslims	11.76	12.41	10.13	5.82	7.73	10.08	10.57
Sikhs	1.23	0.99	0.25	0.25	0.50	0.27	—
Unidentified	3.43	0.74	1.77	0.51	0.75	0.80	—
Total	100	100	100	100	100	100	100

* includes Banya/Jain, Bhumihar, Kayasth, Khatri, Tyagi, and Sindhi
† includes Lodhi, Gujjar, Chauhan, Kashyap, Kacchi, Muraon, Rajbhar, Nishad, Koeri, Baghel, Saini,
Gadarya, Shakya, Teli, Chandel, and others
‡ includes Khatik, Ahirwar, Kol, Kori, Dhanak, Dhobi, Kevat, Goud, Sonkar, and others
Source: Fieldwork conducted by author. I am especially grateful to the Congress-party office for
sharing its data with me.

is evident from the rather large proportion of OBCs in the legislative
assembly that were elected in 1991 and 1996, when respectively the
Congress and the Bharatiya Janata Party (BJP) won the most seats. The
party variable has remained very powerful, however, insofar as the composition of the state government has been concerned. Though all winning parties have increased OBC representation in the Vidhan Sabha
(lower house of the legislative assembly), they have not given ministerial berths to OBCs in a similar manner.

During the 1980s, the last years of the Congress era, the proportion of
the upper castes among the government members stood above 50 percent, with a share of 8.6 to 13.5 percent of OBCs and a larger share from
the Scheduled Castes (15.6 to 21.6 percent) and Muslims (8.9 to 14.3
percent)—a clear reflection of the resilience of the party's "coalition-
of-extremes" pattern. There is no doubt about who was really in charge,
as neither of the latter two groups could match the overwhelming percentage of the upper castes. Mulayam Singh Yadav's Janata Dal gov-

ernment in 1989 did not make a major change because the party "inherited a vast number of former Congressmen from the Rajput community. Clearly the Janata Dal was not an OBC party in a way the SP [Samajwadi Party] was to become."[20] But things did change in 1993, when Mulayam Singh Yadav's SP and Kanshi Ram's BSP formed a ruling coalition. For the first time, the percentage of OBCs holding posts as government ministers was in proportion to their share of the state's population. The following government, which took office in June 1995 under the chief ministership of the BSP's Mayawati Kumari with the support of the BJP, maintained a similar balance. Yet while the BJP was able to form the government on its own, it replicated the pattern set by the Congress governments of the 1980s, with the proportion of upper castes holding ministerial positions above 50 percent. Nevertheless, OBC ministers still cornered nearly 20 percent of positions, "an indication that the trend towards greater inclusiveness cannot be reversed."[21]

The notion that the OBCs form a "political community"[22] also needs to be qualified. When discussing the rise of the OBCs in north India, and more especially in Uttar Pradesh, we are really speaking of the Yadavs, Kurmis, and Jatavs. In UP, the OBC mobilization of the 1990s was spearheaded by the Yadavs as well as by Mulayam Singh Yadav's rise to power in 1989 and again in 1993, both of which were largely due to the support of his own caste. His reservation policy in the administration also favored Yadavs over other castes. Out of the 900 teachers appointed under his second government, 720 were Yadavs. In the police, over one-third of the newly selected candidates were also Yadavs. In 1993, only 8 percent of his party's MLAs were Kurmis (while one-third were Yadavs), and in 1996 the share of Kurmis was down to 3 percent (versus the one-quarter who were Yadavs). This policy alienated other OBCs, particularly the Kurmis. As a result, 75 percent of Yadavs voted for Mulayam's Samajwadi Party in the 1996 assembly elections, while the Kurmi votes were spread between the BJP (37 percent) and the BSP (27 percent).[23]

The BSP also experienced a meteoric rise in UP politics in the 1990s (from 8.7 percent of the valid vote in the 1991 general elections to 24.7 percent in 2004). Yet the BSP can also be considered to be the instrument of one caste, the Jatavs, who have been the main beneficiaries of affirmative-action programs in terms of education and quotas in the administration. According to the census, the literacy rate among the Scheduled Castes rose from 7.14 percent in 1961 to 10.2 percent in 1971, to 15 percent in 1981, and then to 27 percent in 1991. In education, the Chamars have benefited more than any other Dalit caste from this progress because of their relative affluence due to their activity as shoemakers; some of the leather workers became artisans or even traders. Jatavs also made progress because of their sheer numbers: They constituted 56.6 percent of the UP's Scheduled Castes population in

TABLE 4—CASTE COMPOSITION OF CERTAIN GOVERNMENTS IN UTTAR PRADESH, 1982–1999 (IN PERCENTAGES)

CASTES & COMMUNITIES	02/1984 INC	03/1985 INC	01/1987 INC	01/1990 JD	06/1991 BJP	12/1993 SP-BSP	06/1995 SP-BSP	03/1997 BSP-BJP	11/1999 BJP
Upper castes	64.40	51.30	57.10	50.00	51.61	6.70	6.25	17.40	47.00
Intermediate castes	—	—	—	—	3.22	—	6.25	8.70	0.86
OBCs	8.90	13.50	8.60	14.30	19.35	40.00	43.75	26.10	29.90
Scheduled castes	15.60	21.60	20.00	14.30	16.13	33.30	31.25	30.40	8.60
Muslims	8.90	10.80	14.30	21.40	—	—	—	—	4.30
Unidentified	2.20	2.70	—	—	9.67	20.00	12.50	17.40	8.60
Total	100	100	100	100	99.98	100	100	100	99.30
	n=45	n=45	n=35	n=14	n=31	n=15	n=16	n=23	n=117

INC–Congress party; JD–Janata Dal; BJP–Bharatiya Janata Party; SP-BSP–Samajwadi Party/Bahujan Samaj Party
Source: Fieldwork by Jasime Zérinini-Brotel as published in Jaffrelot and Zérinini-Brotel, "Post-'Mandal' Politics," 157 (see note 19).

1991 (versus Pasis, who constituted 14.6 percent). The Jatavs' level of education and their demographic strength enabled them to corner large shares of the quotas reserved for the Scheduled Castes in the education system and the bureaucracy.[24] The BSP cadres first came from this new Dalit elite, who were not offered any avenue for upward mobility in the Congress party.[25]

Surveys indicate that most BSP voters come from the Chamars, who had been the mainstay of the RPI when the party made some headway in UP in the 1960s.[26] Since the mid-1990s, the BSP has won about three-fourths of the Chamars vote, a major achievement in a state where this group represents the largest caste. Unsurprisingly, in 2002 the Jatavs became one of the *jatis* with the largest percentage of MLAs in the UP assembly (12.3 percent), more than the Yadavs. Naturally, the BSP is the party with the biggest contingent of Jatav MLAs, but other parties have nominated candidates from this caste in order to resist the rise of the BSP.

Uttar Pradesh offers a clear picture of the growing assertiveness of subaltern groups in Indian politics. In the wake of the Mandal affair and over the last fifteen years, OBCs and Dalits have gained a new political influence that is evident from their increasing representation in the state assembly. But this trend needs to be qualified. First, the SP and the BSP are the only parties to give large ministerial responsibilities to these groups. The BJP and to a lesser extent the Congress, which remains more Dalit-oriented than OBC-oriented, contented themselves with giving tickets to candidates from the lower castes at the time of elections to win the subalterns' votes. Second, all the OBC castes and the Dalit *jatis* are not profiting by the ongoing "plebeianization" of politics: The Yadavs (who rally around the SP) and the Jatavs (who support massively the BSP) are the main beneficiaries.

Where Is Indian Democracy Headed?

India is inventing a unique route toward democracy. The country has been a political democracy since the 1950s, but until the 1990s, the ruling elite—whichever the party in office—came from the same dominant classes and castes. India is probably the first country in which a formal, institutional democracy has been gaining social substance through a *quiet* transfer of power. In most other societies, such a shift has implied a revolutionary and violent phase: The people have gained power by rising up against the ruling, traditional elite. In India, democracy had already been granted to the country by the elite, but the elite had monopolized power for decades. The revolution is now passing through the polling booth: It is by voting that the subalterns have been rising to power because they are large in numbers and have stopped supporting local notables. Indeed, illiterate Dalit peasants have been voting in larger numbers than Delhi-based executives.

At the state level, long-term developments prepared the ground in the south and the west as early as colonial times, before reaching the north. In the 1970s, for instance, the reservation policies of socialist leaders like Karpoori Thakur in Bihar were significant in propelling lower-caste mobilization. Yet the true catalyst of this change was the Mandal affair, after which lower castes realized on a pan-Indian basis that as OBCs they had common interests—namely, quotas—and that the upper castes would not give them this share of the spoils if they did not organize and unite in the political sphere. Even though these changes occurred in the 1990s, they stemmed from a long maturation, due to a) political conscientization by Ambedkar and socialists, including Lohia; b) major socioeconomic changes such as the Green Revolution, which gave birth to *kisan* politics; and c) affirmative-action programs, which helped Dalits to acquire some education and jobs in the bureaucracy.

The Hindi belt was the crucible of this silent revolution of the 1990s. In contrast, states that played a pioneering role in lower-caste mobilization, such as Maharashtra and Karnataka, are now lagging behind the north in terms of political representation of the lower castes, because dominant castes are still in command.

Yet one needs to take a nuanced view of the rise to power of the subalterns of north India. First, this rise has been unevenly spread, with some states being more progressive than others. Second, if all parties are now prepared to nominate low-caste candidates at the time of elections, the BJP and the Congress—to mention the two largest parties only—are still reluctant to give them ministerial portfolios or responsibilities within the party apparatus. Third, it does not concern all the caste groups; the Yadavs, Kurmis, and Jatavs have been the most obvious winners. An outer circle of OBCs—the Most Backward Classes, as they are officially known in Bihar—and Dalits tend to regroup *against* the "upper OBCs" in Bihar and UP, where they give some of their vote to the Janata Dal (United) and the BSP, respectively.[27]

The democratization of Indian democracy needs also to be qualified from a more general point of view. The subalterns are gaining power in the elective assemblies and through quotas in the bureaucracy, but these institutions do not matter as much as before. The decision-making process ignores the Parliament more and more, as is evident from the economic reforms, which have been imposed by a clique of technocrats and have not been properly debated by the MPs. The state apparatus is shrinking, whereas the private sector is flourishing—so much so that the lower castes may well have quotas in bodies which are becoming empty shells.[28] Incidentally, this is one of the reasons why the upper-caste middle class abstained from demonstrating in the street in 1992 when the Supreme Court cleared V.P. Singh's decision to implement the Mandal Commission's report: They did not care any more for the public sector, the corporate sector (which had started to benefit from the 1991 economic liberalization) being much more promising. They even started to lose interest in the democratic process as a whole: The urban middle class does not vote in large numbers anymore. The subalterns are taking over, but the middle classes can have their concerns fixed in other ways, such as by approaching those in office directly and circumventing the democratic institutions. For Indian democracy, the real danger lies more in this changing mentality of the elite than in any revolutionary threat from below.[29]

NOTES

1. On the "Congress system," see Rajni Kothari, "The Congress System in India," *Asian Survey* 4 (December 1964): 1161–73.

2. Pranab Bardhan, *The Political Economy of Development in India* (Oxford, Blackwell, 1984).

3. For more details, see the first part of Christophe Jaffrelot, *India's Silent Revolution: The Rise of the Lower Castes in North India Politics* (New York: Columbia University Press, 2002).

4. For more details, see Christophe Jaffrelot, *Dr. Ambedkar and Untouchability Fighting the Indian Caste System* (New York: Columbia University Press, 2005).

5. Unsurprisingly, Myron Weiner's interpretation of the Congress as a party open to emerging elites is based on case studies all selected out of the Hindi belt. See Myron Weiner, *Party Building in a New Nation: The Indian National Congress* (Chicago: University of Chicago Press, 1967).

6. Paul R. Brass, "The Politicization of the Peasantry in a North Indian State," *Journal of Peasant Studies* 8 (October 1980): 3–36.

7. Christophe Jaffrelot, "The Changing Identity of the Jats in North India: Kshatriyas, Kisans or Backwards?" in Sujata Patel, Jasodhara Bagchi, and Krishna Raj, eds., *Thinking Social Science in India: Essays in Honour of Alice Thorner* (New Delhi: Sage, 2002), 405–21.

8. For a more detailed comparison of *kisan* politics and OBC politics (or quota politics), see Christophe Jaffrelot, "The Rise of the Other Backward Classes in the Hindi Belt," *Journal of Asian Studies* 59 (February 2000): 86–108.

9. The lower and the intermediate castes form two categories which must be carefully differentiated because the latter, even though they belong to the Shudras, in many cases largely coincide with the dominant landowning castes. The socio-economic status of intermediate castes also varies between the two states.

10. See V.P. Singh, "Towards a Just Society," abridged version from the first address to the nation, 3 December 1989; and V.P. Singh, "Independence Day Address, 15 August 1990," in Surendra Mohan, H.D. Sharma, and V.P. Singh et al., eds., *Evolution of Socialist Policy in India* (New Delhi: Janata Dal, 1997), 356–65.

11. See Zoya Hasan, *Quest for Power: Oppositional Movements and Post-Congress Politics in Uttar Pradesh* (Delhi: Oxford University Press, 1998).

12. In contrast to all the others, the Scheduled Castes are still counted in census data, because the quotas that they are awarded in the framework of affirmative-action programs are adjusted according to demographic trends.

13. Kanchan Chandra pertinently argues that Jatavs or Chamars are composed of an amalgamation of smaller, separate castes. Certainly, all identities are con-structed—sometimes for material advantages such as quotas in the bureaucracy—and caste groups are no exception. But it does not mean that these categories of "Jatavs" and "Chamars" are not realities for those who want to be identified that way. See Kanchan Chandra, *Why Ethnic Parties Succeed: Patronage and Ethnic Head Counts in India* (Cambridge: Cambridge University Press, 2004).

14. Ram Manohar Lohia, "Towards the Destruction of Castes and Classes (1958)," in Ram Manohar Lohia, *The Caste System* (Hyderabad: Ram Manohar Lohia Samata Vidyalaya, 1979), 79.

15. Lohia tried to justify this stand in 1958 by saying, "Let the backward castes ask for two or three shifts in schools and colleges, if necessary, but let them never ask for the exclusion of any child of India from the portals of an educational institution." See Lohia, "Towards the Destruction of Castes and Classes," 104.

16. For more details, see T.J. Byres, "Charan Singh (1902–87): An Assess-ment," *Journal of Peasant Studies* 15 (January 1988): 139–89; and Paul R. Brass, "Chaudhuri Charan Singh: An Indian Political Life," *Economic and Political Weekly,* 25 September 1993, 2088.

17. Lewis P. Fickett, Jr., "The Politics of Regionalism in India," *Pacific Affairs* 44 (Summer 1971): 201–203.

18. Ian Duncan, "Levels: On the Communication of Programs, Levels, and Sectional Strategies in Indian Politics with Special References to the BKD and the RPI in Uttar Pradesh and Aligarh District (UP)," unpubl. Ph.D. diss., University of Sussex, 1979, 156 and 175.

19. Zoya Hasan, "Power and Mobilization: Patterns of Resilience and Change in Uttar Pradesh," in Francine R. Frankel and M.S.A. Rao, eds., *Dominance and State Power in Modern India: Decline of a Social Order,* vol. 1 (Delhi: Oxford Univer-sity Press, 1989), 182.

20. Jasmine Zérinini-Brotel as published in Christophe Jaffrelot and Jasmine Zérinini-Brotel, "Post-'Mandal' Politics in Uttar Pradesh and Madhya Pradesh," in Rob Jenkins, ed., *Regional Reflections: Comparing Politics Across India's States* (New Delhi: Oxford University Press, 2004).

21. See Jaffrelot and Zérinini-Brotel, "Post-'Mandal' Politics."

22. These data draw from a pre-poll survey by the CSDS. See Yogendra Yadav, "Reconfiguration in Indian Politics: State Assembly Elections 1993–95," *Eco-nomic and Political Weekly,* 13 January 1996, 96.

23. *India Today* (New Delhi), 31 August 1996.

24. Radhika Ramaseshan, "Dalit Politics in U.P.," *Seminar* (New Dehli), Janu-ary 1995, 73.

25. Kanchan Chandra underlines that "Congress leaders themselves readily acknowledge that the representational blockage for Scheduled Castes elites in their own party pushed them towards the BSP." See Chandra, *Why Ethnic Parties Suc-ceed,* 187. Sudha Pai has shown that the BSP activists belonged to a new generation of young, educated Dalits. See Sudha Pai, *Dalit Assertion and the Unfinished*

Democratic Revolution: The Bahujan Samaj Party in Uttar Pradesh (New Delhi: Sage, 2002), 96.

26. In 1962, the electoral slogan of the RPI was *"Jatav Muslim bhai bhai, Hindu kaum kahan se aye?"* (*Jatavs* and Muslims are brothers, where do the Hindus [community, nation] come from?), cited in Duncan, Ph.D. diss., 286.

27. Quotas should be systematically designed for Dalits only, otherwise the upper OBCs and the upper Scheduled Castes will continue to monopolize the existing reservations and translate these socioeconomic advantages into political influence.

28. See Sukhdeo Thorat, Aryama, and Prashant Negi, eds., *Reservation and the Private Sector* (New Delhi: Indian Institute of Dalit Studies and Rawat Publications, 2005).

29. The government is in a position, if it wishes, to defuse through social programs the resurgence of the Maoist movement known in India under the name of Naxalism. Also see Jaffrelot, "The Depoliticisation of the Indian Middle Class," in Christophe Jaffrelot and Peter Van Der Veer, eds., *Patterns of Middle Class Consumption in India and China* (New Delhi: Sage, 2007).

II

The State

5

FEDERALISM'S SUCCESS

Subrata K. Mitra

Subrata K. Mitra is professor of political science at the South Asia Institute, University of Heidelberg, Germany, and a visiting fellow at the Centre for the Study of Developing Societies in New Delhi.

India's federal structure has grown in complexity during the sixty years since independence. The uneasy assortment of provinces directly ruled by the colonial government and native princely states whose rulers chose to join India has become a robust federal union with twenty-eight states and seven union territories. The provinces, particularly since their reorganization on the basis of mother tongue, have become cohesive cultural and political units, effectively cooperating through a broad spectrum of federal bodies. These institutional changes are underpinned by growing popular trust in federal institutions. These achievements suggest two major puzzles.

First, while there is no denying the growing depth and complexity of India's federal institutions, what remains unclear is why India's federalism—a modern institution of exogenous provenance ensconced within a traditional society—*should* work at all. If the problems of governance in transitional societies arise from the hiatus between modern institutions and traditional society, then federalism—itself a modern institution based on a written constitution, states' rights, and judicial mediation in case of conflict of interests—should have been undermined by political practice, rather like it has been in neighboring Pakistan. Despite having been to the brink of collapse time and again, the federal structure has pulled back to continue as before.[1] Where does this resilience come from?

The second puzzle derives from the record of unseemly political behavior particularly evident at the regional level. After all, if Indian federalism is the shining success that many claim it to be, then why do state governments—an integral part of the federal institutional design—produce chief ministers[2] whose communal, corrupt, and venal regimes have excessively misused the power and autonomy granted to federal units? Considering that the states are an integral part of the federal structure and process, then why does the sum of parts, many of them damaged political goods by any reckoning, add up to the functioning whole? What federal "brakes" operate to localize the damage and stop it from spiraling upward and spreading horizontally, without at the same time compromising the principle of federal balance?

I argue in this chapter that the fortuitous combination of structure and agency best explains the success of federalism in India. India's political geography, simultaneously marked by regional diversity and crossregional cultural links and social networks, provides the countervailing pressures of regional autonomy and interregional bonds that are essential for a robust federal system. Both tendencies have been reinforced in the Indian case by the political process that characterized British colonial rule and Indian resistance to it. Masters of indirect rule through intermediaries, the British utilized a system of governance that required the transfer of enough autonomy to regional and local units so as to provide some substance to their symbolic identities while simultaneously binding them together within the "steel frame" of colonial rule. The colonial tactic of "divide and rule" found its match in the resolve of the leaders of the freedom movement to "unite and oppose"—a strategy that combined institutional participation with rational protest. In retrospect, thanks to the insuperable political and administrative skills of leaders like Mohandas Gandhi, Jawaharlal Nehru, and Sardar Vallabhbhai Patel, the anticolonial movement also evolved into a government-in-waiting. The second historical moment came after independence. When the Muslim League—the main balancing factor against the hegemonic ambitions of the Indian National Congress (Congress party)—left India for Pakistan, the void was quickly filled by a succession of strong regional leaders who kept the expanding power of the central leaders in check.

This essay narrates the story of this evolution in terms of four empirical arguments, involving the political culture, institutional design, context, and policy process of federalism in India. These arguments draw on Douglass North's core insight regarding what makes institutions work.[3] The essay asserts that the success of a federal system is contingent on the perceived interest of federating units to stay within a federation rather than to strike out on their own. These arguments, discussed in detail below, suggest that the preponderant role of the union in India's federal design responded to the need for unity in the wake of independence and the scope for transfer of resources from the rich to the poor, thereby enhancing the legitimacy of the new postcolonial state. This was reinforced by the countervailing tendencies of Indian politics that gave federal institutions the necessary room to maneuver as well as a successful track record on which to draw once the binding mechanism of the "one dominant" phase of Indian politics—the period from 1947 to 1967 when the Congress party ruled supreme in all centers of power in India—was over. Following the liberalization of India's economy in 1991, interstate competition transformed the states from "clients" into competing stakeholders who have since discovered a new *raison d'être* for federalism in the vast, rapidly expanding Indian market with its global reach.

What should propel rational actors toward federal institutions rather than away from them? Institutions, we learn from North, are "humanly devised constraints that shape human interaction." They achieve legitimacy and strength by "reducing uncertainty" and "providing a structure to everyday life."[4] In a quickly changing political situation of the kind that one can expect in transitional societies, institutional durability depends on whether the institutions can provide a bridge between the indigenous political tradition and exogenous political designs through which the state attempts to shape them. The provision of incentives—material, symbolic, and punitive—to abide by the federal rules of the game is of crucial significance. Crafty political leaders and their equally disingenuous followers can be constrained by rules only when they perceive compliance to be in their best interests. North puts it succinctly: "The resultant path of institutional change is shaped by: 1) the lock-in that comes from the symbiotic relationship between institutions and the organizations that have evolved as a consequence of the incentive structure provided by those institutions; and 2) the feedback process by which human beings perceive and react to changes in the opportunity set."[5] Based on this conjecture, the subsequent analysis examines the strength, resilience, and effectiveness of India's federalism in terms of the culture, design, context, and policy process that underpin it.

Measuring Federalism's Success

Limitation of space does not permit a detailed analysis of the functioning of India's federal institutions. These include designated ones such as the Rajya Sabha (the Council of States, Parliament's upper house), which represents states' interests at the union level, as well as more specialized ones like the Finance Commission, an independent body appointed by the president to maintain a fair and efficient division of revenues between the center and the states, and the Planning Commission and Election Commission, whose responsibilities indirectly affect the vitality of federal processes. One indication of the extent to which the economies of the states are affected by federal institutions is the provisions of sharing the national income. From 1998 to 2002, all the states together raised only 49.2 percent of their current spending from their own taxes. The rest was raised through a variety of mecha-

TABLE 1—INTEREST IN CENTRAL AND STATE GOVERNMENT
(IN PERCENTAGES)

ARE YOU MORE CONCERNED/INTERESTED ABOUT/IN WHAT THE GOVERNMENT IN DELHI DOES OR WHAT THE (NAME THE STATE GOVERNMENT) DOES?	1971	1996	1999
Neither	24.9	39.7	26.0
Central government	21.0	11.0	14.8
Both	14.5	20.9	26.7
State government	18.9	23.0	25.6
Don't know, not applicable, other	20.7	5.4	6.9

Source: Centre for the Study of Developing Societies (Delhi), National Election Studies 1971, 1996, 1999.

TABLE 2—LOYALTY TO REGION FIRST AND THEN TO INDIA
(IN PERCENTAGES)

WE SHOULD BE LOYAL TO OUR OWN REGION FIRST AND THEN TO INDIA. DO YOU. . . ?	1971	1996	1999
Agree	67.1	53.4	50.7
Disagree	22.3	21.0	21.4
Don't know, no opinion	10.6	25.6	27.9

Source: Centre for the Study of Developing Societies (Delhi), National Election Studies 1971, 1996, 1999.

nisms such as tax devolution, grants (both plan and nonplan), and special loans from the Reserve Bank of India. These transfers were made on the basis of complex criteria that took into account distributive justice (the extent of poverty or special circumstances such as natural disasters, terrorism, and population size) while rewarding evidence of efforts at self help. High-income states covered 66.8 percent of their current spending with their own resources, middle-income states covered 55 percent, and low-income states covered 38.8 percent.[6]

The findings from survey research show that enough profits from macro financial transactions have trickled down to the level of the mass public to bring the federal process a measure of legitimacy. A series of National Election Studies measured the interest of the Indian electorate in the political system at the central, regional, and local levels, as well as loyalty to the respective political arenas. Results are presented in Tables 1 and 2.

Analysis of these findings reveals a growing interest in regional matters from 1971 to 1999 (see Table 1). A notable and steady increase can be seen in the group of respondents who are equally interested in both levels of government. This table shows more and more people taking an interest in what their own region does while the focus on the center has somewhat declined. The most remarkable increase has been in the public's interest in *both* central and regional government, accompanied by a stark decline in the percentage of those without an opinion. This

TABLE 3—TRUST IN LOCAL, STATE, AND CENTRAL GOVERNMENT
(IN PERCENTAGES)

HOW MUCH TRUST/CONFIDENCE DO YOU HAVE IN THE GOVERNMENT?	A GREAT DEAL	SOMEWHAT	NO TRUST AT ALL
Local government	39.0	37.8	23.2
State government	37.2	43.6	19.2
Central government	35.2	42.5	22.3

Sources: Centre for the Study of Developing Societies (New Delhi), National Election Studies 1996. Subrata K. Mitra and V.B. Singh, *Democracy and Social Change in India: A Cross-Sectional Analysis of the National Electorate* (New Delhi: Sage, 1999), 163.

can be interpreted as evidence of the internalization of the federal norm in that section of the electorate, which appears to see the power-sharing arrangement as a part of normal center-state relations.

Based on the results presented in Table 2, one could infer that loyalty first and foremost to the regions is in steady decline. Tables 1 and 2 show that both arenas are increasingly perceived as legitimate venues of political action which need not be mutually exclusive. Regional political forces, having established themselves in the states as well as at the central level, have turned the issue of the relationship between national and regional identities from one of exclusive choice into one of inclusiveness. This has been accelerated through India's vigorous media and thriving telecommunications market.

Finally, the horizontal and vertical expansion of federal processes through the creation of new federal units that strategically coopt regional and local dissidents and produce new stakeholders through the women's quota in the local *panchayats* (village councils) has brought greater legitimacy to the Indian state and cohesion to the Indian nation. Some evidence of trust in all three levels of government is presented in Table 3.

The breezy confidence with which some Indians explain the seeming contradictions of their country with reference to the political culture of "unity in diversity" has been sorely tested during the times of violence at partition of the country in 1947, sporadic intercommunity riots, and the separatist movements and mass insurgencies that afflict Kashmir and the northeast. Still, without a culture of compromise, consensus, and accommodation, the main hypothesis of structure, agency, and new federal design will not succeed.

To meet the cultural hypothesis at least halfway, I suggest a modification of the folk theory of unity in diversity into unity *and* diversity. All Indian religions have their specific concepts of a macro, binding structure. Each also has unique ways of accommodating latent conflicts of belief and practice, resulting in regional and local diversity. The same practice has been adopted by modern institutions like political parties and trade unions which, under the umbrella of a modern macro ideology and manifesto, embrace considerable divergence in doctrine and practice.

The legacy of federalism under British rule can be best understood through this modified cultural angle. The preindependence attempts by the British to institute a federal state, seen as biased in favor of the Muslim League, were perceived by the Congress party as an attempt to weaken the center. This path dependency of the preindependence context led to a "union of states" (the word federation is not to be found in the Indian constitution) with the dual purpose of limiting the tyranny of the majority and of generating strength through union.[7] The *swadeshi* federalism—guaranteeing both unity and diversity—was more acceptable than the British design, which was perceived as an instrument to stymie the spirit of nationalism.

Combining Strength with Democracy

Looking back to the partition riots, which cast their long shadow on the deliberations of the Constituent Assembly, one can see the reason for the top-heavy institutional design of federalism that emerged. But what explains its continuation once the immediate peril had passed? Comparative federal theory tells us that a durable federal design derives its resilience from its success at reconciling the contradictory goals of freedom with cohesion and diversity of political cultures with effective collective action. Usually, one can assume such a design to be the product of a context with a tradition of political bargaining among autonomous units, and of a political culture leavened with the history of a "social contract" which so richly textures the political experience of Western federal states. None of these *a priori* conditions prepares the student of comparative federalism for the Indian case. With a constitution that is more the result of a transfer of power than of a concerted, organized quest for independent statehood based on a contract, India stands apart from the world's major federations. After the Seventy-third Amendment to the constitution in 1993,[8] India developed a three-tier system of government wherein authority is divided between the central level, the federal units, and about five-hundred thousand village councils.

With a clear, constitutionally guaranteed division of power[9] effectively policed by an independent Supreme Court, direct elections to the *panchayats* and central and regional governments monitored by an independent Election Commission, and the capacity of the political process to sustain a dynamic balance between the levels of government, India exhibits many of the features of federalism. But India's membership in this exclusive club remains a matter of some dispute.[10] The political evidence with regard to the characteristics of a federal process[11] is present and can be seen from K.C. Wheare's brief review of the condi-

TABLE 4—THE STRUCTURE OF INDIA'S FEDERATION

LEVELS OF GOVERNMENT	JURISDICTIONS		
	EXECUTIVE	LEGISLATIVE	JUDICIAL
Union	President-in-Council	Parliament (Lok Sabha & Rajya Sabha)	Supreme Court
State (central law prevails in case of conflict)	Governor-in-Council	Assembly	High Court
District and below (rule-making power depends on the state assembly)	Collector	Zilla Parishad	District Courts

tions of effective federalism that suggests four necessary conditions for a federal design.[12] The first requires at least two levels of government, each with independent spheres of administrative and legislative competence. This condition is more than fulfilled by the Seventy-third Amendment, by which India actually has three levels of government. The federal division of powers allocates responsibility for matters of national importance to the union government, regional matters to the state governments, and issues of national importance that nevertheless are of regional and local character to the concurrent list on the understanding that in case of conflict, the national law should prevail. Residuary powers are allocated to the union government. Second, the constitution recognizes the principle of *independent tax bases,* though with the combination of democratic pressure for tax reduction on land, education, and healthcare, which fall under the scope of state legislation, states have lost out on the financial front, and expansion of the economy has benefited the central government more. Third, a written constitution from which each side derives its legislative power makes sure that boundaries are clearly demarcated. Fourth, there must be a system of independent judicial courts to arbitrate between the center and the constituent units.

Thus, in terms of the classic features of federal states, the Indian constitution fulfills the necessary conditions (see Table 4). Yet the Achilles' heel of the institutional arrangement lies in its financing. The federal division of powers gives the union jurisdiction over taxes that have an interstate base while taxes with a local base are allotted to the states. The more flexible and lucrative sources of revenue—income tax, corporation tax, customs duty, and excise duties—are allocated to the union list. The constitution, however, recognizes the states' position of financial weakness and provides a number of mechanisms to help them meet their deficit. The constitution provides three methods for the transfer of resources from the center to the states, including: 1) the transfer of net proceeds from certain taxes and duties such as stamp duties, duties on

toilet and medicinal preparations, estate duty on nonagricultural property, duties of succession to property other than nonagricultural land,
and taxes on railway fares and freight; 2) the compulsory sharing of
certain taxes like income tax; and 3) permissive sharing of excise taxes,
as well as conditional and unconditional grants-in-aid. The mechanisms
for balancing the financial might of the union government and the needs
of the states are the Finance Commission, a quasi-judicial body appointed by the president for the duration of five years, and the Planning
Commission, whose recommendations are discussed by the National
Development Council.

The institutional arrangements of federalism, carrying the double
legacy of the euphoria of independence and the fear of disintegration in
the face of the partition riots, show abundant evidence of a bias in favor
of the union. The central Parliament enjoys the extraordinary power of
legislation on state subjects that affect the national interest when authorized by the Rajya Sabha.[13] The consent of states is not required for
alteration of their names or boundaries. The overwhelming financial
power of the union, already mentioned above, gives the union government the edge when it comes to coercing state governments. Similarly,
the comprehensive authority of the Union Planning Commission, very
much Nehru's brainchild and an instrument of central initiatives with
regard to development projects, plays an additional role in regard to
central directives and guidance. The governor, formal head of the state
government, was designed to be a central appointee rather than an elected,
local official. The All India Services, a legacy of the British Raj, remains under central control. Finally, the emergency provisions in articles 352, 356, and 360 have become very much a part of everyday
politics and not just the exception. In consequence, Wheare, voicing
the skepticism of many experts, describes the Indian case as "a quasi-
federation—a unitary state with subsidiary federal features rather than a
federal state with subsidiary unitary features."[14]

The ambivalent legal position that the Indian constitution accords
to the constituent states of the union must appear startling to the feder-
alist. The construction of the union did not result from a decision by a
group of independent political units to shed bits of their sovereignty
out of mutual interest to create a federal state. The Indian union and the
provincial governments were simultaneous creations of the Constituent
Assembly in which the latter did not have any special representation.
Furthermore, the central government gradually shifted the boundaries
of the units that existed at the time of independence and started to
create new states. The first major redesign of state boundaries occurred
in 1956 and 1957 through the States Reorganization Act, after pro-
longed agitation in South India for a reorganization of states along
linguistic and cultural boundaries.[15]

Despite the misgivings of experts and the asymmetry in the structural relations between the union and the states, regional governments were not the mere minions of the union government. The Indian Supreme Court, vindicating the claims of Watts regarding the importance of an institutional arrangement to guarantee the autonomy of the constituent units,[16] declared that "the fact that under the scheme of our constitution greater power is conferred upon the center vis-à-vis the states does not mean that states are mere appendages of the center. Within the sphere allotted to them, states are supreme. The center cannot tamper with their powers."[17]

Political dominance by a single ethnic group has been the bane of many postcolonial states. The dominance of Pakistani politics by the Punjabi people, or the great sense of insecurity that the Tamil minority of Sri Lanka feels because of the dominance of the Sinhala majority, both in terms of numbers and area, is enough evidence of the potential consequences of the structural asymmetry of the union. In the Indian case, the Supreme Court has confirmed the status of India's federalism as part of the basic structure of the Indian constitution.[18] Thus, the Supreme Court has codified this institutional design which was not expressly laid out in the constitution of India.[19]

Institutional Changes Since Independence

The framers of the Indian constitution were keen on federalism as a functional instrument for the creation of an Indian nation and a strong, cohesive state. The leading politicians of the immediate postindependence state were faced with internal and external threats to India's security and confronted the challenge of development through centralized economic planning. Thus, for both constitutional and political reasons, the institutionalization of federalism in the Indian system appears to have been seriously compromised from the outset. In fact, the apprehension of "fissiparous tendencies" and "balkanization" among the informed observers was so great that the professional predictions for the future of India as a democracy and a federation were pretty grim. Nonetheless, the political process has been able to adapt to this design and in many, though not all cases, to modify it when necessary to safeguard regional interests.

The first phase of federation lasted from the time of Indian independence to the mid-1960s. Nehru cared enough about democracy to face the enormously expanded electorate in the first general election in 1951. The electorate significantly included the Hindu nationalists, one of whom had assassinated Mohandas Gandhi, and the Communists, who had just staged an armed revolution in Telengana in South India. Nehru took the chief ministers seriously enough to write to each of them every month, in an effort to keep them informed and to solicit their opinion in an effort to build a national consensus.[20] The Congress party, which had already embraced federalism by organizing itself into Provincial Congress Committees based on the linguistic regions, institutionalized the principles of consultation, accommodation, and consensus through a delicate balancing of the factions within the "Congress system."[21] It also coopted local and regional leaders in the national power structure[22] and sent out Congress "observers" from the center to mediate between warring factions in the provinces, thus simultaneously ensuring the legitimacy of the provincial power structure in running its own affairs and the role of central mediation.

The second phase of Indian federalism began with the fourth general elections in 1967, which drastically reduced the Congress party's overwhelming parliamentary strength to a simple majority and saw half of the states moving from Congress control into the hands of opposition parties or coalitions, causing a radical change in the nature of center-state relations. No longer could an imperious Congress prime minister benevolently "dictate" to a loyal Congress chief minister. Even as the tone became more contentious, however, the essential principles of accommodation and consultation held during the crucial period of transition from 1967 to 1969. The Congress-dominated center started cohabiting with opposition parties at the regional level. The tenuous balance was lost once the Congress party split in 1969 and Indira Gandhi, her party reduced to a minority in Parliament, adopted a strategy of radical rhetoric and authoritarian leadership. In consequence, the regional accommodation, which had been possible through the internal federalization of the Congress party, eroded. After the authoritarian interlude of 1975 to 1977 (which in both law and fact reduced India's federal system to a unitary state), the system reverted to the earlier stage of tenuous cooperation between the center and the states.

The third phase in the federalization of Indian politics began at the end of the 1980s. Regional parties, like the Dravida Munnetra Kazhagam (DMK) of Tamil Nadu and the Rashtriya Janata Dal (RJD) of Bihar, have asserted their interests more openly over the past one-and-a-half decades of coalition and minority governments. Even the Hindu-nationalist Bharatiya Janata Party, which led the ruling coalition in the thirteenth Lok Sabha (Parliament's lower house) until 2004, has had to be solicitous in its at least symbolic adherence to the norms of center-state relations established by its predecessors. This has been most evident in its acceptance of the three-language formula in spite of its advocacy of Hindi as India's national language during the long years in the opposition.

The most important phase of financial federalism started with the "big-bang liberalization" of the Indian economy. It has seen a radical transformation from the earlier "ganging up of the states against the center" to a free-for-all competition between all stakeholders—union, states, and megacities—to create conditions that attract investments from home and abroad. This has led to the decline of the center-dominated developmental model that was implemented after independence. By scaling back the state's involvement in the developmental process and as such reducing the functions of the central government, liberalization removed the safety net on which regional governments had depended. As such, the process of liberalization risked opposition from state governments. This opposition failed to materialize. Rob Jenkins even argues that part of the momentum for further liberalization comes from India's regions.[23]

The policies of liberalization launched in 1991 that started to dismantle the draconian rules of the command economy required a new regime to provide coordination in a rapidly changing financial environment. The removal of subsidies and handouts could produce an antireform coalition of leftist parties that must have been aware of the lack of popular support for reform. Why did this antireform wave, in spite of the rhetoric from its leaders, fail to block reform? Jenkins's analysis of the liberalization of coffee pricing makes the point. In 1992, following the first generation of liberalization policies, coffee growers were for the first time permitted to sell 30 percent of their crop in the open market, effectively ending the monopoly control of government coffee boards. The free-sale quota was increased to 50 percent in 1993. In April 1995, in a long-anticipated move, all obligations to the coffee board were removed for "small growers" (those with land holdings of less than ten hectares). Jenkins shows how states with coffee-growing operations, under financial pressure and in search of new sources of revenue, began to tax coffee growers who had received "windfall" profits. The Karnataka government was able to raise resources in this way, justifying the new tax in terms of the responsibility of those who are better off to share some of their gains with the poor and the needy.

These adaptations further delink states' economic fates from one another—contributing to the pattern of provincial Darwinism that "has reduced the effectiveness of resistance among state-level political elites."[24] Thus, *center-state* conflicts have been at least partially displaced by *interstate* competition for inward investment. Lawrence Saez draws attention to changes in institutional arrangements and the process of political coordination of the economy. "[T]he most significant transformation of India's federal system is exemplified by the gradual shift from intergovernmental cooperation between the central government and the states towards interjurisdictional competition among the states."[25]

The Federalization of National Politics

The recognition of political coalitions as the most practiced institutional form of politics in India has reinforced the concept of federalism as the most practical and effective method of center-state and interstate relations. Drawing on the literature,[26] I suggest four general conditions to explain the federalization of India's national politics with regard to the policy process. The first and foremost is "elite accommodation." Next is "public involvement" though it may "complicate the patterns of negotiation for the establishment of a federal system."[27] An atmosphere of "competition and collusion" between intergovernmental agencies is a third condition.[28] In the fourth place, drawing on Riker, Watts mentions "the role and impact of political parties, including their number, their character, and the relations among federal, state, and local branches" as helpful in explaining the dynamism of federal processes.[29]

The pattern of elite recruitment employed by the Congress party during the period of its hegemony (1952 to 1967) where local and regional talent rose to prominence within the party organization and moved horizontally to government, and the subsequent practice of new, upwardly mobile social groups that entered the electoral arena as political parties organized under their own names, revealed a steady expansion of the social base of leadership in India. That satisfies the first two of the conditions mentioned by Watts. The competition for scarce natural resources among bureaucrats and political leaders from Indian states is a good example of the third condition at work.

With the decline of the Congress party, however, intraparty federalization has been supplanted by an entirely different intraparty and interparty system. Nevertheless, even though regional parties are viewed as champions of special interests in the states, leaders who aim to become national figures hope to place the region in the larger context of the nation. Eventually, as members of national coalitions of regional parties, they start to pose as national leaders, ready to compromise and conciliate among conflicting regional interests. This places a measure of restraint on political impropriety and policing by coalition partners who do not wish to have their own political futures ruined through a partner's misconduct. The elevation of Laloo Prasad Yadav from Bihar to the railway ministry in the central government is a case in point.[30] Thus even as the dominance of the Congress party has declined, the multiparty system that replaced it has produced the same institutionalized method of regional conflict resolution within a national framework.

The social origins of these "new regionalist" champions who become born-again nationalists following the logic of the Indian political process help to identify the dynamic process that sustains the federal system in India. These new regionalists (who should be distinguished from the old regionalists who were given to taking non-negotiable positions during the period of Congress dominance) are likely to be upwardly mobile educated males, the erstwhile "bullock capitalists"[31] who have now graduated beyond exclusive reliance on agriculture to other avenues of upward mobility. The new regionalists are busy in the construction of India's center from the periphery.

Having established themselves locally, regionalists have now set their sights on constructing the kind of nation that they want. They are using their alliances with similar forces from outside their region to define the nature of the national community in their own way. Recent events in different parts of the country have demonstrated that the pursuit of these goals cannot only coexist with similar aspirations elsewhere but that regional movements can, in fact, reinforce one another by pooling their political resources. Hence the unprecedented scenes of political leaders from one part of India campaigning for regional parties in other parts of the country. The Congress system incorporated local and regional interests at lower levels of the internally federalized system; the new element in Indian politics makes these processes of consultation a systematic way of drawing from people in India's outlying areas and weaves them into different ways of defining what the nation is about and who has the legitimate right to speak in its name.

As one can see from both the 1999 and 2004 Lok Sabha elections and the subsequent government coalitions, regional parties have become part and parcel of government-formation processes even at the central level.[32] As in the case of the 2004 government-formation process, some regional politicians have been able to secure more than their fair share of influence at the central level. While the 21-member RJD secured only two cabinet-rank ministries, the DMK, despite its limited strength of only 16 legislators, was allocated three cabinet ministries. At the same time, the RJD was able to secure a first tentative success with the inclusion of a "Backward States Grant Fund"—of which Bihar would be a major beneficiary—in the Common Minimum Programme of government after the 2004 elections.[33] This exposes the ambiguous nature of the federal bargaining process, where office means influence above and beyond the limits of the portfolio that a politician is allocated. Thus while some regions can hope that their interests are represented through regional power brokers at the central-government level, other states fear being left behind whenever their regional parties are not included in the national-government coalition.

The political processes of the 1990s show the integration of federal norms in the game plans of local and regional political leaders. Rather than taking a mechanical, anti-Delhi stance as their only *raison d'être*, the new breed of ambitious, upwardly mobile leaders of India have learned to play by the rules even while they challenge them, and thus have developed for themselves a new federal space in which the nation and the region can coexist. As Mitra and Lewis show, the integrative power of this model is at its best in Tamil Nadu, where a federal "deal" can be struck with specific actors such as the DMK.[34] But when the actors themselves are fragmented or not a part of the negotiation (as in

Kashmir), the model is no longer very effective in producing a legitimate federal solution.

The Resilience of India's Federalism

The high mortality rate of federalism in changing societies leads one to ask: has India just been lucky? I have argued that while chance, in the form of helpful structural conditions, has certainly played a positive role in the success of India's federalism, the agency of the post-independence leaders and their successors in terms of choice, strategy, and design has provided a useful complement. Looking back, one can admire the prescience with which the framers of the Indian constitution equipped the Indian state to respond to the demands for autonomy through the dual mechanisms of individual and group rights, as well as the federal division of powers in normal times and the effective union of powers in the times of emergency.

During the first phase of India's constitutional development, some of these instruments were useful in empowering political majorities below the level of the national state through the effective enactment of provincial administrations. The second phase of constitutional development through the states reorganization of 1956–57 created linguistically homogeneous states and counterbalanced the likely chauvinism. In its third phase, the process of constitutional development of federalism initiated by the Seventy-third Amendment of 1993, India has witnessed the deepening of the power-sharing principle by the statutory power now accorded to village councils. Finally, the liberalization of the Indian economy has produced an atmosphere where state governments have emerged as stakeholders in the new economic order rather than clients of an almighty union, dependent on a handout to balance their budgets.

These institutional changes of India's federation explain the fusion of modern and traditional political cultures, historical contingency, and the fortuitous historical legacy of great political events like the partition of India. During the critical years of transition from British rule and the consolidation of popular democracy in India, the Congress party provided the link between the modern state and the traditional society. Congress rule, both at the center and in the states, provided informal channels of communication and the balancing of national, regional, and sectional interests. The politics of coalitions that has replaced Congress hegemony has given a public voice to the new debate on the nature of the nation. In consequence, the search for regional allies has now become an imperative for all national parties.

The new group of highly visible and effective regional leaders, drawing on their power bases in the states which often include people from India's periphery (in terms of religion, elite caste-status, or geographic distance from the center), are able to generate a different concept of the nation-state that is better suited to the spirit of our times. When speaking in the national mode, regional leaders do not count out the need to be well-informed and decisive in the defense of the security and integrity of the nation. But in terms of actual policies, they are much more willing and (in view of their social bases) able to listen to the minorities, to regions with historical grievances, and to sections of society that entered the postindependence politics with unsolved, preindependence (in some cases, premodern) grievances. It is thanks to these political "fixers"—culture brokers who mediate between the union and the regions—and the emerging multiparty democracy of India that politics is not merely an anomic battle for power and short-term gain but the release of pent-up creativity and visions that provide a fertile and cohesive backdrop to the realignment of social forces. Far from being its antithesis, the region has actually emerged as the nursery of the nation.

The constitutional, legislative, and policy instruments that India has drawn upon to reach the positive outcomes in the development of federalism have an important implication for the comparative analysis of the federal process. Whereas old institutionalists, such as Wheare, prescribed a given set of institutions as the necessary and sufficient basis of a federal state,[35] neoinstitutionalists show the importance of being pragmatic in devising the institutions appropriate to specific cultural, religious, and historical contexts.[36] The creation of subregional states like Gorkhaland (a result of protracted negotiations between the Congress government of New Delhi, the communist government of Bengal, and the Gorkha leadership) and, more recently, the creation of three new states in the regime of the NDA (considered opposed to further divisions of India) is in every sense a genuine and unprecedented innovation, guided by the heuristic notion of power-sharing and solid, political common sense. The rules of the federal system, rather than being exogenous to the federal process, have become endogenous to it.

In contrast to India, in Pakistan, also a successor state with the British legacy of an English-educated elite schooled in the grammar of parliamentary politics for almost as long as the Congress party, federalism has followed a different trajectory. The undoing of federalism and consequent split of the Pakistani state in 1971 came through the combination of short-sighted leaders and trigger-happy generals, without the balancing factor of the regional and local leaders—the unshaven and ill-clad power brokers who throng the corridors of power in Delhi and the state secretariats. It is true that India, whose government-in-waiting was already forged in the 1930s and whose links with the constituencies remained intact even as the partition wrenched the leaders of the Muslim League from their political soil in India, held the better cards. But faced with the example of leaders like Nehru who, rather than taking short-term advantage of the preponderant role of the union and using this power to promote partisan advantage, used it with judicious discretion, taming the obdurate satraps of larger regions and reassuring the weak and insecure states of the rightness of their just demands, one has to admit that the Indians played their federal cards rather well. Of course, as the fragile state of the northeast and continued dissension in Kashmir show, the parallel processes of federalization and national integration are far from complete. A consideration of the Indian achievements from the dark days of the partition riots of 1946–47, or the rising secessionist movements of the critical 1980s, however, shows that India's unfolding federalism is both robust and resilient.

NOTES

1. The anti-Hindi agitations in Madras in the 1950s were based on the fear of domination by north India and formed the basis of a movement for a separate state to be called Dravidstan. Similar anti-Delhi feelings were roused in West Bengal for much of the 1960s and 1970s, in Punjab in the 1980s, and, currently, in Kashmir and in the northeast.

2. Some of the notable examples of regional autonomy being used for purposes that stand contrary to the norms of the Indian state can be seen in the cases of chief ministers Narendra Modi, Laloo Prasad Yadav, Kumari Mayawati, and Jayalalitha Jayaram. The issue is why this regional habit of violating the constitution does not trickle upward to the center, reducing its legitimacy and integrative role, as is the case in other countries such as Nigeria.

3. Douglass C. North, *Institutions, Institutional Change and Economic Performance* (Cambridge: Cambridge University Press, 1991).

4. North, *Institutions, Institutional Change and Economic Performance,* 1.

5. North, *Institutions, Institutional Change and Economic Performance,* 7.

6. M. Govinda Rao and Nirvikar Singh, "Asymmetric Federalism in India," Paper 567, Department of Economics, University of California–Santa Cruz, 1 April 2004, *http://repositories.cdlib.org/ucscecon/567.*

7. Article 1 of the Indian Constitution of 1950 puts it this way: "India, that is Bharat, shall be a Union of States."

8. In addition, the vertical expansion of the federal structure—to which a third tier was recently added through the inclusion of India's half-million villages, with constitutionally mandated authority and financial autonomy and an obligatory minimum of 30 percent of seats for women—deserves careful attention. This has turned the federal process into a major source of legitimization and democratization of power in India.

9. Following Indian usage, the constituent units of the Indian federation will be called states and state will refer to the central state.

10. Watts, in his comprehensive study of federal systems, counts 23 states as full federal states but one senses a certain reluctance to admit India as a full member of this club. "India and Malaysia, marked by deep-rooted multilingual, multicultural and multiracial diversity, have nevertheless managed to cohere for half and a third

of a century respectively, but are at a critical phase in their development." Ronald L. Watts, "Federalism, Federal Political Systems and Federations," *Annual Review of Political Science, 1998* (Palo Alto, Calif.: Annual Reviews, 1998), 117–37.

11. Following the usage of Watts, federal process is used in this chapter as a descriptive category that refers to the presence of a "broad genus of federal arrangements" in a political system. These characteristics, which could in principle be composed into a scale, are drawn from the definition of a federation as "a compound polity combining constituent units and a general government, each possessing powers delegated to it by the people through a constitution, each empowered to deal directly with the citizens in the exercise of a significant portion of its legislative, administrative and taxing powers, and each directly elected by its citizens." Watts, "Federalism, Federal Political Systems, and Federations," 117, 121.

12. K.C. Wheare, *Federal Government,* 4th ed. (New York: Oxford University Press, 1964).

13. Article 249.

14. K.C. Wheare, as cited in Durga Das Basu, *Introduction to the Constitution of India* (New Delhi: Prentice Hall, 1985), 58.

15. For an assessment of linguistic and cultural diversity and its impact on federalism in India, see Subrata K. Mitra, "Language and Federalism: The Multiethnic Challenge," *International Social Science Journal* (March 2001): 51–60.

16. Watts, "Federalism, Federal Political Systems, and Federations," 126.

17. *S.R. Bommai v. Union of India,* 1994 (3) SCC 1, 216.

18. A similar arrangement can be found in the German constitution (the *Grundgesetz* or Basic Law) which does not specify the number of states which constitute Germany and allows for the alteration of boundaries—albeit only with the consent of the people living the territory concerned (Article 29)—but declares the abolition of federalism, i.e., the division of the country into constituent units as such, as beyond the power of parliament to amend (Article 79, Sec. 3, *Grundgesetz*).

19. Nonetheless, the alteration of boundaries, not least in the recent case of the creation of the state of Jharkhand out of Bihar, have invited protest on several occasions and this instrument, while creating opportunities for greater autonomy for certain ethnic or linguistic groups, has also placed constraints on the political process.

20. These letters, which are a veritable treasure trove on the politics of the early postindependence decades, are now available in a four-volume set. Jawaharlal Nehru, *Letters to Chief Ministers, 1947–1964* (Delhi: Oxford University Press, 1985).

21. Rajni Kothari, *Politics in India* (Boston: Little Brown, 1970).

22. Arend Lijphart, "The Puzzle of Indian Democracy: A Consociational Interpretation," *American Political Science Review* 90 (May 1996): 258–68.

23. Rob Jenkins, *Democratic Politics and Economic Reform in India* (Cambridge: Cambridge University Press, 1999).

24. Jenkins, *Democratic Politics and Economic Reform in India,* 132–33.

25. Lawrence Saez, *Federalism Without a Center: The Impact of Political and*

Economic Reform on India's Federal System (Delhi: Sage, 2002), 215.

26. William H. Riker, "Federalism," in Fred I. Greenstein and Nelson W. Polsby, eds., *Handbook of Political Science,* vol. 5 (Reading, Mass.: Addison Wesley, 1975), 93–172; Watts, "Federalism, Federal Political Systems, and Federations," 128.

27. Watts, "Federalism, Federal Political Systems, and Federations," 128.

28. Watts, "Federalism, Federal Political Systems, and Federations," 130.

29. Watts, "Federalism, Federal Political Systems, and Federations," 130.

30. "Laloo Prasad Yadav, India's railway minister, was known during the 15 years that he and his wife, Rabri Devi, were successive chief ministers of the state of Bihar, for his earthy realism and rustic lifestyle, which included keeping cows in the garden of his official residence. He was also famous for failing to improve the lot of one of India's poorest and most lawless states, and for a raft of corruption charges that put him in jail five times. In May 2004, he was made railways minister in Delhi. . . . Mr Yadav is a wily and disarming politician and has confounded his critics by becoming one of the country's most successful railway ministers." See "India's Railway Minister with Big Ambitions," *The Economist* (London), 29 July–4 August 2006, 54.

31. Lloyd I. Rudolph and Susanne Hoeber Rudolph, *In Pursuit of Lakshmi: The Political Economy of the Indian State* (Chicago: University of Chicago Press, 1987), 49–55.

32. The BJP-led NDA coalition under Atal Bihari Vajpayee initially consisted of 16 parties in the Lok Sabha, out of which only the BJP was a national party, and the cabinet included many veteran regional politicians. In the fourteenth Lok Sabha, the 10-party coalition led by the Congress party under the name United Progressive Alliance and supported by the Left parties included only two national parties, INC and NCP. Of the cabinet ministers, two key portfolios, Information Technology (Dayanidhi Maran) and Railways (Laloo Prasad Yadav), have been allocated to regional figureheads.

33. "UPA Government to adhere to six basic principles of governance," *The Hindu* (Chennai), 28 May 2004, *www.thehindu.com/2004/05/28/stories/ 2004052807371200. htm.*

34. Subrata K. Mitra and R. Alison Lewis, eds., *Subnational Movements in South Asia* (Boulder, Colo.: Westview, 1996).

35. Wheare, *Federal Government.*

36. North, *Institutions, Institutional Change and Economic Performance*; Watts, "Federalism, Federal Political Systems, and Federations."

6

THE RISE OF JUDICIAL SOVEREIGNTY

Pratap Bhanu Mehta

Pratap Bhanu Mehta *is president of the Centre for Policy Research in New Delhi. His most recent publications include* The Burden of Democracy *(2004) and* India's Public Institutions *(coedited with Devesh Kapur, 2005). His essay "Hinduism and Self-Rule" appeared in the July 2004 issue of the* Journal of Democracy. *This essay originally appeared in the April 2007 issue of the* Journal of Democracy.

The Indian Supreme Court's chief duty is to interpret and enforce the Constitution of 1950. Running to more than a hundred-thousand words in its English-language version, this document is the longest basic law of any of the world's independent countries. It contains, at latest count, 444 articles and a dozen schedules. Since its original adoption, it has been amended more than a hundred times, and now fills about 250 printed pages. It is fair to say that the Supreme Court, operating under the aegis of this book-sized liberal constitution, has by and large played a significant and even pivotal role in sustaining India's liberal-democratic institutions and upholding the rule of law.[1] The Court's justices, who by law now number twenty-six, have over the years carved out an independent role for the Court in the matter of judicial appointments and transfers, upheld extensive judicial review of executive action, and even declared several constitutional amendments unconstitutional. The Court upon which they sit is one of the world's most powerful judicial bodies, and yet precisely because of this its career has been and remains shadowed by irony and controversy, with implications for democracy that are both positive and problematic.

A simple issue-wise scorecard of the Court's contribution to maintaining liberty and the rule of law might begin by noting that the Court has generally upheld basic freedoms associated with liberal democracy, albeit with some glaring exceptions. The Court has a relatively weak record when it comes to questioning executive action in cases of preventive detention. While the Court has generally upheld the right to

free expression, it has given the state more leeway in banning books—
particularly those held to offend religious sensibilties—that officials
fear may threaten public order. During the period of emergency rule
declared at the instigation of Prime Minister Indira Gandhi from June
1975 to March 1977, the Supreme Court shrank from its duty and—in a
now universally condemned decision—chose supinely to concur with
the executive's suspension of the writ of *habeas corpus*.

Besides protecting the basic liberties that put the "liberal" in India's
liberal democracy, the Court has helped to ensure the polity's democratic character by safeguarding the integrity of the electoral process.
The Court has acted to curb the central government's tendency to misuse Article 356 as a pretext to sack elected state governments and install "president's rule" instead. Supreme Court interventions have also
promoted democratic transparency by making political candidates meet
fuller norms of disclosure.

The Supreme Court's record in promoting decentralized governance
is mixed. On the one hand, the Court has ensured the integrity of Indian federalism by pronouncing that the central government cannot
dismiss a state government without a high threshold of public justification. On the other hand, courts across the country have been less
receptive to the claims of lower tiers of government against state governments. The Supreme Court has so far proven unable to clarify the
law in this area. While the social and economic rights that the Constitution lists were not at first deemed justiciable, the Supreme Court has
managed over the years to apply a more substantive conception of
equality that justices have used to uphold rights to health, education,
and shelter, among others. To one degree or another, the executive
branch has responded by at least trying to make provisions for the
guarantee of these rights.

The Court's greatest judicial innovation—and the most important
vehicle for the expansion of its powers—has been its institution of Public-Interest Litigation (PIL). In PIL cases, the Court relaxes the normal
legal requirements of "standing" and "pleading," which require that
litigation be pressed by a directly affected party or parties, and instead
allows anyone to approach it seeking correction of an alleged evil or
injustice. Such cases also typically involve the abandonment of
adversarial fact-finding in favor of Court-appointed investigative and
monitoring commissions. Finally, in PIL matters the Court has expanded
its own powers to the point that it sometimes takes control over the
operations of executive agencies.

The PIL movement has allowed all kinds of public-interest matters to
be heard, and given hundreds of poor people a route by which to approach the Court. While PIL cases to date have had mixed success at
shrinking poverty or correcting injustices, the provision of a forum to
which citizens marginalized by the corruptions of routine politics can

turn has arguably given serious moral and psychological reinforcement to the legitimacy of the democratic system.

In the Shadow of Irony

The Indian Supreme Court's undeniable contributions to democracy and the rule of law, to say nothing of its reachings for power in service of these aims, are shadowed by three profound ironies. First, even as the nation's most senior judicial panel engages in high-profile PIL interventions, routine access to justice remains extremely difficult. India's federal judicial system has a backlog of almost twenty million cases, thousands of prisoners are awaiting trial, and the average time it takes to get a judgment has been steadily increasing. There is a saying in India that you do not get punishment after due process—due process *is* the punishment.

The second irony is that even as the Supreme Court has established itself as a forum for resolving public-policy problems, the principles informing its actions have become less clear. To the extent that the rule of law means making available a forum for appeals, one can argue that the Court has done a decent job. To the extent that the rule of law means articulating a coherent public philosophy that produces predictable results, the Court's interventions look less impressive.

The third irony is that the Court has helped itself to so much power—usurping executive functions, marginalizing the representative process—without explaining from whence its own authority is supposed to come. In theory, democracy and constitutionalism can reinforce each other, but in practice their relationship is complex and even problematic. The question of where one begins and the other ends has taken on global significance in light of the widely observed trend toward "post-democracy," according to which representative institutions are losing power to nonelected centers of decision making the world over. In India, unelected judges have effectively replaced the notion of the separation of powers among three governmental branches with a "unitarian" claim of formal judicial supremacy. The concept of the rule of law is supposed to legitimate this claim, but whether judicial supremacy—either as such or as exercised by the Indian Supreme Court—actually upholds the rule of law remains an open question.

In order to understand how this situation has come about, it is helpful to know that in India, the power of judicial review is more or less explicitly spelled out in the 1950 Constitution,[2] and that this Constitution has a dual goal. On the one hand, as a basic law in the liberal tradition, it seeks to check the power of government and to safeguard individual rights and liberties. On the other hand, it is the work of framers who believed, with good cause, that their country needed a state with the capacity to intervene massively in society in order to overcome structural injustices grave enough to threaten liberal democracy itself. So the Constitution allows the courts to intervene in the cause of what might be loosely termed "social reform." Moreover, judges have gradually widened the definition of rights held to be constitutionally "justiciable." Hence the scope of judicial intervention can include everything from civil liberties to urban planning. This constitutional practice, which licensed the courts to intervene, was bound to generate a promiscuity that would be the cause of some resentment.

That resentment has a history. In the early postindependence years, the Supreme Court tried to block land-reform legislation, virtually denied that the Constitution requires substantive due process, and gave serious scrutiny to government regulation of publications.[3] The government's response was typically to seek a change in the letter of the Constitution, which helps to explain why India's basic law is so heavily amended.[4] During the late 1960s and early 1970s, the judiciary struck down major planks of Indira Gandhi's development agenda, including her scheme for nationalizing the banks. This era also saw the Court make its first strong claim that Parliament may not, even via amendment, override the fundamental rights elaborated in Part II of the Constitution. Later, the Court would extend and revise this claim to argue that the legislature may not, through amendment, override the "basic structure" of the Constitution—a structure of which the judiciary has insinuated itself as the custodian. Yet when Prime Minister Gandhi declared her State of Emergency on 25 June 1975, suspended Article 21 of the Constitution (which provides that no person shall be deprived of personal liberty except according to the procedure established by law), and had hundreds of people detained by executive order, the Supreme Court overruled nine High Courts and upheld her actions. That decision is now unanimously regarded as one of the worst in Indian judicial history.[5]

Despite Indira Gandhi's court-packing schemes and other efforts to exert arbitrary executive influence over judicial appointments, the courts emerged from her premiership stronger than ever. For during those years judges framed far-reaching interpretations that would lay a constitutional basis for future judicial bids to curb the powers of the two other branches. The Supreme Court, moreover, managed to legitimize itself not only as the forum of last resort for questions of governmental accountability, but also as an institution of governance. The Court's PIL initiatives—an innovation influenced by Gandhi's populist political style—allowed judges to make policy and demand that executive officials carry it out by closing businesses on environmental grounds, building new housing for slum dwellers, and even maintaining particular college courses.

The second big moment for the judiciary was securing its own independence in matters of filling the Supreme Court. The Constitution's

Article 124 is ambiguous on judicial appointments, calling for consultation between the executive and the judiciary but leaving it unclear who has the final say. While the original idea seems to have been to steer a middle ground between the British practice of executive appointment and the U.S. practice of legislative confirmation, in practice the appointments system became increasingly messy and allowed the executive to "pack" the judiciary.

In a decision in *The Third Judges' Case* (1993), the Supreme Court held that the power to name new judges to the highest bench rests primarily with the chief justice and the next four most-senior justices of the Supreme Court itself.[6] Extensive consultations with the executive are required, but in the end the Court's highest-ranking jurists have the lion's share of the appointment power. As critics have pointed out, this process gives the public no sense of the criteria used in naming justices and no forum in which the merits of prospective Supreme Court judges can be openly weighed and debated. Thus the Court may have secured its autonomy at a cost to its transparency and perhaps its legitimacy as well.

The Rule of Laws or the Rule of Men?

Although most studies of Indian politics pay almost no attention to the courts, disputes between the judiciary and the other two branches have been as important a fact about Indian political life as any. Judges have struck down hundreds of state and national laws. During the first 17 years of the Supreme Court's existence, when it was supposedly in its restrained period, it struck down 128 pieces of legislation. Of the first 45 constitutional amendments, about half were aimed at curbing judicial power. The most recent amendment, number 104, is designed to reverse the result of the *Inamdar* case,[7] in which the Court ruled unconstitutional the central government's effort to control who is admitted to half of all the seats in private institutions of higher education every year, and to set the fees that these schools could charge.

If the frequency of amendments meant to reverse Supreme Court decisions is significant, so is the legislative assumption that amendments are needed at all. Court decisions may infuriate Parliament, in other words, but Parliament thinks that they cannot simply be ignored. Even during the 1975–77 emergency, the government took care to curtail the authority of the courts by formally legal means. This deference has ensured that even constitutional amendments have not been able to alter the basic structure of the Constitution and the *formal* allocation of powers within it.

The foregoing suggests that there is a profound inner conflict at the heart of Indian constitutionalism. The question, "Who is the Constitution's final arbiter?" admits of no easy answer. The Court has declared itself to be the ultimate judge, and has even assumed the power to override duly enacted constitutional arrangements. Yet in a polity where parts of the Constitution can be amended by as little as a majority vote of each of the two houses of Parliament, there is no reason to suppose that a court decision regarding the constitutionality of a particular matter will suffice to remove it from the political agenda. In India, Parliament and the judiciary have been and are likely to remain *competitors* when it comes to interpreting the Constitution. It is by no means settled who has the final word. The decisions of each are episodes in an iterative game of action-response-rejoinder that can be played out any number of times. Parliament can pass a law, the courts can strike it down, Parliament can try to circumvent the courts by amending the Constitution, the courts can pronounce that Parliament's amendment power does not apply to the case, and so on.

It is true that the 1990s saw no full-scale parliamentary assault on the courts' interpretation of what the "basic structure" doctrine requires, but that was an accidental side effect of a fragmented political system in which no one party could achieve dominance in Parliament. Should any party gain enough parliamentary heft to wield the amendment power, the judicial-legislative tussle will almost certainly resume, and it is impossible to predict what the outcome will be, either in the nearer or the longer term.

In the event of a political consensus, such as the one that backs reservation quotas designed to aid members of the so-called Other Backward Classes, the judiciary can be readily overruled. (Parliament has passed no fewer than five amendments meant to thwart judicially imposed restrictions on how the reservations policy is implemented, and the judges have had to go along.) But it is possible that in the near future this kind of overturning of judicial decisions through constitutional amendment will itself become subject to judicial scrutiny. In India, the supremacy of any branch of government is not simply a result of a one-time-only act of constitutional design, but must be secured through an ongoing struggle.

Furthermore, the Court's institutional task is not only to resolve this or that current conflict over constitutionality, but also to preserve the legitimacy of constitutional review as such over the long haul. Indian jurists have, for the most part, been keenly aware of the dilemmas that can lurk here. Justices seem routinely to anticipate the effects of particular decisions on the Court's popular authority. This makes the Court's major decisions, however the Court itself chooses to present them, something other than purely straightforward applications of high constitutional principles or values. Most judgments, in fact, are the result of a delicate and *political* process of balancing competing values and political aspirations; they seek to provide a workable *modus vivendi* rather than to articulate high values.

This is not the place to argue the point at length, but I would submit that most Supreme Court decisions can be read as accommodations or balancing acts of this sort. Even *Golak Nath,*[8] arguably the strongest Court ruling to date vindicating the sanctity of fundamental rights, made a retrospective exception for three constitutional amendments relating to property rights that the decision might otherwise have invalidated. Similarly, *Kesavananda,*[9] while making a statement whose strong drift was that Parliament cannot amend the "basic structure" of the Constitution, was nonetheless deliberately vague about exactly what counts as part of that "basic structure." The *Mandal* decisions on affirmative action showed the Court balancing different pressures rather than giving a principled argument. The justices enlarged the scope of affirmative action, but less than some states wanted. With few exceptions, the courts in general have tread very gingerly regarding certain classes of religious disputes. Judges go to unusual lengths to show that, while they may recommend the reform of certain religious practices, they are not antireligious. Jurists have interpreted Indian secularism itself as a kind of *modus vivendi* rather than as a set of clear principles.

Moreover, the courts have often shied away from taking firm stands on the hottest religious disputes. One such controversy, the *Babri Masjid* case, has languished in various courts for fifty years. When the executive sought an advisory opinion from the Supreme Court, the justices took two years to rule that the matter belonged at the appeals-court level. In more narrowly political matters as well, the Supreme Court has been wary of upsetting the apple cart. Thus the justices have used vague insinuations of corruption as the basis for upholding the political parties' decision to end secret balloting when state legislators vote to send representatives to the Rajya Sabha (House of States), the upper chamber of the Indian Parliament. One may look in vain for a constitutional principle in this judicial bow to political consensus.[10]

In short, the Court's concern for its own authority has led it to read the political tea leaves with care. The judicialization of politics and the politicization of the judiciary turn out to be two sides of the same coin. It is no accident that Indian constitutional law has been relatively unstable, or that the same courts which appear assertive in some areas seem weak in others: strong enough to spark the passage of many constitutional amendments meant to confound judicial rulings, but so easygoing that no major politician has ever been charged in any of the numerous corruption cases that the Supreme Court has been supervising for years. The legitimacy and power that India's judiciary does enjoy most likely flow not from a clear and consistent constitutional vision, but rather from its opposite. The Supreme Court in particular has given enough players enough partial victories to leave them feeling as if they have a stake in keeping the game of political give-and-take going. This, more than any ringing defense of principle, is the Court's signal contribution to Indian democracy.

The Uncaused Cause?

It is hard to say what are the necessary and sufficient conditions under which independent judicial review will arise and take hold. It used to be a common argument that successful constitutional judicial review is caused and required by strong federalism. Federalism requires a "referee" to protect complex boundary arrangements, the logic ran, so each unit of a federation will, despite incentives to deviate, support the creation and maintenance of some central institution designed to identify and stop noncompliance by others. The logic of this argument was never very persuasive. Why would it necessarily be the case that a state involved in a dispute with the central government would support the creation of another arm of the central government to resolve the dispute? As it turns out, the nature of the federal arrangement in India has turned on *how* judicial power is exercised, and judicial review has often eroded rather than strengthened federalism. In the case of India, one could argue that the nature of judicial scrutiny of the center's intervention in the states has influenced the character of federalism itself.

When it comes to defining the federal character of the Indian polity, legislatures and executives have largely followed the judiciary's lead. One-party dominance in New Delhi has often been fingered as the culprit in the weakening of federalism during the 1970s and 1980s, but a simpler explanation points to the courts. The Supreme Court's 1977 advisory opinion permitting the dissolution of nine state governments in favor of so-called president's rule weakened Indian federalism, and before long additional state legislatures had been dissolved. The Court's 1994 ruling in the *Bommai* case made it clearer than before that there must be "substantial constitutional" reasons for dismissing a state government, and has led the central government to be warier about imposing presidential rule on the states.[11] Thus it seems that the character of judicial review can determine the nature and scope of federalism rather than the other way round.

An analogous argument can also be made about the "separation of powers" hypothesis. This suggests that, as with a robust division of powers among different levels of government (central and state), a strong separation of powers among the various branches of government will encourage judicial power and independence.[12] The general presumption has been that in parliamentary systems, where the executive rises directly from the legislature, judicial review will be weak. Yet strong judiciaries replete with doctrines of judicial review are appearing in such parliamentary countries as Australia and Canada, neither of which has traditionally had a strong separation of powers. This has been happening, moreover, even in polities where there has been no change in the formal distribution of powers.

The actions of judges themselves, and not federalism or the separation of powers, most cogently explain changes over time in the exercise of judicial power. Court rulings are the main means for institutionalizing judicial review. In India as elsewhere, it is not simply the formal allocation of powers but an evolving constitutional jurisprudence that has enhanced the powers of judicial review. I am not sure we have or can have a general theory of the conditions under which constitutional law will evolve in the direction of wider powers of judicial review. In democratic societies especially, it seems that the degree of independence which a judiciary asserts is itself a creation of judicial power. The thought that "judicial review causes itself" is probably as good as any answer to the puzzle of judicial power.

The history of judicial power and its exercise in India suggests that the separation-of-powers doctrine is a highly misleading metaphor. It is still invoked all the time, of course, but in reality it offers neither an accurate empirical description of how actual courts work, nor a plausible conceptual account of any government. Policy making has become a routine part of the judicial role in many contexts, and adjudication likewise now belongs in many countries and in many ways to the realm of administrative functioning. The traditional distinction that holds legislatures to be forums for the balancing of interests and courts to be forums of principle is far less obvious than it seems: India's judges do as much balancing as India's lawmakers do. The Supreme Court, strikingly, has given up any formal pretense to the doctrine of the separation of powers, and one would be hard pressed to name a single recent case in years where the Supreme Court simply said: This does not lie within our jurisdiction or domain of competence. Even in instances where the Constitution *specifically* prohibits the courts from inquiring into the proceedings of Parliament and the several state legislatures (Articles 122 and 212), the courts have disregarded the ban.

On the conceptual level, the plausibility of the separation-of-powers metaphor breaks down as soon as one asks: "Who polices the boundaries between different branches of government?" Each branch will want to patrol the borders on its own terms, rendering any idea of "separation" merely rhetorical. Indeed, I would submit that "independence" is not something that inheres in any branch of government; instead, claims to independence are a political resource that is deployed in specific contexts.

A resonant phrase contrasts the rule of law with the rule of men. In more prosaic legal terms, the Supreme Court of India is given to pronouncements that all the branches of government are "under the Constitution," suggesting that all legitimate power has its source in a legal or constitutional order that somehow regulates the conduct of men. But who decides what this legal and constitutional order requires in any given case? The answer is: some group of men! This is a way of saying that there is no such thing as a rule of law which is not also a rule of men, for men will decide what law is. If this is the case, then the separation-of-powers doctrine implodes. It is not something that can be deduced from a formal legal order. Instead, it will be subject to the vagaries of the contending wills of men, or in short, politics.

The Legitimacy of Judicial Intervention

India is not the only democracy where judges have been coming to play an unprecedented governing role. The expansion of the authority enjoyed by unelected bodies has been a staggering worldwide trend in recent years. From waste management, clean air, and education policy to property rights and religious liberty as well as many administrative matters—it is hard to think of a single issue relevant to politics or policy on which the courts of India have not left their mark. The Supreme Court has set itself up as the final arbiter of the Constitution, scrutinizing even amendments made to that document by Parliament.

The weakness of the political process provides fertile soil for judicial activism, and judges keen to compensate for their failure to defend democratic principles during the 1975–77 emergency have avidly taken up the task of preserving the republic. In many instances, the executive has almost invited the judiciary to play a leading role. State governments often seek judicial dispensation as a source of political cover when unpopular decisions have to be made. But such power as the Indian courts have acquired mostly confirms the dictum that power flows to those who choose to exercise it. In decision after decision, be it the authority to review constitutional amendments or the mode of appointing judges, the Supreme Court has created its own powers.

Judicial activism can mean many things: scrutiny of legislation to determine constitutionality, the creation of law, and the exercise of policy prerogatives normally reserved for the executive. But whatever its form, judicial activism raises two questions: Is it legitimate? And is it effective? The democrat in all of us is rightly suspicious when a few people (mostly older and mostly male, as it happens) assume such broad powers over our destiny without much accountability. At least, we ruminate, we can throw the politicians out once in a while, but judges are mostly shielded from accountability. And yet our impatience with a debilitating political process whose usual results are inaction or unsatisfying compromises makes us thankful for an assertive judiciary. At least the judges and their decrees can protect our rights, clean our air, call our politicians to account, and so forth. It is hard not to feel the pull of both sides of the argument. And it must be an unenviable task for judges to steer a middle course between usurping too much power on the one hand, and doing too little to sustain the fundamental values of constitutional democracy on the other.

But the prickly question remains: What legitimizes judicial activism and makes it an exertion not of mere power, but of just authority? One possible answer is that judicial activism is justified to the extent that it helps to preserve democratic institutions and values. After all, transient majorities in Parliament can barter away our democratic rights, and representative institutions are so often burdened with the imperatives of money, power, and inertia that to call their decisions democratic and in the public interest is often something of a joke. If judges use their power to restore integrity to the democratic process, to make our rights (including social and economic ones) more meaningful, and to advance the public interest, then an assertive judiciary can be both a shield and a sword of sorts for democracy. This is the most plausible defense of an assertive judiciary.

The trouble is, however, that there is no reason to assume that judges any more than politicians will always protect our liberties. A student of the Indian scene need only recall the judiciary's "no show" during the state of emergency and hands-off approach to preventive detention since then. Less dramatically but still seriously, the courts in ruling after ruling have been diluting the impact of two democratizing amendments (numbers 73 and 74) by insisting that unelected bureaucrats have more power than local elected officials. And can anyone who cares about the democratic legitimacy of the decisions that govern us look on unconcerned as judges decree the right level of air pollution, the appropriate amount of school fees, the height of dams, or the types of fuel that local buses and trains can burn? Judges are often guilty of both populism and adventurism. Representative institutions are, after all, the essence of democracy, and judges do not stand in the same relation to us as legislators. It may be that we cannot trust representative institutions, but it would be stretching logic to pretend that the guardianship which the courts exercise over policy is synonymous with democracy.

But faced with the messy abdications of politics, should we not simply dispense with self-indulgent qualms about democratic authority and be more pragmatic? Does not judicial activism do good? Does it not produce outcomes that we desire? How one answers these questions depends in part on what one thinks of as the public interest. Defenders of the judiciary often focus on the few success stories that result from judicial decisions. Yet there is a glaring lack of concrete, empirical data on the effects of court interventions. Courts can proclaim new rights as much as they want, but the proclamation of rights by itself does not produce results.

This is not to deny the few instances so far in which the Supreme Court's intervention has done real and even remarkable good. Court rulings have had a lot to do with progress toward making schooling an

implementable constitutional right, for example, and judicial monitoring has improved school-meal programs with good effects on both nutrition and education. But these were both instances where government
and society were willing to meet the Court more than 90 percent of the
way. In the case of other rights—the right to health, for instance—judicial declarations have had little effect. Courts may achieve certain results such as lowering air pollution, but whether they achieve those
results in a cost-effective manner is another question. And whatever the
costs of such decisions, do we have reason to believe that courts distribute them fairly?

Court interventions could be judged successful if they were fostering a constitutional culture wherein certain fundamental values and
aspirations become authoritative constraints on the behavior of governments and citizens alike. But the judiciary's own overreaching and
arbitrariness are making it hard for courts to be what the U.S. political
theorist Ralph Lerner once called "republican schoolmasters,"[13] who
teach voters and officials to internalize respect for the rule of law as a
goal rather than to see the law as a mere tool for manipulation. Indeed,
the more the judiciary expands its ambit of intervention, the more judges
become subject to the charge that their actions are arbitrary.

There are many other reasons to doubt that the Courts alone can be
bringers of social change. The judiciary itself is in deep disrepair. The
civil-justice system gives the impression of being an arena where the
law is subject to discretionary manipulation rather than being a conduit
of justice. Its massive case backlog alone is shocking. The Supreme
Court's efforts to foster a more robust constitutional culture suffer from
the Court's penchant for seeking hazy accommodations among competing interests rather than settling issues on clear, decisive principles.
Perhaps the U.S. jurist Learned Hand was right when in 1942 he wrote:

> You may ask what then will become of the fundamental principles of
> equity and fair play which our Constitutions enshrine; and whether I seri-
> ously believe that unsupported they will serve merely as counsels of mod-
> eration. I do not think that anyone can say what will be left of those
> principles; I do not know whether they will serve only as counsels; but this
> much I think I do know—that a society so riven that the spirit of modera-
> tion is gone, no Court can save; that a society where that spirit flourishes
> no Court need save; that a society which evades its responsibility by thrust-
> ing upon the Courts the nurture of that spirit, that spirit will in the end
> perish.[14]

The eminent Indian legal scholar Upendra Baxi once memorably
called judicial activism a dire cure for a drastic disorder: "chemotherapy
for a carcinogenic body politic."[15] And certainly judges have an important role to play in strengthening our democracy. But they will have to
exercise great discretion and resist the intoxication which comes from

the view that judges are the last, best hope of the republic. As Judge Hand also observed, during a great world war in which freedom was at stake and just a few short years before India began its life as an independent republic: "Liberty lies in the hearts of men and women; when it dies there, no constitution, no law, no court can save it; no constitution, no law, no court can even do much to help it."[16]

NOTES

1. India's courts by and large fit into a single three-tiered system, with the Supreme Court at the apex. Each state has a High Court, with District Courts below it. The Supreme Court, established in 1950 as a successor to the Federal Court, has broad powers. Under Article 131, it exercises original jurisdiction in cases involving the government and appellate jurisdiction in a variety of cases. Under Article 132, it rules on cases involving constitutional interpretation; under Article 133, it exercises jurisdiction over civil cases that involve a substantial question of law with general importance. In addition, it is an appellate court for some criminal cases, has the power to grant special leave to appeal, has writ jurisdictions over questions of fundamental rights, and has the authority to issue advisory opinions. The High Courts act as courts of first and second appeals in civil matters; in addition, they have extensive writ jurisdiction and act as superintendents for subordinate courts.

2. The warrant for judicial review comes from a combined reading of Articles 13, 32, and 142. Article 13(2) provides that "The State shall not make any law which takes away or abridges the rights conferred by this Part and any law made in contravention of this clause shall, to the extent of the contravention, be void." Articles 32 and 226 give any person the right to move the Supreme Court or the High Court, respectively, for the enforcement of fundamental rights guaranteed in Part III of the Constitution. Finally, Article 142 provides that the Supreme Court "may pass such decree or make such order as is necessary for doing complete justice in any cause or matter," and such decree or order is "enforceable throughout the territory of India." Article 142, especially the phrase "complete justice," has given the judiciary a virtual license to intervene in any matter whatsoever. In addition to these textual enablers, the Court has over the years created its own powers in a number of domains.

3. At the same time, however, the Court's thwarting of the government was not absolute: The justices tended to uphold the state's preventive-detention orders.

4. Different parts of the Constitution can be amended in three ways: 1) by a simple majority of all members of Parliament present and voting; 2) by a two-thirds majority of Parliament subject to a quorum requirement of 50 percent; and 3) by two-thirds vote of Parliament as above, followed by ratification via a two-thirds vote of at least half the state legislatures. In each case, presidential assent is required before an amendment can become law.

5. *ADM Jabalpur v. Shivakant Shukla AIR* 1976 SC 1207.

6. See *S.P. Gupta v. Union of India and Others (First Judges Case)* AIR 1982 SC149; 1981 Supp(1)SCC87; *Supreme Court Advocates-On-Record Association and Anr. v. Union of India* AIR 1994; SC268; (1993) 4 SCC 441.

7. *P.A. Inamdar and Others v. State of Maharashtra* AIR 2005 SC 3226; (2004) 8 SCC 139.

8. *Golak Nath and Others v. State of Punjab and Anr.* AIR 1967 SC 1643.

9. *Keshavanda Bharati and Others v. State of Kerala* AIR 1973 SC 1461; (1973) 4 SCC 225.

10. *Kuldip Nayar v. Union of India and Others* W.P. (C) Nos. 217, 262, 266, and 305 of 2004 JT 2006 (8) SC 1 (not yet published in AIR or SCC).

11. *S. R. Bonmai v. Union of India* (1994) 3 SCC 1.

12. For a statement of this view, see John Ferejohn, "Law, Legislation and Positive Political Theory," in J.S. Banks and Eric Hanushek, eds., *Modern Political Economy: Old Topics, New Directions* (Cambridge: Cambridge University Press, 1995), 208.

13. Ralph Lerner, "The Supreme Court as Republican Schoolmaster," *Supreme Court Review 1967* (Chicago: University of Chicago Press, 1967), 127–80.

14. Learned Hand, "The Contribution of an Independent Judiciary to Civilization," in Irving Dillard, ed., *The Spirit of Liberty: Papers and Addresses of Learned Hand,* 3rd ed. (New York: Alfred A. Knopf, 1960), 181.

15. Upendra Baxi, "Introduction" to S.P. Sathe, *Judicial Activism in India* (Oxford: Oxford University Press, 2001), 3.

16. Learned Hand, "The Spirit of Liberty," in Dillard, *The Spirit of Liberty,* 190.

7

POLICE AGENCIES AND COERCIVE POWER

Arvind Verma

Arvind Verma *is associate professor of criminal justice and director of the India Studies Academic Program at Indiana University. He is a consultant to the Bureau of Police Research and Development of the Government of India and has served as managing editor of* Police Practice and Research: An International Journal.

Maintaining order has always been perceived to be a challenge in India. The large, diverse population with its divisions of class, caste, region, religion, language, and culture has been seen as a threat by the Mughal, the British, and even the Indian rulers—a greater threat than that from hostile neighbors. Rulers of India therefore have not hesitated in using a variety of coercive mechanisms to maintain their hegemony and power. The British, concerned about the threat from the masses, especially after the First War of Indian Independence (known to the British as the Sepoy Mutiny) in 1857, devised the ultimate coercive mechanism, an armed police system that could deal expeditiously with riots, demonstrations, and disorder.[1] The postindependence leaders also found this force a useful instrument and continued the system unchanged despite the infamy of the "khaki force."

Indeed, India's democratically elected governments went further in strengthening the coercive powers of the police system. In February 1950, less than a month after promulgating a new constitution, the government of Jawaharlal Nehru enacted the Preventive Detention Act which allows for the imprisonment of people suspected of posing a threat to society. With this act, India became the first democratic country to create a prevention clause—an action that evoked considerable opposition in the Parliament and the Indian National Congress (Congress party) itself.[2] In retrospect, this act appears mild compared to other coercive legislation that was to follow. Ironically, as Indian democracy matures and rule of law becomes the governing principle of the country, governments from both the left and the right have added to the powers of the enforcement agencies. Furthermore, they have not hesitated in applying coercive powers to administer their writ in the country.

This chapter first will examine the nature of repressive laws that have been devised by successive Indian governments over the course of independence. In particular, it will look into the nature of policing and legal mechanisms that give coercive powers to the executive. Second, it will present evidence of the abusive application of these legal instruments and explore situational factors that suggest deliberate recourse to repression by the executive. It will then debate the need for and the application of such powers in the democratic functioning of Indian society. I will argue that Indian policy makers, particularly the executive branch, have readily used coercive powers and in so doing have sacrificed long-term interests for short-term expediency. The chapter will conclude with the implications of coercion for the democratic polity of India.

The Tool of Coercion

All modern states exercise coercive powers. Beginning in the sixteenth and seventeenth centuries, the modern states in Western Europe "asserted their own legal and political sovereignty . . . [insisting] that they were the sole jurisdictional authority within their territory and that those living in it were subject to the state's authority simply by virtue of that fact."[3] At present, all states have centralized their authority and power, created legal mechanisms of coercion, and asserted their power to enforce domestic order. The Indian state is no different in this regard. Even though there is evidence of "unity in diversity," the state has armed itself with extensive powers to ensure that there is no challenge to its authority and territorial sovereignty from its diverse constitutents.

The foundation of these coercive powers was laid by the British when they began taking control of the reins of government after their victory at the Battle of Plassey in 1757. Yet it would take them almost a hundred years to forge a formidable mechanism to rule India. The Police Act V of 1861, enacted in the aftermath of the war of 1857, was deliberately designed to maintain the British Raj in which the suppression of the people was the first priority of the police. "The new police was so shaped in personnel, powers and procedures as to be a terror to the law abiding citizen."[4] The police force was designed to produce a fear of authority in the population and to establish itself as the first line of internal defense.[5] The British feared that lower subordinates would establish long-term relations with the citizens and thus dilute the symbolic hegemony of the Raj.

The British administrative officers, numbering less than one thousand in the combined jurisdiction of what is now India, Pakistan, and Bangladesh, exercised power only indirectly through the Indian Civil Service, the Imperial Police (IP), and other elite services. The leadership was not legitimate in the eyes of the people but imposed from above by the crown. The bulk of responsibilities were entrusted to the natives who filled the subordinate ranks. Direct recruitment into the IP ranks was closed for native people as late as 1921 and even then the number of Indians in these services was kept disproportionately low. Furthermore, a conscious class distinction between the superior and subordinate officers was strictly enforced.

In addition to the artificial separation between British and Indian policemen, there was also an enforced infallibility attributed to the leaders of the IP.[6] The Police Act and all subsequent department rules were framed so that the authority of senior officers could neither be questioned nor disobeyed. Section 23 of the Police Act V of 1861, for example, describes the *duty* of the police personnel "to obey all orders lawfully given by the officers." Ostentatious pageantry was another intentional emblematic form of authority. The daily parade and salute to the commanding officer, the sentry at the superintendent's gate, and the armed escort for British officers' tours were symbols that placed the officers on a high pedestal. This style of governance created a setting in which the administrators were placed far above their subordinates and this distance was deliberately maintained.[7]

On the other hand, the ill-trained and poorly paid subordinates were let loose upon the people. The citizens endured daily humiliations and oppression from the bureaucracy. The only relief from the marauding army of government servants came from the senior officers who alone could control and discipline them. Yet the aura of the senior officers was such that no citizen dared to approach them. The British, through their inspections and administrative mechanisms, would occasionally find a corrupt officer and punish him. This maintained the façade that the British were concerned about the welfare of the citizens and would act if the complaint reached them. The fact that they insulated themselves and only in rare cases took action reflected their indifference and poor administrative arrangements.

Apart from the symbols of power that kept the citizens subdued, the British developed a deliberate administrative style that would ensure that no citizen dared to challenge the Raj. The police, for instance, were housed in barracks away from the general population. Most police units of a district were situated in Civil Lines, an area off limits to the native population. The officers were not encouraged to mix with civilians for fear that they would develop close relationships and empathize with them. A strict rule of keeping officers at a station for a limited period was developed wherein every member of the police force, from the lowest constable to the highest-ranking officer, was transferred every three years.

Independence did not change police administration. From the beginning, Prime Minister Nehru and Deputy Prime Minister Sardar Vallabhbhai Patel were involved in dousing the fires of partition and religious fanaticism. According to David Arnold, after independence in

1947, hardly any significant change in police methods and attitudes occurred.[8] Communal violence and unprecedented civil unrest before and after India's independence compelled the national and provincial governments to defer any plans for a transformation of the police to a later date. After the initial euphoria of independence faded, protests and demonstrations began to challenge the Nehru government. Thereafter, Indian governments always felt besieged and threatened by the rising aspirations of the people. As such, the colonial model of police was seen to be useful in keeping order in the country and no changes were sought by any successive government.

Problems maintaining law and order became immensely more complicated after the Congress party began to lose power in the provinces. From the 1970s on, growing incidents of extremism, large-scale protests, demonstrations, and riots have so threatened the state that despite the recommendations of the National Police Commission (1979–83), no government has seen any reason to reform and build a localized civilian police system. The concept of a police force that would work with the people without frequent recourse to its coercive powers remains illusory to this day.

Successive governments, recognizing the critical necessity of maintaining order, have funded additional armed units to deal with public disturbances while remaining indifferent to their ultimate consequences.[9] The number of specialized armed police battalions at both the central and provincial levels has been increasing rapidly since the 1960s. These armed police forces, meant largely for "public-order" duties, far outnumber the units engaged in crime-control tasks. The need for more antiriot units has been justified on the grounds that the number of "lawless" situations is increasing. There is some justification to this claim. In 2004, for example, there were 68,608 cases of riots and arson affecting public safety forming 32.9 percent of violent crimes registered by the police. Additionally, riotous mobs were responsible for more than 38.5 percent of injuries caused to police officers on duty.[10]

The seriousness of public-order problems has also meant that the police have not hesitated in the use of force against citizens. In 2004, there were 791 incidents of police shootings in which 420 civilians were killed and 257 persons sustained injuries.[11] Indeed, confronting large crowds has become a daily duty of the Indian police and, not surprisingly, they routinely resort to coercive powers during their operations.[12] Volatile social, economic, ethnic, religious, and political conditions have made modern India stress "order" more than due process. The ideal of a civilian police force has not yet materialized in practice.

Police and Coercive Powers

Apart from the system of armed policing, police personnel have also been empowered with formidable powers of arrest, search-seizure, and preventive detention. The Indian laws have conferred a vast amount of unbridled discretion to the police officers that enables them to coerce people to an extraordinary degree. The general powers of arrest as provided in Sections 41 to 56 of the Criminal Procedure Code (CrPC) describe the conditions under which a police officer may arrest any citizen without seeking a warrant from the magistrate.[13] Thus Section 54 of the CrPC states that "any police officer may arrest . . . without a warrant . . . such person who has been concerned in any cognizable [indictable] offence or . . . against whom . . . reasonable suspicion exists of his being so concerned . . . [and] in whose possession anything is found which may reasonably be suspected to be stolen property." As the abovementioned clause suggests, the law has left the determination of the grounds for making the arrest entirely at the discretion of the police officer. Even in subsequent clarifications, what constitutes *reasonable suspicion* has not been spelled out and is said "to depend upon circumstances of the particular case."[14] Furthermore, clause four of this section has extended this discretion and has stipulated that no formal (citizen) complaint is necessary for a police officer to arrest a person under this provision.

It is not imperative that an arrest should be made only on commission of an offense. Police have been given authority to arrest an individual even to *prevent* the occurrence of a crime. Thus Section 151 of the CrPC states that "a police officer knowing of a design to commit any cognizable offence may arrest . . . the person so designing, if it appears to the police officer that the commissioning of the offence cannot be otherwise prevented." Though in a subsequent clarification the courts have stated that "where no emergency for arrest which this section contemplates is shown to have existed, the attempt to arrest on part of the police is not only 'not strictly justifiable by law' but is illegal."[15] Yet police officers have still been given broad optional powers under this section. In a subsequent decision the judges have clarified that "[i]t is not open to the Honorable Court exercising jurisdiction . . . to go into the question whether in fact the police officer was justified in concluding that the necessity contemplated by this section really existed. The discretion is vested solely in the police officer and that discretion cannot be questioned."[16] The judgment of whether a person is likely to commit an offense and whether that offense cannot be prevented without resorting to arrest is entirely that of the police officer. It is no wonder that even in maintenance of law and order police make constant use of this provision on grounds that the persons concerned are likely to cause affray or rioting, which are cognizable offenses.

Additionally, Section 61 CrPC permits the police to keep a suspect in custody for a maximum period of 24 hours, after which the person has to be released or brought before a magistrate. Utilizing this provision, Indian police arrest a person under Section 151 CrPC and release him after a few hours without bringing any formal charges. Such legal provisions are extraordinary, for they give the police unquestioned powers to detain any citizen for a short period of time.

The provisions of search are equally discretionary in their nature and provide extensive coercive powers to the police. Section 165 CrPC states that "whenever an investigating officer has *reasonable* grounds for believing that anything . . . may be found at any place . . . and that such thing cannot in his *opinion* be obtained without undue delay . . . he may after recording the reasons . . . cause search to be made . . . even by a subordinate officer, duly authorized by him."[17] Again, Indian law merely uses the term "reasonable grounds" for providing authority to the police officer, who can conduct this search if in his *opinion* there is no time to seek a search warrant. Even in later clarification, the courts have held that once it is found that the evidence of the recovery of articles is reliable, "the illegality of the search however does not make the evidence of seizure inadmissible."[18] The fact that search was illegal would not vitiate trial and furthermore, "conviction on basis of discoveries made in such search can be made."[19] Thus, in sharp contrast to American jurisprudence,[20] Indian lawmakers have permitted police to make use of even illegal searches in the course of their investigations. In fact, section 166 CrPC extends the power to have searches performed outside the jurisdiction through a police officer from that area. Consequently, Indian police rarely attempt to obtain search warrants for they can easily search a place under any *current* ongoing investigation. Undoubtedly, the Indian police have a wide range of coercive and discretionary powers which escape judicial scrutiny.

Even in the registration of a cognizable offense the law ends up giving vast coercive powers to the police. Under Indian law, a criminal case begins when information about the commission of a crime reaches a police officer. The law stipulates that a verbal complaint should be reduced to writing under Section 154 CrPC: "All information, relating to the commission of a cognizable offence, shall be reduced to writing and . . . substance thereof entered in a book kept as prescribed by the government" (called the First Information Report [FIR]). The word "shall" implies that an officer has no discretion but is required to register a case if a complainant makes a statement. Although this provision may appear innocuous, it has several serious implications. First, investigation by the police can only be done for a cognizable crime. A noncognizable criminal incident is a minor infraction of the law for which police cannot arrest a person except by order of the court. On the other hand, in all cognizable incidents the police have the power to arrest without a warrant. All major crimes are cognizable offenses under the Indian Penal Code of 1860. Yet the police officer may change a few nuances of the statement made by the complaint to make a complaint into a cognizable crime. This discretion is significant since in the name of a cognizable offense the officer becomes empowered to make an arrest. This difference in a statement could then be used for extortion and corrupt practices. Causing a simple hurt, for example, is deemed noncognizable under Section 323 Indian Penal Code (IPC), but by adding in the statement that the offender blocked the path while assaulting the victim, Section 341 IPC (causing obstruction) could be added to the charge which then becomes a cognizable offense. The police thereafter have powers to arrest the offender even though the incident was a minor infraction.

Furthermore, the law places considerable importance on the FIR. The courts accept this police document without corroboration. All subsequent evidence, whether oral or written in the crime-investigation diary, has to be corroborated since the law makes the assumption that the police story cannot be trusted. Indeed, under Section 162 CrPC, the statement of a witness can only be used by the police to contradict the witness in court and declare the witness hostile if he or she deviates from the story told earlier to the police. In the recent murder case of socialite Jessica Lal, witnesses—including her close friend—were declared hostile by the prosecution for changing their statements. The court only believes the FIR because of the assumption that the police have no knowledge of the incident and thence cannot tailor the story to strengthen the prosecution.

Since 1860 the Indian police have developed mechanisms to circumvent these legal restrictions. A common strategy is not to record the FIR immediately as provided by section 154 CrPC. Invariably, the police officers hear the complaint, go to the location of the incident, contact witnesses, and collect evidence before writing the FIR. They try to incorporate as much evidence in the FIR as possible since it helps to strengthen the case. Supervising officers too turn a blind eye towards this circumvention of the law. This is contrary to law but a common practice in the country. Unfortunately, this leaves the Station House Officer (SHO) in a dominant position. The SHO determines the nature of the complaint, when to register the complaint, and which criminal incident to register and which one to ignore, thus exercising extraordinary discretion.

All these organizational practices lead to corruption and misuse of authority. Indeed, citizens commonly experience considerable problems in registering a case at the police station. Frequently, the SHO has to be pressured by a senior officer or bribed to lodge the complaint. Furthermore, many complaints are not recorded or the gravity of an offense is minimized so the police can claim that crime is under control. This minimization of crime is a serious and widespread problem at all the police stations in the country. The power of the state never seems more formidable than when making a simple complaint to the police.

The discretion afforded police officers under other Indian laws has also been extraordinary. Section 3 of the National Security Act enables a detention order to be passed if the detaining authority "is satisfied with respect to any person that such an order is necessary." The Indian courts have not developed proper procedures that may require evidence of specific conditions to assess how the decision was made by the authority. Largely, the judiciary has left the decision to the executive on the grounds that the court cannot substitute its own opinion for that of the detaining authority by applying an objective test to decide the necessity of detention for a specified purpose.[21] In Anil Dey vs. State of West Bengal, the Supreme Court reaffirmed that "the veil of subjective satisfaction of the detaining authority cannot be lifted by the Courts with a view to evaluating its objective sufficiency."[22] Consequently, the police have been arbitrary in exercising their powers of detention.

Preventive-Detention Laws

Despite the formidable policing system and the draconian powers of even the lowest constable, the rulers of India have remained apprehensive about the challenge to their authority. The British, in addition to designing the armed police, kept adding more repressive powers to deal with emerging threats to their authority. "To the British must go the dubious distinction of having introduced preventive detention in India as early as 1793. The East India Company Act of that year authorized the Governor of Fort William and such other officers as he thought fit to secure and detain in custody any person or persons suspected of carrying on . . . any illicit correspondence dangerous to the peace or safety of any of the British settlement or possession in India."[23]

Subsequently, the Bengal State Prisoner's Regulation Act was enacted, which was to have a long life as "Regulation III of 1818." This provided, for "reasons of State," the indefinite confinement of individuals against whom there was no "sufficient ground to institute any judicial proceeding." Furthermore, by invoking the concept of born criminals the British added formidable coercive powers to the existing arsenal of laws governing the country. The notorious Criminal Tribes Act (Act XXVII of 1871) was devised to deal with people "whose ancestors were criminals from time immemorial, who are themselves destined by the usage of caste to commit crime, and whose descendants will be offenders against the law, until the whole tribe is exterminated or accounted for in the manner of thugs."[24] This law essentially criminalized almost 13 million people and empowered the police to maintain surveillance and control their movements. Many other repressive laws were enacted that empowered the police to apprehend anyone suspected of antigovernment activities without a warrant. As the Indian freedom movement gathered momentum, the British passed a series of acts in the name of "national security": the Vernacular Press Act of 1878, the Newspapers (Incitement to Offences) Act of 1908, the Explosives Substances

Act of 1908, the Prevention of Seditious Meetings Act of 1911, and the Official Secrets Act of 1923.

The threat to internal security did not come only from the people of India. The fear that foreigners would incite people to revolt against the British was addressed by the Foreigners Ordinance of 1914, which restricted the entry of foreigners into India. Further, the Ingress into India Ordinance (1914) allowed the government to indefinitely detain and compulsorily domicile suspects, while the Defence of India Act (1915) allowed suspects to be tried by special tribunals whose decisions were not subject to appeal. These were followed by the notorious Rowlatt Act that provided for the expeditious trial of seditious crimes by a three-judge tribunal. More significantly, the accused were not to have the benefit of either preliminary commitment proceedings or the right of appeal, and the rules under which evidence could be obtained and used were relaxed. Other preventive measures included detention without the levying of charges and searches without warrants.

The trend has continued after independence. Partition and communal frenzy laid the basis for the Punjab Disturbed Areas Act, Bihar Maintenance of Public Order Act, Bombay Public Safety Act, and Madras Suppression of Disturbance Act, all enacted in 1947–48. These laws also targeted antisocial elements by providing a pretext to settle scores and commit mayhem in the name of religion. These were the reasons most commonly cited for the retention of preventive-detention provisions both in the Constitution of India (Article 22) and legislation of the first Preventive Detention Act in 1950.

The colonial practice of using coercive powers could not be abandoned despite the first flush of freedom. The preventive-detention bill was introduced ostensibly to deal with the communist threat. In the words of Patel, the government sought additional powers against those "whose avowed object is to create disruption, dislocation and tamper with communications, to suborn loyalty and make it impossible for normal government based on law to function."[25] When the act was renewed in 1952, Nehru asserted that such powers were needed to act against communal, communist, terrorist, and Jagirdari (landlordism) activities.

The preventive detention was justified through several arguments that are repeated today. First, India is an infant democracy where democratic habits and procedures have neither been widely learned nor understood. Second, these powers deter potential provocateurs, black-marketers, dacoits (robbers), and other criminals. Third, there are parties in the country that have vowed to overthrow a legitimate government by any means. Finally, Indian democracy demands a consensual approach but society is divided by antagonistic loyalties. Such social instability may destroy democracy unless checked in time by preventive actions.[26] Once the Parliament accepted these arguments it did not take long to create additional preventive-detention measures. The Armed

Forces Special Powers Act was enacted in 1958 to control the growing Naga unrest in the northeast. The Maintenance of Internal Security Act (MISA) and other preventive-detention acts such as the Disturbed Areas Act and the National Security Act followed.

Assessment of Coercive Legislation

States that fail in their basic functions of maintaining law and order and providing economic development tend to resort to restrictive legislation.[27] Even when a law is enacted to meet a specific threat of sedition, anarchy, terrorism, or incitement to violence, invariably it has been used for dealing with those found inconvenient to the rulers. The Rowlatt Act was used to detain freedom fighters. The Preventive Detention Act of 1950 was enacted to deal with what Deputy Prime Minister Patel called "the perilous times through which India was passing," but by 1960 it was being used "mainly to curb the activities of habitual goondas [ruffians] in the cities of Bombay and Calcutta."[28] The Armed Forces Special Powers Act enacted in 1958 was intended to quell, in the words of then–Home Minister G.B. Pant, arson, murder, looting, and "dacoity" (banditry) by a certain misguided section of the Naga people. The act was meant to be on the statute book for one year, but it is still in effect 46 years later.

The history of MISA shows well how a law may be designed for one end but serve a different one. Indeed, MISA, far from dealing with antinational elements and making India safe from foreign saboteurs, became the tool for Prime Minister Indira Gandhi to stifle all dissent from her authoritarian rule. The members, supporters, and sympathizers of opposition parties—numbering almost 100,000 and including journalists, scholars, and activists—were booked under MISA and detained without trial for eighteen months or more during the 1975–77 emergency.[29] Many of the detainees were rounded up for opposing sterilization drives or the demolition of slums.

The exercise of the National Security Act has also been arbitrary. According to a report in 1993, of the 3,783 people arrested under this act almost 72.5 percent were released for lack of evidence. It is also reported that between 1980 and 1990 an incredible two-thirds of the 16,000 detentions made under the National Security Act were deemed invalid by either the advisory boards or the courts.[30] The application of the Terrorist and Disruptive Activities Act (TADA) is equally illustrative. Enacted to control violent militancy and an insurgency in Punjab, it was used far more in Gujarat and Maharashtra to deal with ordinary criminal offenders. Despite its stringent provisions, its objectives were rarely pursued diligently. By 1992, only 434 out of 52,998 arrestees could be convicted. Tellingly, in Punjab the rate of conviction was a measly 0.37 percent. Clearly, TADA did little to combat insurgency in Punjab.

Furthermore, members of Parliament seem to have little interest in the consequences of their legislation. Only eight members participated in the debate on a two-year extension of TADA.[31] When the Essential Services Maintenance Act (ESMA) was passed in 1980, Home Minister Gyani Zail Singh was unable to explain its provisions. In 1985, when the act came up for renewal, only thirteen members participated in the discussion.

The coercive powers of these laws have largely targeted the common people who end up facing dehumanizing incarcerations and unending trials. It is not surprising that with India's armed model of policing the violations of human rights by police officers are substantial. Police are notorious for using "third degree" methods on suspects to extort confessions, money, and information. Torture is routinely practiced in most police stations and death in police custody is a frequent phenomenon. According to the National Crime Records Bureau (NCRB), during the year 2002 there were 84 deaths and three cases of rape among people in police custody.[32] Not surprisingly, the National Human Rights Commission (NHRC) reports a larger number of custodial deaths than the NCRB (a police organization). According to the 2002–2003 annual report of the NHRC, 183 people died in police custody between 1 April 2002 and 31 March 2003. More seriously, NHRC also received 83 complaints of police killing suspects in false encounters.[33] The police practice of getting rid of suspects through staged encounters is unfortunately all too common. Suspects against whom the police are unable to bring substantial evidence or those who are perceived to be dangerous are simply murdered. In the 1980s, when the Uttar Pradesh police were under pressure to deal with the growing menace of dacoity, officers began to liquidate gangs falsely claiming that they were defending themselves when attacked by the dacoits.

The encounters became an institutional strategy during the Punjab insurgency. The police killed a large number of terrorists and their sympathizers after K.P.S. Gill became chief of the Punjab police. Indeed, this became a major issue following allegations of large-scale cremations of people killed during alleged "encounters." These were "extra-judicial executions" after which the police conducted hasty and "secret cremations" claiming that the bodies were "unidentified." The Supreme Court, after examining the report submitted by the Central Bureau of Investigation, observed: "The report indicates that 585 dead bodies were fully identified, 274 partially identified and 1238 unidentified. Needless to say, the report discloses flagrant violation of human rights on a mass scale."[34]

Inquiries against the armed forces, particularly those operating in the northeastern states and in Jammu-Kashmir, have also revealed several instances of fake encounters. Police-staged killings remain so blatant and widespread that the NHRC has advised state governments to treat this matter with special consideration. Torture, illegal detention, unlawful arrest, and false implication are far too common. The misbehavior of police personnel against ordinary citizens, particularly weaker groups, is ubiquitous. It is little wonder that most citizens fear police officers and distrust the institution as a whole.

Preferring Coercion to Democratic Negotiation

Indian leaders have also seemed ambivalent about opening a dialogue with their opponents. In a democracy, it is necessary that the government and the political parties engage all sections of society in discourse, even those opposed to their policies. Yet the trend in India has been to ignore emerging problems. Furthermore, the preference has been to use repression to browbeat activists rather than to listen to their concerns and negotiate for the larger good. The current left-wing extremism in Bihar (central India comprising Bihar, Jharkhand, Chhattisgarh, parts of Orissa, West Bengal, and Andhra Pradesh) and the unrest in the northeast illustrate this issue.

Bihar. It is well understood that the rise of Naxalism (a Maoist movement) has been a response to the feudal nature of Indian society where upper castes dominate every aspect of life—from politics to education to social relations.[35] It took almost four decades for the Naxals to grow into a guerrilla force of more than 10,000 well-armed cadres and to create a "liberated" zone stretching from Nepal to Andhra Pradesh. "The Revolutionary Corridor (RC) [now] extends from Nepal across six Indian States, including Bihar, Chhattisgarh, Jharkhand, Andhra Pradesh, Orissa and Madhya Pradesh. This entire area has been identified in Maoist literature as the Compact Revolutionary Zone (CRZ)."[36]

The exploitation and mortification of the poor, especially the Scheduled Castes and Scheduled Tribes, has been a major factor in their support for these extremist groups. For marginalized peoples, the system of "begar" and sexual exploitation of women have been major causes of resentment against the upper castes. Begar is a form of unfree labor where the poor are forced to work in a system of bondage. Despite the provisions of the Minimum Wages Act, pay is minimal and intermittent. Furthermore, sexual exploitation of poor women is a personal humiliation that emphasizes their powerlessness. As late as the 1970s in central Bihar, it was a common "custom" for a bride to spend her first married night at the landlord's house. Despite the ugly practice of untouchability, the upper castes never hesitated in sexually assaulting the women of Scheduled Castes. Since the police were always aligned with the moneyed and the powerful, very few cases of rape were ever registered. Governments and political leaders remained indifferent to these crimes. It was this matter of abject dishonor that drove the lower castes to the Naxalites who promised to combat the feudal lords.

The government's failure to implement fair and equitable land reforms that could improve the economic conditions of the poor peasants further exacerbated the situation. The Bihar government attempted to undo the damage of the permanent land settlement by passing the Bihar Land Reforms Act in 1950. This act abolished the private interests in lands, forests, fisheries, mines, and other natural resources and transferred ownership to the state. To avoid the provisions of this act, many landlords transferred or fragmented their holdings and had them registered in *benami* (illegal) names, such as those of their dogs, horses, or fictitious family members. The government and ruling party, consisting mostly of upper-caste politicians, were apathetic toward the implementation of land reform and did not use the power of the state to ensure an equitable land distribution. The Land Ceiling Act came into force in 1962, for instance, but the notices to landlords for seizure of their land had still not been served as late as 1970. In fact, no more than 9,700 of an estimated 100,000 to 150,000 acres of surplus land were collected by the government.[37]

Other laws, such as the Minimum Wages Act of 1948 (amended in 1975), the Bihar Consolidation of Holdings and Prevention of Fragmentation Act of 1956 (amended in 1970), and the Bihar Money Lenders Act of 1974, met the same fate. Most of the laws were inadequately drafted and left legal loopholes for landowners. This legislation displayed good intentions but there was no serious attempt to implement them. The nexus between politicians, government agents, and the landed upper-caste gentry in not implementing these laws was clear. The National Commission on Agriculture stated that the authorities in Bihar have reduced the whole package of land-reform measures to a sour joke by their abysmal failure to implement the laws.[38] The government also remained apathetic toward the security of the poor who were forced to agitate for higher wages and to obtain land for cultivation. Media reports of upper-caste landlords attacking rebellious poor people became ubiquitous. The carnage at Parasbigha in 1977 and the killings at Pipra, Sikandarpur, and Lahsuna were all perpetrated to teach the restless poor some grim lessons. In none of these cases did the police take meaningful action against the culprits. Successive governments remained indifferent to these problems and ignored demands to change social relations. Several administrators who attempted to enforce the laws were summarily transferred and the cases they brought were dismissed.

Government indifference to the poor and weak sections of society and its misuse of coercive powers provided fertile ground to the leftist extremist groups seeking to gain support and build their strength in the region. Government failure to engage social activists and to prevent social conflicts soon transformed central India into a killing field. The violence perpetrated by the Naxalite groups prompted the upper castes to organize their own militias. Private armed groups such as the Bhoomi Sena, Lorik Sena, Brahmarshi Sena, Shoshit Dalit Samajvadi Sena, and

Shoshit Mukti Sena gained considerable notoriety in Bihar.[39] The notorious Bhoomi Sena and Ranbir Sena killed more than 200 people—38 in one massacre at the village of Poonpoon—over the course of few violent years. In retaliation, the Maoist Communist Center selected an isolated village called Senari and massacred 34 upper-caste men by slitting their throats on 3 March 1999.[40]

In the past 25 years, Bihar has become synonymous with anarchy, strife, mismanagement, corruption, and the killing fields. The Naxalites are running a parallel administration where any challenge to their authority is met with a swift, murderous assault. The state has become increasingly lawless and is failing on every socioeconomic index of development. Despite all its coercive powers the police appear helpless against the growing strength of the Naxalite groups. The attack on Jehanabad jail in November of 2005 and another recent one on a jail in Orissa look like battles in which the guerrilla army attains victory over the state.[41] There also seems to be little evidence of an enlightened policy that may soon end this orgy of violence in central India. The lure of a violent ideology seems to be rooted primarily in a sense of alienation arising from the injustices and exploitation that people suffer. Instead of attempting to solve the socioeconomic problems that Naxalites exploit to attract people to their violent cause, governments continue to use repression to deal with the situation. Consequently, the situation continues to deteriorate in these regions.

Assam. The extremism in the northeast provides another illustration of the government's preference for coercion over negotiation. Since the partition in 1947 the influx of migrants from Bangladesh (previously East Pakistan) has been a serious sociopolitical problem in the region. The Congress governments, both at the center and in the northeast states, ignored the problem despite clear evidence of changing demographics, political instability, and the rising apprehension of the local people. In 1979 the All Assam Students Union (AASU) and the All Assam Gana Sangram Parishad (AAGSP) began a mass movement to seek the deportation of illegal migrants and their deletion from the voters' list. The government displayed little interest in these problems, fueling anger and protest. The agitation gained strength as government employees joined the movement and brought the administration to a grinding halt. It did not take long for other groups to exploit the situation and provoke a violent turn toward secession. The militant United Liberation Front of Assam (ULFA) emerged in 1979 to demand independence from the Indian Union.[42] By 1980, the army had to be deployed and most of the state, with the exception of the Cachar and the North Cachar Hills districts, was declared a disturbed area. The region then came under the Assam Disturbed Areas Act of 1955 and the Armed Forces (Special Powers) Act of 1958.

Despite evidence of considerable support for the antiforeigner issue and demands for revision of the voters' lists, the central government forced elections to the state assembly in February 1983. The government refused to revise the voters' lists and ignored demands to track down foreigners who might participate in the elections using false identities. The consequences of the government's decision were grim. On February 18, more than 3,500 Bangladeshi settlers, including women and children, were massacred in Nellie. This was perhaps the largest mass murder perpetrated in India in a single day.

It was only with the advent of Rajiv Gandhi in 1985 that the Assam accord was signed. Nevertheless, the issue of foreigners has not been settled, and resentment continues to simmer in the region. All the political parties have voiced concern about the influx of illegal migrants from Bangladesh but no serious attempt has yet been made to identify and expel illegal residents. The matter has also been communalized with the BJP making it a Hindu–Muslim issue. The region remains embroiled in violence and unrest, with little prospect for peace.

An Alternative to Coercion

A staggering number of laws that sanction the use of coercive powers have been enacted in India. Short-circuiting the due-process system has largely insulated the enforcement agencies from judicial scrutiny and has provided encouragement for them to act illegally and irresponsibly. The evidence presented above suggests that the Indian state has not been willing to learn that repressive measures only marginally assist in meeting objectives and are more often misused. Nevertheless, whether it is the Congress government introducing the Preventive Detention Act in 1950 or the Bhartiya Janata Party promoting the Prevention of Terrorism Ordinance in 2002, all political parties have added to the arsenal.

The argument that extensive coercive legislation is unwarranted because powers provided under the "normal" laws of the land are sufficient to deal with dangerous situations has not been accepted by the political leaders. As described above, there is substance to this argument since Indian laws do provide extraordinary discretion to police officers in matters of arrest, search, and seizure. On the other hand, police officers point to the inadequacy of these provisions and to the reasons why most cases fail in the courts. The failure to convict terrorists in Punjab and Kashmir and the never-ending trials in the Bombay bomb-blast case are cited as evidence of weaknesses in Indian laws. The undue delays in court proceedings and the high standards of evidence demanded by the judges are also mentioned as reasons why few offenders are brought to justice and why they easily get out on bail to commit more crimes.

Furthermore, there is no denying the fact that India faces extraordinary threats from terrorism, sedition, and hostile external powers. In fact, as K.P.S. Gill argues: "Terrorism, organized crime, caste and communal violence, the immense and increasing criminalization of politics, the growing numbers of poor and rootless, accumulating pressures of population and consumerism on limited natural and national resources, and a widening area of abject non-governance—once associated only with Bihar—have all combined to make internal security the most urgent issue of our time."[43] The dangerous threats in Jammu, Kashmir, the northeastern states, and the central regions together with the extortion, kidnapping, smuggling, bootlegging, and drug trafficking of the organized mafia present formidable challenges to the police agencies. Yet the courts appear to be impervious to the seriousness of the situation. "In nearly 14 years of strife in Jammu and Kashmir (J&K) there have been just 13 convictions in cases related to terrorism, of which eight concern relatively minor offences such as illegal possession of arms or illegal border crossings."[44] During the period of terrorism in Punjab, the entire civil and judicial administration broke down. The judges were reluctant even to issue warrants and to appear in person to hold the bail hearings of suspects arrested by the police. The civil and judicial administrators completely abdicated their duties and the entire responsibility for dealing with terrorists was left to the police.

Even today, the courts continue to release hardened offenders on bail; despite well-publicized reports of the misuse of bail provisions, judges rarely act to cancel a suspect's release. It is little wonder that offenders like Shahbuddin in Bihar and Munna Bhaiyya in Uttar Pradesh continue to expand their power base despite the ongoing prosecution of more than two dozen serious cases against each of them. Accordingly, the police demand for more stringent laws to deal with organized crime and terrorism is understandable. The extraordinary threats to the survival of democratic governance in the country demand stringent powers for the enforcement agencies: Otherwise, it is impossible to deal with offenders. Consequently, the enactment of coercive acts does not seem perverse within the context of the country.

Many of the problems enumerated above are directly linked to the policies of the state and its inability to devise suitable remedial measures within the democratic framework of the system. The Indian state itself has been almost criminal in the handling of a variety of problems. The inequitable distribution of wealth, the failure to stop the exploitation of the weaker sections of society, and the inability to provide security has enabled opportunistic groups to find support for their violent ideologies. In most regions of the country, the government machinery has often sided with the rich landlords and thus destroyed its neutrality. The poor no longer trust the police or the government agents to give them justice. They seek recourse elsewhere, which in turn leads to a cycle of violence and repression.

The best alternative to coercive powers is to prevent social unrest through the development of prudent and fair policies that assure people of economic and social justice. Despite India's visible economic growth, the fruits of development are limited, which leads to resentment and frustration with government policies. The political leaders should recognize the need to negotiate and involve everyone in the developmental process. Those who advocate violence should be dealt with firmly but according to the due process of law. The police should not resort to brutality or illegal means since this further alienates the people. The leaders and the enforcement agencies need to display faith in the rule of law and adopt policies that promote human rights.

Perhaps the best way to limit and control the application of coercive powers is through the reform of the police force and the criminal-justice system. At present, the police are highly politicized and demoralized. A radical reform of internal-security forces that imparts the skills and knowledge to create a lawful society is necessary. This need has been articulated by many police officers and a writ petition to implement the recommendations of the National Police Commission (NPC) has been filed in the Supreme Court.[45] Groups of active and retired Indian police officers have demanded complete overhaul of the police apparatus.[46] All the recommendations, including the one by the NPC to limit political interference in police affairs, have been ignored. The feeling persists that political leaders are unwilling to relinquish control of the police and that they do not hesitate to misuse these powers for their partisan purposes. A committee under the chairmanship of the jurist Soli Sorabjee has recently convened to propose a new Police Act.[47] The committee is still deliberating and it remains to be seen what comes from these efforts.

Failure to reform the police compounds the problem of governance. Indeed, the failure to improve the criminal-justice system is making it more and more difficult for the government to maintain order and handle the serious threats of organized crime and terrorism.[48] A focus on the short-term need to maintain order rather than looking into the underlying nature of problems invariably results in repression. It needs to be understood that the objectives that the police must safeguard in an independent India are based on democratic ideals and freedom. The present police system does not subscribe to these ideals and was not created to do so. The state cannot function through coercion, and urgent criminal-justice reforms cannot be postponed indefinitely. A system in which cooperation rather than coercion forms the basis of the state's relationship with the people must be found.

NOTES

1. Anandswarup Gupta, *The Police in British India: 1861–1947* (New Delhi: Concept Publishing Company, 1979).

2. David H. Bayley, *Preventive Detention in India: A Case Study in Democratic Social Control* (Calcutta: Eastend Printers, 1962).

3. Helen Thompson, "The Modern State and Its Adversaries," *Government and*

Opposition 41 (Winter 2006): 25.

4. Gupta, *The Police in British India,* 74.

5. Arvind Verma, *The Indian Police: A Critical Evaluation* (Delhi: Regency Publications, 2005).

6. David Cannadine, *Ornamentalism: How the British Saw Their Empire* (New York: Oxford University Press, 2002).

7. Arvind Verma, "The Cultural Roots of Police Corruption in India," *Policing: An International Journal of Police Strategies and Management* 22 (September 1999): 264–79.

8. David Arnold, "Police Power and the Demise of British Rule in India 1930–47," in David M. Anderson and David Killingray, eds., *Policing and Decolonisation* (Manchester: Manchester University Press, 1992), 42–61.

9. S.K. Ghosh, *Keeping the Peace: For Whom the Bell Tolls* (New Delhi: Ashish Publishing House, 1988).

10. National Crime Record Bureau, "Crime in India 2004," *http://ncrb.nic.in/ crimeinindia.htm.*

11. Ghosh, *Keeping the Peace,* 463.

12. Upendra Baxi, *The Crisis of the Indian Legal System* (New Delhi: Vikas Publishers, 1980).

13. B.B. Mitra, *The Code of Criminal Procedure,* 13th ed. (2 vols., Calcutta: Eastern Law House, 1960).

14. AIR 1950 M.B. 83.

15. Gaman v. Emp. AIR 1930 Lah. 348–349.

16. Om Prakash, 51, CrLT 143 Mad.

17. Emphasis added.

18. AIR 1965 Orissa 136–137.

19. AIR 1955 NUC M.B. 3862 DB.

20. Mapp vs. Ohio's exclusionary rule.

21. AIR 1975 SC 550 Khudiram Das v. State of West Bengal.

22. AIR 1974 SC 832.

23. Vinay Lal, "Anti-Terrorist Legislation: A Comparative Study of India, the United Kingdom, and Sri Lanka," *Lokayan Bulletin* 11 (July–August 1994): 15.

24. Anand A. Yang, ed., *Crime and Criminality in British India* (Tucson: University of Arizona Press, 1986).

25. Bayley, *Preventive Detention in India,* 12.

26. Bayley, *Preventive Detention in India,* 23.

27. AIR 1965 Orissa 136–137.

28. Bayley, *Preventive Detention in India,* 29

29. Bipan Chandra, *In the Name of Democracy: JP Movement and the Emergency* (Delhi: Penguin Books India, 2003).

30. Seminarist, "Time to End Abuses," *Seminar* 512 (April 2002).

31. Arun Jaitley, "Let us not Abdicate Our Responsibility," *Seminar* 512 (April 2002).

32. Ghosh, *Keeping the Peace,* 450.

33. National Human Rights Commission Annual Report 2002–2003, 53, *www.nhrc.nic.in.*

34. Seminarist, "Time to End Abuses," Reference Case No.1/97/NHRC.

35. Arun Sinha, *The Struggles of the Poor* (London: Oxford University Press, 1991).

36. "Nepal Terrorist Groups—Communist Party of Nepal-Maoist," South Asia Terrorism Portal, *www.satp.org/satporgtp/countries/nepal/terroristoutfits/index.html.*

37. Vinod Misra, *The Flaming Fields of Bihar: A CPI (ML) Document* (Calcutta: Prabodh Bhattacharya Publisher, 1987).

38. Arvind N. Das, *Agrarian Unrest and Socio-economic Change 1900–1980* (Delhi: Manohar Publications, 1983).

39. Kanhaiah Bhelari, "Waking Up to Death," *The Week* (Kochi), 14 December 1997.

40. Harinder Baweja and Sanjay Kumar Jha, "Inside the Bloodland," *India Today* (New Delhi), 5 April 1999, 20–24.

41. "Out of Isolation," *The Telegraph* (Calcutta), 27 March 2006, *www.telegraphindia.com/1060327/asp/opinion/story_6018398.asp.*

42. National Human Rights Commission Annual Report 2002–2003.

43. K.P.S. Gill, "The Imperatives of National Security Legislation in India," *Seminar* 512 (April 2002).

44. Gill, "The Imperatives of National Security Legislation in India."

45. Prakash Singh and Others vs. Union of India and Others, Writ Petition (Civil) No. 310 of 1996.

46. See the discussions at *indiatopcop@yahoogroups.com.*

47. Arvind Verma, "To Serve and Protect," *India Together,* 10 January 2006, *www.indiatogether.org.*

48. Atul Kohli, *Democracy and Discontent: India's Growing Crisis of Governability* (New York: Cambridge University Press, 1990).

III

Society

8

THE ROLE OF CIVIL SOCIETY

Niraja Gopal Jayal

Niraja Gopal Jayal *is professor of law and governance at Jawaharlal Nehru University in New Delhi. She is also senior fellow at the Nehru Memorial Museum and Library in New Delhi.*

For the past six decades, India has been relatively successful at sustaining its democratic institutions. The country has held regular and reasonably free and fair elections; institutionalized a multiparty system and adversarial politics; and maintained the other trappings of a democratic society, such as free speech and free media. Yet Indian democracy is also seriously flawed, most notably in its failure to ensure the provision of minimum basic needs to all its citizens, which leads to a denial of the conditions under which the equal rights of citizenship may be meaningfully exercised. One crucial ingredient of both the successes and the failures of Indian democracy has been civil society.

In the success story of Indian democracy, the role of civil society is self-evident as an element in the political framework of liberal-democratic institutions, a vigorous public sphere, a tradition of public debate, and a free press. But civil society is also part of the narrative of the failures of Indian democracy: In the absence of political parties performing the sort of interest-aggregating functions that they do in established democracies, large sections of citizens remain outside the scope of organized civil society. More often than not—particularly with respect to development-oriented nongovernmental organizations (NGOs)—these citizens become *objects of* civil society action, rather than *participants in* civil society.

The lack of consensus on the precise meaning and the empirical referents of the concept of civil society has not prevented the term from being widely, and even loosely and indiscriminately, deployed in Indian political discourse. This essay sidesteps the definitional issues and contentious taxonomies that characterize this field, building instead on the distinction proposed by Michael Foley and Bob Edwards[1] between two versions of the civil society argument: the first emphasizing associational life and civic participation, and the second conceptualizing civil society as a sphere independent of the state and a site of resistance to potentially tyrannical state power.

The empirical referents of these two versions are relatively easy to identify, but they exclude two types of civil society that are significant in contemporary India, not only in terms of the pervasiveness of their activities but also their size. The first of these is the very large number of NGOs working in the development sector. The second may be described as "uncivil society," for want of a better phrase. It may not be as large as the first in terms of the number of organizations, but one organization alone—the Rashtriya Swayamsevak Sangh—is said to be the largest volunteer organization in the country, with a membership of 1.3 million. Such organizations may attempt to organize communities around an identity that definitively excludes other communities, propagates intolerance, and is not averse to the use of violence. Together, these four categories—civil society as civic associations (CS-1), civil society as a counterweight to the state (CS-2), the development sector (CS-3), and uncivil society (CS-4)—provide a theoretically plausible and practically manageable way of approaching the vast sphere of Indian civil society.

All four types of civil society have their lineage in colonial India. The first strand is exemplified by the organizations formed in the middle of the nineteenth century, which advocated social reform, questioned the indignities of the caste system, campaigned against child marriage and female infanticide, and favored widow remarriage and women's education. Such demands for social reform were addressed not only to society but also to the colonial state, in the form of demands for progressive legislation. By the third quarter of the nineteenth century, several organizations had been established in the major Indian cities, advocating liberal ideas and clamoring for the introduction of Western education in India.

The press too had grown, so that by 1905, the circulation of English-language newspapers alone was 276,000—up from 90,000 in 1885—suggesting that a large number of Indians were educated in English, most of whom were lawyers, teachers, and journalists. This intelligentsia of educated, middle-class professionals formed the membership of associations such as the Indian Association, the Bombay Presidency Association, and the Poona Sarvajanik Sabha. These were Westernized discussion groups, mainly created to petition the government to support modern education and to reform the colonial administration so that it would hire Indians. This is arguably the pedigree of the modern public sphere in India. Social movements represent a more contemporary form of CS-1. While the term "association" may be a misnomer for such movements, there is a similarity of civic purpose in the claims of social citizenship that they advance and the transformative goals that inspire them.

Founded in 1885, the Indian National Congress (Congress party) was the logical culmination of the developments signified by the associational life of the mid–nineteenth century, and gradually came to occupy almost the entire space that could be described as civil society in the sense of a counterweight to the state (CS-2). The party was a vast umbrella organization that assimilated and accommodated diverse social groups and interests, creating a network of organizations which were united in their desire to work for a free India. Richard Sisson argues that this rise of associational life was an important cultural basis of democratization in the preindependence period because it was based on a secular-associational model, rather than on caste or religion.[2] As its demand for self-government gradually crystallized, the Congress party came to represent opposition to the colonial state, whose legitimacy the party fundamentally questioned and attacked.

The third strand of civil society in India—related to the tradition of voluntarism—can be dated to the first decade of the twentieth century. Around that time, there emerged a number of social-service organizations which drew inspiration from ideals of active citizenship, patriotism, and character-building. These groups included the Arya Samaj, the Servants of India Society, the Theosophical Society, and the Seva Samiti.[3] The "constructive programme" of Mohandas K. Gandhi—which emphasized the spinning and wearing of *khadi* (handloomed) cloth, village reconstruction, basic education, and the upliftment of the Dalits (earlier disparagingly known as the "untouchable" castes)—could also be seen as part of this strand as well. While the programs of associations such as the Servants of India Society were ostensibly philanthropic, they carried strong political overtones in emphasizing loyalty and duty to one's homeland. By contrast, Gandhi's "constructive programme" supplied the nonpolitical dimension of his leadership of the national movement, and was implemented by organizations outside the Congress party, such as the Harijan Sevak Sangh.

Finally, what we today describe as uncivil society (or CS-4) historically originated in colonial times, though it has arguably taken a more openly uncivil form in recent years. The Hindu Mahasabha (formed in 1915) and the Rashtriya Swayamsevak Sangh (RSS or the National Volunteers' Union, formed in 1925) were both inspired by the vision of a Hindu nation. The RSS projects itself as a charitable social-service organization but has been the driving force behind the politics of religious hate and exclusion. With an estimated membership of 1.3 million, it is said to be the largest noncommunist organization in the world.

Civil Society in Postcolonial India

The first two decades after independence were years of relative quiescence. The popular consensus that had underlain the massive mobilization of the national movement was simply transferred to the state structures, which were administered by the Congress party. The party therefore enjoyed a unique though essentially inherited legitimacy. The state and mainstream political processes played a dominant role in the definition of Indian society and in the twin projects of nation-building and development. There was a widespread consensus that saw the state as the engine of development, and thus there was little scope for oppositional civil society. Even the establishment of institutions such as universities was undertaken by the state.

Gandhi had wanted the Congress to disband as a political party once independence had been obtained and to convert itself into the Lok Sevak Sangh, an organization for the welfare of the people. In the words of Lloyd and Susanne Rudolph, "As a man of civil society, Gandhi targeted the statist face of the party. . . . Gandhi's stance problematised the state more fundamentally than most proponents of civil society in Europe or America."[4]

Unsurprisingly, this idea found few takers within the Congress, and the Gandhian voluntary organizations—working to promote spinning, village industries, cow protection, and the upliftment of the "untouchable" castes—remained aloof from the pursuit of political power. Vinoba Bhave, the Gandhian initiator of Bhoodan (donation of land), traveled across India for fourteen years; he persuaded many landowners to voluntarily give up some of their land for redistribution to the landless, collecting 4.2 million acres of land.

The next spurt of voluntary activity was observed during the drought of 1966 and the subsequent food crisis. At this time, several groups of volunteers were involved in famine-relief work in the state of Bihar, and many of these were led by workers of the Sarvodaya (literally, "improvements in the quality of life for all") movement, most notably by Jayaprakash Narayan. After the famine, many of these groups stayed on to carry out development work in the rural areas.

Many other university-educated young people, disillusioned with the development process and the failure of radical-left politics, established voluntary organizations in the countryside, often inspired by the writings of E.F. Schumacher and Paolo Freire. Examples of this include the Social Work and Research Centre, established in Rajasthan in the early 1970s, which taught people to use local productive skills to create a self-sustaining economy; Kishore Bharati, a program to promote innovations in rural education set up by a molecular biologist in Madhya Pradesh; and the Vidushak Karkhana, which combined the search for appropriate technology with participatory social action. In a parallel development, foreign organizations such as Oxfam and Christian Aid began working in India on poverty relief and development. This was a period in which CS-3 was preeminent, as disillusionment with state-led development was giving rise to the early development NGOs.

The conception of CS-2—civil society as a counterweight to potentially tyrannical state power—was reinvented during the national emergency declared by Prime Minister Indira Gandhi in 1975. The revival
and consolidation of civil society in this sense was provoked by repressive state action, not unlike the experience of civil societies in Eastern
Europe that emerged in response and resistance to state power. Although
the immediate provocation for the declaration of the emergency was an
adverse court judgment on the electoral malpractices committed by
Prime Minister Gandhi, it was substantially a response to widespread
social, political, and economic unrest that was fuelling mass mobilization and countrywide strikes. This discontent was expressed in the growing power of the Nav Nirman Movement led by Narayan, which called
for "total revolution" and "partyless democracy."

From 1975 until the government's defeat in the election of 1977, the
emergency provisions of the constitution remained in force, suspend-
ing the fundamental rights and civil liberties of citizens, muzzling the
press by censorship, and making possible the arbitrary arrest of political opponents by the use of a preventive-detention clause (thereby dis-
allowing recourse to the law courts). This brief episode of authoritarian
rule in India's otherwise respectable record of political democracy left a
lasting legacy of popular awareness of civil liberties and political rights,
including the freedom of the press. It also saw the consolidation of
associations such as the People's Union for Civil Liberties and its later
offshoot, the People's Union for Democratic Rights, which adopted a
more radical view of what constituted basic rights.

In the 1970s, the civic-associational space of CS-1 was inhabited by
a large number of entities that were given the appellation of "non-party
political formations" by Rajni Kothari, but were also described as
"grassroots movements" and, a decade later, as "new social movements."
These movements targeted various forms of injustice: They challenged
the patriarchal ordering of society; questioned subordination on the
basis of inherited caste status; mounted protests against unjust displacement by dam projects, mining projects, and missile ranges; provided
critiques of the conventional paradigm of development; and articulated
newer and more egalitarian visions of the social order. That global dis-
courses exercised an influence on local protest was nowhere more visible than in the feminist and environmental movements, the best-known
example of the latter being the Narmada Bachao Andolan (NBA, or
Save the Narmada Movement), which has been campaigning tirelessly
for two decades against the social and environmental impacts of the
dam on the Narmada River.

The so-called new social movements in India are not, as in the West,
postmaterialist movements of the middle classes. Although young
middle-class individuals have often acted as catalysts in the articula-
tion of such movements, they remain essentially movements of the dis-

advantaged who struggle for survival and claim a right to only the most basic needs. One example of this is the Chipko movement in the Himalayan region, which gained prominence in the 1970s and was overwhelmingly represented as an ecological movement, though equally compellingly also interpreted as a feminist and peasant movement. The claims of such movements are generally addressed to the state, couched in the vocabulary of rights and justice, and they invariably point to the hollowness of democracy, insofar as it tends to consolidate the power of the already influential and is unreceptive to the claims of the poor and powerless.

Civil Society and Democracy in India

Given the diversity and vast number of organizations that constitute civil society in India today, it is hardly surprising that their relationship to democracy is varied. Some components of civil society are more strongly associated with democracy than others. For instance, of the wide and diverse set of organizations that inhabit CS-1—ranging from neighborhood associations to organizations campaigning for communal harmony to social movements with a transformative agenda—neighborhood associations are far less likely to have as strong an association with democracy as social movements, in whose activism the social shades into the political. In the following pages, aspects of each of the four types of civil society that have been identified will be further examined, in terms of each type's contribution to democracy.

Civic associationism. The different segments within this category vary widely in their relationship to democracy, and in this section, three subtypes will be discussed in terms of this relationship, in descending order of the strength of that link. Those most strongly linked with claims of substantive democracy are the social movements with an emancipatory and transformative vision. In two major campaigns in 1989 and again in 1990–91, the Narmada Bachao Andolan mobilized tens of thousands of poor people who were being threatened by displacement. Despite repression by the Gujarat state government, the movement followed mainly Gandhian modes of protest, such as fasting, long marches, the boycott of state institutions and personnel (including census-takers and election officials), and the threat to commit mass suicide by drowning when the waters rose to engulf their villages. Although the struggle has yielded only incremental gains, more than any other such movement it has placed the question of alternative and more humane paradigms of development onto the national agenda.

Another example of a mass movement with a transformative vision is the Ekta Parishad (Unity Forum), with a membership of more than a hundred-thousand people, working chiefly in the states of Madhya Pradesh and Chhattisgarh, with some spillover in the states of Bihar and

Orissa. The Ekta Parishad has sought to mobilize the poor, mostly tribal people, around the issue of ownership of, control over, and access to natural resources such as water, forests, and land, which are the mainstays of the livelihoods of the poor. It has also campaigned for the reorganization of the village economy, decentralized decision making, social legislation for minimum wages, the release of bonded laborers, and greater accountability. Sustained pressure on the government has helped the Parishad to secure fishing rights, *nistaar* rights (traditional rights for people living in the villages in protected areas), cultural rights for the tribal communities, and a ban on logging by the timber mafia.[5]

A very different type of democratizing initiative that has been translated successfully into national legislation is the right-to-information campaign of the Mazdoor Kisan Shakti Sangathan (MKSS, or Organization for the Empowerment of Workers and Peasants). Starting from the local level in Rajasthan, the MKSS worked relentlessly to demonstrate that pervasive corruption and a lack of information made it impossible for the legitimate rights of the poor workers and peasants to be secured. While the demand for legal recognition of the right to information was a central part of its battle for transparency and accountability, the MKSS also innovated methods of public audit, such as the *jan sunwai,* or people's hearing. These are forums in which local officials and elected representatives are held to account by the people of the village, in the presence of invited intellectuals or distinguished public figures. Responding to the MKSS campaign, nine states passed right-to-information acts, some of which have been in existence for more than five years. In 2005, Parliament passed the Right to Information Act (RTI). All government (and government-funded) departments now have a public-information officer, who is required to respond to applications under the RTI Act within 30 days, or else face a penalty. The initial exclusion of file notings from the remit of the Act has also recently, though somewhat controversially, been reversed.

The three movements described above—the NBA's struggle against the dam and for proper rehabilitation of the displaced, the Ekta Parishad's work for restoring customary rights over natural resources to vulnerable tribal communities, and the MKSS's campaign for the right to information—illustrate different ways in which social movements have sought to expand the landscape of social rights for ordinary citizens, and particularly for vulnerable groups which lack the capacity to claim an effective voice in India's democratic polity.

A second and more Tocquevillian type of associational life has been highlighted in the context of ethnic conflict in India. Ashutosh Varshney has shown how organized networks of civic engagement in select Indian cities—some prone to Hindu-Muslim violence, and others which, even in the presence of the same objective conditions as are likely to trigger conflict, remain relatively peaceful—can actually play a conflict-preventing role.[6] These include a variety of forms of associational life, including business and trade associations, trade unions, and professional associations as well as the more quotidian forms of engagement between communities. Of course, Varshney's account of ethnic peace and conflict, driven as it is by a civil society explanation, gives less analytical weight to the role of the state and politics in manufacturing identity and triggering conflict.

The third and final subtype of civic association is the neighborhood association. In recent years, associations of this type have begun to participate more actively in civic matters. In the capital of India, New Delhi, they were actually organized and energized by the state government, which in 2001 launched a governance initiative called Bhagidari (defined as a Citizen-Government Partnership, or a form of public-private partnership in which the private element is supplied by citizens). It was expected that the enormous range of civic problems in the city—from overflowing sewers and litter to poor roads, traffic jams, and vehicular pollution—could be more effectively addressed with the participation of ordinary residents than by government action alone. The citizens were encouraged to organize themselves in elected Residents' Welfare Associations (RWAs) and Market and Traders' Associations.

There are about 1,700 such associations in Delhi, with a total membership of approximately three million (a fifth of the capital's population). These groups were provided with technical expertise and the wherewithal to implement programs of water harvesting, community involvement in crime prevention and detection, and the creation and maintenance of parks and community centers. They were also involved in the policy initiatives to reform electricity distribution and change the way in which the house tax was computed. In many of these areas, the RWAs proved to be effective agents of change. In July 2005, however, a 10 percent hike in the power tariff spurred the RWAs to mobilize *against* the state government, which had to roll back the increase. This was a Pygmalion situation, where the associations dubbed as partners had simply outgrown their creator and acquired lives of their own. Whether or not RWAs can be seen as agents of democratization in any grand sense, they have certainly brought a greater awareness of civic issues to urban citizens who now have a higher propensity to debate and agitate on these issues.

Civil society as a counterweight to the state. In times of "normal" democratic politics, with the robust practice of adversarial politics in the legislatures, CS-2 tends to provide a relatively stable framework for the expression of dissenting opinions and critical analysis of public issues. During the emergency declared in 1975, the personal and political liberties of citizens, hitherto taken for granted, came under threat for the first time. It was in response to this crisis that the civil-liberties movement underwent a process of profound renewal in the mid-1970s.

In subsequent decades, members of this movement investigated abuses
of power by the police, including episodes of torture and "encounter
deaths" (a euphemism for what are often suspicious killings by the police) of so-called terrorists. The concerns of some sections of the civil-
liberties movement widened to include the democratic rights of victims
of involuntary displacement or of communal violence, the nonpayment
of workers' dues, the struggles for legal entitlement to land, and so on.

Following the brief authoritarian interlude that lasted from 1975 to
1977, the media played an important role in creating awareness of the
"excesses" of the emergency, especially the curtailment of the freedom
of speech and association and the program of forced sterilization for
population control. While the print media was always under private
ownership, radio and television programming at the time was completely
under government control. The credibility of government-owned media
was never particularly high; at the time of the emergency, it plummeted.
Privately owned newspapers had to submit to censorship, and any tru-
culence on their part was punished with disconnection of electricity
and the withdrawal of government advertising which, in the days pre-
ceding the liberalization of the economy, was a substantial threat. Some
newspapers expressed their dissent symbolically by leaving the editorial columns of the paper blank or by framing the front page with a
funereal black border.

The dismantling of state control over the electronic media in the early
1990s led to a phenomenal expansion in satellite television. The penetration of television in India has more than doubled that of the print
media in both rural and urban areas. In urban areas in 2001, there was 80
percent penetration of terrestrial television and 63 percent of cable and
satellite television. Even the rural areas had 34.3 percent cable penetration. "Politics after television," to invoke the title of Arvind Rajagopal's
book,[7] have not been the same. Rajagopal's reference is to the phenomenon of "retail Hindutva," or the shaping of public sentiment by Hindu-
nationalist ideas. The screening of the serialized Hindu epic the *Ramayana*
by the state-owned channel Doordarshan could be seen to have violated
a secular taboo. Rajagopal shows that Doordarshan helped to create an
audience that—cutting across lines of region, caste, and language—became receptive to the lure of Hindu-nationalist ideology, the political
benefits of which subsequently went to the Bharatiya Janata Party.

The freeing of the airwaves brought into being the phenomenon of
the 24-hour news channel. Parliamentary proceedings began to be
beamed into people's homes, from the long debates on no-confidence
motions against an incumbent central government, to the distressing
spectacle of members of the Uttar Pradesh state legislative assembly
breaking furniture and hurling microphones at each other. The news
channels have regularly grilled and exposed the doublespeak of politicians; conducted hidden-camera sting operations exposing the corrup-

tion of ministers and political-party functionaries; and mounted campaigns against the denial or miscarriage of justice in high-profile murder cases where the powerful and wealthy have been allowed to roam freely without any regard for the principle of the rule of law. In all these ways, a tradition of public debate has been fostered, even if it has on occasion run to excess and resulted in trial-by-the-media rather than by the appropriate judicial institution. The effectiveness of such media exposures in securing the resignation of a politician or a more responsible verdict by a court has been a heady elixir—sometimes producing opinionated journalism and hubris—and is a potentially dangerous weapon with no safeguards to ensure that it will be used responsibly and accountably.

Development NGOs. There is no completely reliable estimate of the size of the nongovernmental sector in India today. According to one survey, there were 1.5 million NGOs in 2001, although another estimate claims the figure is 200,000. Not all NGOs receive foreign funding, but those that do have to be registered under the Foreign Contribution Regulation Act of 1976. In 1995–96, there were 16,740 such associations registered with the Home Ministry; by 2004–2005, the number had almost doubled to 30,321. The amount of reported foreign funding (only half the associations complied with the annual reporting requirement) increased threefold in the same period to INR62.57 billion. Contrary to the expectation that the money spent on fixed costs and establishment expenses would be minimal in service-oriented organizations, such expenses actually constitute anywhere from 35 percent to 70 percent of the money received from abroad. In 2004–2005, establishment expenses totalled INR22.61 billion, rural-development activities accounted for INR15.64 billion, and relief rehabilitation for victims of natural calamities was INR10.85 billion, while the welfare of children and the construction of schools and colleges accounted for approximately INR7 billion each.[8]

The development-NGO sector is not merely vast, it is also extremely diverse. Much of it is engaged in service delivery in the fields of primary education, primary health care, water and sanitation, microcredit, technology, and environmental conservation. The relation of this development sector to democracy is clearly ambivalent. As an appendage to, and often even a franchise of the state, the NGO sector is perceived to be an apolitical successor to the older voluntary sector which belonged organically to *civil society,* rather than to the "third sector."

Indeed, the very term NGO often conveys derision, chiefly because of the scale and sources of funding of NGOs, which are usually ample and come from foreign donors. By contrast, social movements are seen as closer to the people, for whom and with whom they struggle, backed by slim resources. These movements proclaim the authenticity of their commitment to the grassroots and their representation of its interests, in

sharp contrast to the more technocratic, protocorporate mold of the bet-
ter-funded NGOs. Social movements often have leaders from the middle
class who have deliberately shed their class affiliations, but the development NGOs have become institutions in which middle-class youth
actively seek careers and competitive pay packages.

This is obviously not true of all NGOs, many of which are not engaged in service delivery and have transformative goals. India's
panchayats[9] have a quota of one-third for women representatives, and a
large number of NGOs have been engaged in capacity-building programs, many of which have been funded by the government and foreign
donors. In central India, an NGO called Prakriti has been recruiting and
training women workers as *panchayat sakhis* (friends of the *panchayat*),
who in turn motivate and empower the elected women representatives
so that may more effectively perform their representative roles. The
panchayat sakhis assist the elected women in withstanding pressure
from rural elites as well as from the local bureaucracy; asserting their
rights of participation in public life; making *panchayats* more responsive to women's needs; and learning how to mobilize financial resources
for local development needs. While the *panchayat sakhis* are paid workers, each of whom travels to each of the many *panchayats* in a district,
the success of this model has inspired former women representatives to
volunteer their services as *gram sakhis* for the same sort of work at the
village level. Now, not only women but even men elected to the
panchayat for the first time seek out the *gram sakhis* to help them understand the laws and obtain information about development programs
and how to access them. Like many other NGOs engaged in this sort of
work, Prakriti also helped to strengthen the participation of women
citizens at every level of the *panchayat* structure, from the *gram sabhas*
(village assemblies) upwards.

Uncivil society. The inelegant phrase "uncivil society" describes a
range of organizations which are legally registered as and purport to be
"social-service" organizations, or organizations for the promotion of
culture. The Rashtriya Swayamsevak Sangh and the Vishwa Hindu
Parishad (VHP) claim to be organizations of this sort, but the culture
with which they are engaged equates Indian-ness with Hinduism, and
an important component of their ideology of Hindu nationalism is the
cultivation of prejudice against minorities who are inevitably projected
as antinational. As members of what is called the Sangh Parivar, the
clutch of organizations affiliated with the Bharatiya Janata Party, they
supply the ideological foundations of the party's political program.

RSS cadres are trained in a strict disciplinary regimen that includes
physical exercise and moral sermons. They are trained to be useful foot
soldiers in situations of intercommunity violence. The VHP is led by a
physician with a specialization in oncology, and has played the central
role in gruesome violence against Muslims, as well as tribals who have

converted to Christianity. VHP translates to "World Hindu Council," and this global nomenclature indicates its popularity with the Indian diaspora which funds it generously. On the whole, there is little ambiguity about the relationship of such organizations to democracy: Their ideas and activities are patently illiberal, exclusionary, and intolerant of cultural difference. As such, they are completely antithetical to the fundamental values of democracy. It is interesting to note that, in 2001, the top receiver of foreign funding in India was a little-known Hindu religious NGO in Gujarat. Indeed, 13 out of 25 receivers of such funds were religious organizations, both Hindu and Christian.

Issues Facing Civil Society Today

As we have seen, the relationship between civil society and democracy is contingent upon the segment of civil society about which we are speaking, and it is also contingent upon the definition of democracy that we adopt. There are at least five sets of issues that merit closer attention.

Whose civil society? Civil society in India speaks with an urban, middle-class accent, and its language is generally English. The upper classes have little use for civil society and the lower classes little access to it. Media campaigns are more likely to be frenzied when they involve a middle-class victim of injustice or violence, rather than suicides by indebted farmers or the everyday exploitation of the poor. None of this applies to social movements, however, partly because of their links to the grassroots and partly because they do not view people as objects upon which to act.[10]

India's political parties are plagued with serious problems, including the lack of inner-party democracy; their tendency to function as family firms rather than as secular associations of people who share a political worldview; and above all their tendency to define the political agenda in ways that encourage populist solutions. Middle-class people, writes John Harriss, have "responded to their impotence in the political sphere by devoting their energies to activism in civil society, and in doing so de-valorise party political activity."[11]

Even so, the question of whether civil society *should* perform a representative role, or *can* be constructed in a way that makes such representation possible, permits of no easy answers. Is the fact that the interests of large sections of citizens are not represented by civil society a flaw in civil society or a comment on the quality of political representation in a democracy? Given that, as Neera Chandhoke argues, the civil society argument is insensitive to power equations between unequally endowed groups, perhaps we should recognize that "all that civil society affords is the provision of both a site as well as the values, which can help us to battle with the inequities of the sphere itself."[12]

One recent attempt at bringing the concerns of grassroots civil society into the domain of public policy was the establishment of the National Advisory Council (NAC) in 2004 under the chairpersonship of Sonia Gandhi, the president of the Congress party. The members of the NAC included many prominent civil society activists and individuals who have worked tirelessly to empower the poor, such as Aruna Roy of the MKSS and Jean Drèze of the Right to Food Campaign. The 2005 passages of the Right to Information Act and the National Rural Employment Guarantee Act (guaranteeing a minimum of a hundred days' worth of employment to families in rural areas) is substantially the result of the efforts of these individuals. Nevertheless, the NAC provoked some cynical commentary about how civil society had *become* the state. An unrelated political controversy rendered the NAC headless in 2006, and it is currently in limbo.

The politics of the nonpolitical. In the days before the vocabulary of civil society gained currency, the Indian political scientist Rajni Kothari used the term "non-party political formations" to describe movements and organizations that would today be categorized as civil society groups. This term remained standard currency for decades, and continues to color the way in which civil society is perceived, especially by activists. As such, the term *political* in the phrase "non-party political formations" remains a badge of honor.

There is a dual opposition here in relation to politics. On the one hand, some sections of civil society wear their politics on their sleeve, disdaining the apolitical character of NGOs. For these groups, civil society must necessarily be engaged in fighting for the rights of the oppressed and in seeking to transform society fundamentally by making it more just and equitable. This entails dirtying their hands in the field, in the local soil. On the other hand, organizations engaged in service delivery, particularly tasks franchised out by the state, are clearly not seen to be deserving of the mantle of such noble virtue. The essential difference is that the first type of groups involve the people as *participants* in the struggle, while the second casts people as beneficiaries and clients, as *objects* of but not subjects in activism.

Yet there is also a tendency for some sections of civil society superciliously to position themselves as "clean" alternatives to the "dirty" business of politics. Still, the lure of politics may sometimes lead these organizations to seek a political role, as the recent example of Loksatta shows.[13] Loksatta (literally, Rule by the People) is an NGO led by a physician who worked as a civil servant for seventeen years, and then resigned to set up an NGO describing itself as "a nonpartisan people's movement for reforms in the governance structure." Loksatta is a membership-based organization, with a hundred thousand enrolled members, which has focused on fighting corruption and the criminalization of politics, as well as on agitating for electoral reform. Over the last ten

years, it has trained citizens in techniques of "informed assertion" to
enable them to fight corruption in public institutions, and has conducted election-watch exercises in the state of Andhra Pradesh. In October 2006, Loksatta announced that it would become a political party.
From its role as a watchdog on the state, Loksatta has now decided to
participate in mainstream politics—the final goal of which is to control
and direct the state.

Civil society and accountability. While civil society tends to be
somewhat self-righteous in the watchdog role it has assumed in holding
the state to account, how accountable is civil society itself? That this
question is increasingly being asked is not unrelated to the phenomenal expansion in the number of development NGOs, and the answer to
the question therefore varies greatly depending on the type of civil
society organization that is being considered. With respect to NGOs,
the question of sources of funding is of paramount importance. How
autonomous are NGOs funded by the state, industry, or foreign donors?
If NGOs do their funders' bidding, and their accountability is to the
funding agencies alone, can they really be described as belonging to
"civil society" in the Tocquevillian sense of the term?

Service-delivery NGOs often function as state franchises[14] and public-service contractors, as well as implementers of state-designed and
state-funded development programs that states themselves lack the capacity to implement. Some NGOs are prone to cooption by the state in
ways other than funding, such as through involvement in policy networks and consultative positions on official bodies. The scale of state
funding for NGOs raises a legitimate question about their nomenclature: Exactly how *non*governmental are they?

In terms of organizational culture, NGOs funded by foreign donors
tend to be vulnerable to the dual impact of local organizational culture
and the donor agencies which fund them. While the former leads to the
reproduction of local biases within the organization, the latter encourages NGOs to expand and structure themselves similar to donor agencies, with the attendant dangers of bureaucratization. Even as they demand transparency and accountability from public agencies, NGOs have
resisted attempts to make their own functioning more transparent.

In the case of the media, the chief accountability concern arises from
the issue of private ownership. Majority stakes in the media are today
owned by industrial and business houses, which therefore enjoy enormous financial and political clout. The temptation is ever-present to
use the media to further private interests or to support friendly or useful
political groups and individuals. It is common knowledge that, over the
last decade, the balance of power between the media baron and the
marketing department, on the one hand, and the journalist, on the other,
has shifted. In such a situation, biases in both reportage and editorial
opinion are only to be expected.

A regulatory framework for civil society? The lack of accountability is often blamed on the absence of a regulatory framework for civil society. According to Indian law, all voluntary agencies with seven or more members are required to register under the Societies Registration Act of 1860 or, in the case of religious and charitable organizations, as a trust under the Indian Trusts Act of 1982. Those receiving foreign funding are registered with the Ministry of Home Affairs, and their funding is monitored in accordance with the Foreign Contributions Regulation Act (FCRA) of 1976, which was enacted during the 1975 emergency in response to allegations that foreign money was being used for subversive activities. In 1981, when she returned to office, Indira Gandhi set up the Kudal Commission to investigate the activities of Gandhian organizations and to harass them. There was a tightening of the FCRA provisions in 1984, as a result of which 142 voluntary organizations were banned from receiving foreign funds. It is said that Indira Gandhi's suspicion toward the voluntary sector stemmed from her belief that such groups, especially the Gandhian organizations, had conspired to bring about the collapse of her government following the emergency.

When Rajiv Gandhi became prime minister, Bunker Roy of the Social Work Research Centre in Tilonia, Rajasthan was appointed to be a consultant to the Planning Commission. He proposed a statutory code of conduct for voluntary organizations, as well as a national council that would monitor and recommend "legitimate" groups to the government. Both moves were fiercely opposed by voluntary groups across the country, which saw in this a covert attempt to institutionalize tighter government regulation as well as patronage of NGOs favored by the state. Taking a leaf out of Indira Gandhi's book, the Bharatiya Janata Party too tried to target unfriendly NGOs which did not share its religious-nationalist vision of politics, by using the FCRA against them. There is clearly a need for a legal and regulatory framework that promotes accountability and financial probity, but also provides protection against politically motivated harassment. Until such a regulatory framework is created, civil society will remain vulnerable to intimidation by the government of the day, and all sections of civil society will have to suffer being tarred with the same brush of suspicion from the lack of transparency and accountability.

The globalization of Indian civil society. The emergence and consolidation of global civil society—from the 1992 Earth Summit at Rio de Janeiro, through the Beijing women's conference in 1995, to the more recent protests against globalization at Seattle and Genoa—has been presented as a response to "the conceits of the state system." While some transnational NGOs and social movements have been effective in bringing about policy changes in multilateral institutions such as the World Bank, global civil society has also been accused of treating citizens of the South in a manner that robs them of their political agency, as when they are told what sorts of rights or democracy they need, and what they should do to become empowered. The links between local and global civil society often tend to be clientelistic, especially when NGOs in the North set up country offices in the South.

In India, the Narmada Bachao Andolan's campaign obtained a great deal of support from global civil society organizations such as Environmental Defense and Oxfam. This also made it vulnerable to the charge, leveled by a hostile central government, of appealing to "foreign" agencies to resolve a domestic dispute, and so engaging in "antinational" activity. This argument failed to recognize that the foreign NGOs were only putting pressure on the equally foreign agencies which were funding the dam. Thus, while links between local and global civil society can be helpful, it is also true that it is the national state to which most civil society claims have to be addressed, and fellow citizens upon whom accountability is enjoined.

Even if sections of civil society are themselves characterized by a democratic deficit, there can be no disagreement that India's robust civil society has been a bulwark of its democracy. That Indian democracy has the resilience to absorb the expression of even extreme and fundamentalist opinions is unquestionably the gift of a self-confident civil society. It is notable that civil society itself is typically threatened only when the democratic peace is disturbed, and with the exception of the period of emergency rule, civil society—including and especially the media—has remained largely free of such attempts at control. This reinforces Michael Walzer's formulation that "only a democratic state can create a democratic civil society, [and] only a democratic civil society can sustain a democratic state."[15]

If civil society is an important part of the success story of India's democracy, it must also share the blame for the imperfections of this democracy, though perhaps to a lesser degree. Social and economic inequalities, which often overlap in Indian society, have made it difficult to realize the full promise of Indian democracy. While civil society has mobilized on such issues, there have been contrary and conflicting tendencies within civil society itself, limiting its ability to secure desired political outcomes. As we have seen, some segments of civil society, such as civil-liberties organizations and the media, are democracy-enhancing—if we interpret democracy narrowly and in formal terms. Other segments, for instance social movements that campaign for social and economic rights, seek to make democracy more substantive. Still others are antidemocratic, such as those segments in "uncivil" society, while development NGOs can be simply democracy-neutral. Different segments of civil society remain trapped within their intrinsic limitations which determine their particular abilities to secure democratic political outcomes.

Nevertheless, the robustness of India's democracy is unquestionably linked to its vast and varied civil society. The widespread dissatisfaction with political institutions that are either inefficient or vulnerable to capture by special interests has led to greater faith being invested in civil society. While much of this current activism is middle class in character, and is conducted through the use of modern technologies such as television, the Internet, or text messaging on mobile telephones, it has laid bare the lack of accountability and responsiveness of public institutions. If social movements were the dominant form of civil society in the 1970s and 1980s, and NGOs characterized civil society in the 1990s, the first decade of the twenty-first century reveals a new version of civil society that is issue-based and led by articulate members of the middle classes. If its predecessors were inspired by the goals of social transformation and development, respectively, the objective of the current phase of civil society action is greater accountability of public institutions.

NOTES

1. Michael W. Foley and Bob Edwards, "The Paradox of Civil Society," *Journal of Democracy* 7 (July 1996): 38–52.

2. Richard Sisson, "Culture and Democratization in India," in Larry Diamond, ed., *Political Culture and Democracy in Developing Countries* (Boulder, Colo.: Lynne Reinner, 1993), 47.

3. For a detailed discussion of these, see Carey Anthony Watt, *Serving the Nation: Cultures of Service, Association and Citizenship* (Delhi: Oxford University Press, 2005). Also see R. Srivatsan, "Concept of 'Seva' and the 'Sevak' in the Freedom Movement," *Economic and Political Weekly,* 4 February 2006.

4. Susanne Hoeber Rudolph and Lloyd I. Rudolph, "The Coffee House and the Ashram: Gandhi, Civil Society and Public Spheres," in Carolyn Elliot, ed., *Civil Society and Democracy* (New Delhi: Oxford University Press, 2003), 378.

5. Amitabh Behar and Aseem Prakash, "India," in Muthiah Alagappa, ed., *Civil Society and Political Change in Asia: Expanding and Contracting Democratic Space* (Stanford, Calif.: Stanford University Press, 2004), 207–208.

6. Ashutosh Varshney, *Ethnic Conflict and Civic Life: Hindus and Muslims in India* (Delhi: Oxford University Press, 2002).

7. Arvind Rajagopal, *Politics After Television: Hindu Nationalism and the Reshaping of the Public in India* (Cambridge: Cambridge University Press, 2001).

8. R. Vaidyanathan, "NGOs Should Practice What they Preach," *Business Line,* 24 August 2006.

9. These institutions of local governance, *panchayati raj,* were established by constitutional amendment in 1992. At all three levels of these institutions of local democracy, from the village to the district, one-third of the seats are reserved for women. Civil society activism has been indispensable to enabling more effective participation by women.

10. There is a view, however, that asserts and laments the "NGO-isation of

grassroots struggles." See Sangeeta Kamat, *Development Hegemony: NGOs and the State in India* (Delhi: Oxford University Press, 2002), 167.

11. John Harriss, "Middle Class Activism and Poor People's Politics: An Exploration of Civil Society in Chennai," DESTIN Working Paper Series No. 05-72, London School of Economics and Political Science, October 2005, 1.

12. Neera Chandhoke, *The Conceits of Civil Society* (New Delhi: Oxford University Press, 2003), 248.

13. Such moves from civil society to mainstream politics are not unusual. In 1984, the Bahujan Samaj Party was formed, building on the legacy of what was essentially a trade union, the All India Backward and Minority Employees' Federation (BAMCEF). Likewise, resignations by disillusioned civil servants who go on to form NGOs are also not unknown, two of the better-known examples being Aruna Roy of MKSS and Jayaprakash Narayan of Loksatta. Such leaders are quite different from those civil servants who set up NGOs upon retirement, which become single-person institutions with secure sources of comfortable funding.

14. Wood's formulation of a "franchise state" refers to the fact that citizens lose their political rights when the delivery of services is entrusted to nonstate agencies which are not accountable to the citizens, but only to the state. Furthermore, if the state devolves responsibility for implementation, to the extent that practice is policy, it loses control over policy itself. See Geof Wood, "States without Citizens: The Problem of the Franchise State," in David Hulme and Michael Edwards, eds., *NGOs, States and Donors: Too Close for Comfort?* (London: Macmillan, 1997), 81.

15. Michael Walzer, "The Civil Society Argument," in Ronald Beiner, ed., *Theorizing Citizenship* (New York: State University of New York Press, 1995), 170.

9

CIVIL SOCIETY VERSUS CORRUPTION

Rob Jenkins

Rob Jenkins is professor of political science at Birkbeck College, University of London. He is author and editor of several books, most recently Reinventing Accountability: Making Democracy Work for Human Development (2005). This essay originally appeared in the April 2007 issue of the Journal of Democracy.

Not least among the achievements of India's sixty-year-old democratic experiment is the sheer durability of its liberal constitutional system. Almost no other country that attained independence in the post–Second World War wave of decolonization has managed continuously to hold free and fair elections, protect and augment fundamental rights, and maintain civilian control of the military.

But many Indians insist that their democracy be held to a higher standard and thus judged against the world's most successful democracies, not the dysfunctional postcolonial countries that happened to come of age at the same historical moment. The relevant yardstick from this perspective—the quality shared by the world's most mature democracies—is the ability to deepen democracy, that is, to make politics more *inclusive* and the state more *accountable*. Democratic deepening in India has undoubtedly been impressive. But as we shall see, it has progressed much further in terms of inclusiveness than with respect to accountability.

Indian democracy's signal achievement has been to broaden the narrow social base on which its representative institutions stood at the time of independence in 1947. India's initial crop of political parties was dominated by English-speaking professionals from elite backgrounds. India's legislatures were disproportionately populated by the richer and better-educated groups in the Hindu social order, the so-called upper castes. The Indian National Congress (also known as the Congress party) dominated the first two decades of postindependence politics, receiving its first major jolt from power in the 1967 state-level elections. Another decade elapsed before Congress first lost power at the national level—to a coalition government that barely managed two years in office, from 1977 to 1979. Congress then ruled for almost the entire 1980s and the first half of the 1990s, at which point India entered its current era of coalition governance.

Throughout the 1970s and 1980s, parties dedicated to advancing the interests of the lower castes emerged on a large scale, a trend that accelerated rapidly during the 1990s. By the mid-1990s, not only was unchallenged Congress dominance a thing of the past; so was control over electoral politics by social elites. What Christophe Jaffrelot calls "the silent revolution"[1]—the process by which India's political leadership became more broadly representative—is an accomplishment of which many Indians are rightly proud. It is against this backdrop that efforts to address the problem of corruption in India must be assessed. For if the success of India's democratic experiment has frequently been justified by pointing to the rise of parties led by and ostensibly dedicated to the advancement of historically disadvantaged communities, the bribe-taking politician has become the preeminent symbol of India's democratic malaise. The persistence of corruption is a constant reminder that democracy is deepening in some respects but not others—that inclusiveness and accountability do not necessarily accompany one another.

Corruption and the Quality of Governance

There is an ambivalent relationship between two analytical tendencies—between the belief that the successful incorporation of nonelites into electoral politics represents a profound deepening of Indian democracy, and the view that pervasive corruption epitomizes how shallow India's democratic pretensions are in practice. On the one hand, it is possible to see these as essentially distinct if conflicting conclusions: Choosing to emphasize one or the other of these two dimensions of India's contemporary political reality would thus indicate nothing more than an inclination to see the glass of democracy as either half full or half empty.

But another way of reconciling these two competing assessments of India's democracy is to argue that they are less contradictory than at first they might appear: Nonelites would not have been able to build parties and consolidate electoral gains—thus making politics more inclusive—had they not engaged in systematic corruption when given the opportunity that even limited shares of state power conferred. Promising voters favored treatment is the stock-in-trade of political clientelism, and to the extent that such transactions take place on a group basis (where politicians are aggregated into parties, and voters into social groups defined by ethnicity), there should be little surprise that the rise of lower-caste politics has relied on the distribution of patronage. This dynamic is of course not limited to parties based on lower-caste identity. Kanchan Chandra calls India a "patronage democracy," arguing that both voters and politicians face almost impossible-to-resist incentives to continue interacting through an identity-based form of clientelism.[2] Pratap Bhanu Mehta has gone so far as to say that corruption has become a key channel of social mobility in India, and that corruption enjoys a kind of popular legitimacy as a result.[3]

Yet even if the distribution of goods, services, and official posts to members of specified groups is accepted as part of the means by which historically disadvantaged communities have taken power in their own right (rather than as junior partners in broader catch-all parties such as Congress), and even if this process is seen to have legitimated much of the routine corruption that is practiced in Indian politics, it does not necessarily follow that public opinion will be forever forgiving of what is still understood as criminal behavior. A convincing case can be made that the emergence of movements against corruption in the 1990s was originally a reaction *against* the notion that corruption was acceptable because it gave subaltern groups the means to build successful independent parties. India's anticorruption movements have since then continued to wage an uphill fight against a potent narrative that excuses graft as an unavoidable accompaniment to democratic deepening under Indian conditions.

That corruption could ever have been regarded as necessary will come as a surprise to observers of democratization in countries other than India. Public-opinion surveys in Latin America, for instance, have cast corruption as a serious obstacle to the consolidation of that region's third-wave democracies. Based on his reading of survey data from several parts of the world, Larry Diamond concludes that, as a result of "mounting citizen disgust with corruption worldwide, the global democratic trend is at greater risk of reversal than at any time since the end of the Cold War."[4] Diamond's analysis contrasts "the wealthy, established democracies of North America, Europe, and Japan" with "the less established democracies, where the legitimacy of democracy is not so deeply rooted." While in the former, corruption undermines faith in politicians, in the latter, "political corruption scandals are much more likely to erode public faith in democracy itself and thereby to destabilize the entire system."[5]

India does not fit comfortably into this typology. Despite its relative poverty, India possesses democratic institutions that have reached levels of consolidation (depending on one's measure) approaching those of the industrialized world. As a result, unlike in many developing-world democracies, corruption in India is not generally considered to be a threat to its democratic regime. Indians have firsthand experience of democracy's ability to weather crises: several wars, periodic economic meltdowns, communal riots, and the two-year internal state of emergency imposed by Prime Minister Indira Gandhi from 1975 to 1977. The Indian case highlights the need to distinguish between the conten-

tion that corruption is undermining popular commitment to India's democratic form of government and the argument that corruption is undermining the quality of governance produced by democratic politics. It is
the latter argument that India's anticorruption activists have sought to
advance over the past dozen or so years.

Pioneers of Anticorruption Activism

Ironically, the work of anticorruption activist groups in Indian civil
society since the mid-1990s stands as one of the strongest indications
that India's democracy is deepening in ways which go beyond the "silent revolution" of expanded political representation for marginalized
social groups.

Corruption was not of course invented in the 1990s, when the first of
two succeeding waves of anticorruption activism was unleashed. Allegations of scandal plagued the 17-year tenure of India's first prime minister, Jawaharlal Nehru. Two of Nehru's ministers resigned under an ethi-
cal cloud, and Nehru was often criticized for indulging corrupt allies
whom many thought he ought to have jettisoned. During the reign of
Nehru's daughter, Indira Gandhi, corruption began to become more ex-
tortionate, a development largely attributable to the wholesale induction of organized-crime figures into Indian politics by Sanjay Gandhi,
Indira Gandhi's son and presumed political heir until his death in a
1980 plane crash.[6]

Corruption remains a staple of political discussion in India. Little
has changed in the two decades since the Bofors affair (a scandal involving allegations of kickbacks in defense procurement) helped to
sink Rajiv Gandhi's government in the 1989 general election. Print and
broadcast media, not to mention parliamentary debates, are filled with
charges of corruption and heated discussions about how best to combat
it. Anticorruption activism is nothing new in India either. One of Nehru's
most forceful detractors throughout his premiership was Ram Manohar
Lohia, a one-time comrade in the freedom struggle who became a key
figure in the development of Indian socialism. Throughout the 1950s,
Lohia railed against high-level corruption "and its pervasive effect on
India's morality and economy."[7] Lohia sought not only to shame political leaders into taking action to punish the most egregiously corrupt,
but also to build a grassroots movement for probity in public office to
overcome what he regarded as growing indifference to corruption. Few
leaders were susceptible to shaming; the movement never materialized.

Throughout the 1990s, India witnessed a seemingly endless proces-
sion of "scams," as the Indian media labeled them—the stock-market
scam, the urea scam, the telecom scam, the sugar scam, the fodder scam,
and others too numerous to mention. There was also the 1996 discovery
of an industrialist's diary that was alleged to show payments to politi-

cians, whose names were indicated by the use of initials. The "Jain Diaries" were captivating both because they appeared to be convincing primary-source documents and because they revealed how readily an entrepreneur could come to see corruption as just another business expense to be recorded.

It was amid this atmosphere that a new type of anticorruption activism emerged in the mid-1990s. Rather than focusing on the collective misdeeds of a ruling party, or directing their energies toward the strengthening of state-accountability institutions such as the auditor-general's office, the oversight committees of Parliament, and the Central Vigilance Commission, some anticorruption campaigners began to chart a different course. The key elements of their new strategy were to expose specific acts of corruption (rather than to condemn broad patterns of misrule); to do so by utilizing the investigative energies of ordinary people (rather than mobilizing in response to accusations leveled by the press or by opposition politicians); and to focus on the local level, where routinized corruption was a daily curse, where the theft of public resources was personal, and where citizens themselves could do the most to expose the precise mechanisms through which corruption took place.

The paradigmatic grassroots movement of the mid-to-late 1990s dedicated to exposing local corruption was the Mazdoor Kisan Shakti Sangathan (MKSS, or Organization for the Empowerment of Workers and Peasants), a people's organization active mainly in the northern state of Rajasthan.[8] The MKSS was based in a rural part of a poor state, and its approach emphasized the impact of corruption on poorer citizens and the direct role that they could play in punishing those who engaged in it.

The MKSS's campaign during the early 1990s to secure the payment of back wages owed to day-laborers on government drought-relief programs revealed the role of corruption in the workers' ongoing predicament. Access even to rudimentary data on local allocations made it clear that officials were billing the government for amounts far in excess of what workers were being paid for building roads, digging irrigation canals, and creating other small-scale public works. But to expose the specific acts of fraud that were involved (wage payments to ghost workers, or the substitution of poor-quality materials for those specified in purchase orders), the MKSS needed access to detailed government financial records, which officials had long kept secret. Among the documents sought were "muster rolls," the forms on which labor supervisors daily recorded the names of workers for each job site, the hours worked, wages owed, and payments made. The information contained in these records could then be crosschecked against other sources of information to reveal discrepancies.

Throughout the late 1990s, MKSS activists faced great resistance when trying to gain access to government-held information. They obtained some documents by appealing to the moral virtue of several mid-level civil servants. Leaks from sympathetic clerks in run-down government offices at the periphery of the rural-development bureaucracy yielded more data. But the information needed to expose specific acts of fraud remained available only on an extremely ad hoc basis. After Rajasthan's state-level Right to Information Act was passed in 2000 (thanks largely to intense MKSS lobbying), activists could seek documents through official channels with greater assertiveness, though ingenious forms of bureaucratic resistance meant that obtaining information remained a struggle.

The MKSS's key innovation, however, was to develop a novel means by which information found in government records could be shared and collectively verified: the *jan sunwai* (public hearing). A *jan sunwai* is a publicly accessible forum, often held in a large open-sided tent pitched on a highly visible spot, at which government records are presented alongside testimony by local people with firsthand knowledge of the development projects that these records purport to document. Key pieces of information from project documents are read aloud. Those with direct knowledge of the specific government projects under investigation are invited to testify on any apparent discrepancies between the official record and their own experiences as laborers on public-works projects or applicants for means-tested antipoverty schemes. Through this direct form of "social audit," many drought-relief workers discovered that they had been listed as beneficiaries of antipoverty schemes despite never having received payments, which presumably were pocketed by the officials who authorized the disbursements. Others learned that certain well-connected villagers, who performed no labor at all, were nevertheless listed as workers and often paid more than those who actually worked. Local people were astonished (and, increasingly, angered) to learn of large payments to building contractors for construction projects that existed only on paper—in project documents held in inaccessible government files.

While citizens have traditionally been relegated to participating in vertical channels of accountability (by voting or engaging in advocacy), the MKSS and other anticorruption groups mobilized poor people to substitute their own investigative energies where horizontal institutions of accountability (state agencies that monitor the performance of other state entities) were demonstrably failing.[9] By participating in popular audits of government spending, people were able to assume new roles as citizen-auditors, blurring the conventional distinction between vertical and horizontal channels of accountability. The MKSS and other groups that emulated its success forged a new, "hybrid" form of accountability.[10] This has subsequently been incorporated, by statute, into Rajasthan's system of local government: Village-level accounts now *must* be subjected to scrutiny by regular village meetings to which all residents are invited. Similar provisions were enacted in other states such as Kerala, and are found in the legislation that in 2005 created one of India's most ambitious antipoverty initiatives, the National Rural Employment Guarantee program.

Thanks to the demonstration effect generated by the work of MKSS and groups like the Bhrashtachar Virodhi Jan Andolan (BVJA, or People's Movement Against Corruption),[11] based in the western state of Maharashtra, the link between access to government-held information and the ability of ordinary people to combat corruption at levels that afflict them in direct personal terms became firmly established in public discourse. Prime Minister Atal Bihari Vajpayee's government enacted India's first nationwide freedom-of-information legislation in 2003. Though used by some groups to open up the workings of government, the Freedom of Information Act's provisions were too forgiving of official secrecy. A coalition of activists subsequently pressed the succeeding government, headed by Prime Minister Manmohan Singh, to produce more substantial legislation. In June 2005 a new Right to Information Act was enacted.

Although the first wave of activism (1995–2000) developed innovative techniques for exposing corruption, its overall impact was limited. The movement's prospects were not helped by a broader discursive shift that had begun to redefine the relationship between corruption and market-oriented economic reform, one of the most controversial issues on the public agenda. When the MKSS began organizing public hearings in the mid-1990s, the debate on reform and corruption seemed to be going their way: It had quickly become clear that market reform would not extinguish corruption. Activists thought that once people came to this realization, they would seek alternatives, and perhaps join a movement that harnessed the potential of ordinary members of the public.

As the 1990s came to an end, however, a new cynicism arose in discussions about corruption. Some began to feel that if India's economy could perform as well as it was despite the prevailing culture of graft, then perhaps corruption was less growth-retarding than commonly thought. Historical accounts of the process by which corruption was tamed in today's wealthy democracies supported this view: Countries like the United States and South Korea brought corruption under control *after* they gained their riches.[12] Thus it was easy to dismiss corruption as a problem that development would solve. By the late 1990s, rising indifference toward corruption started becoming a serious drag on recruitment of new activists.

Anticorruption activism might not have survived this blow had not another twist in the public debate about corruption and reform taken place around the same time. It was not long after the turn of the new millennium that concern increased sharply about the uneven consequences of India's economic reforms. This fueled worries about the political sustainability of reform. To nip rising political discontent with liberalization in the bud, politicians (particularly those up for reelection) poured funds into antipoverty programs. When, in 2003, even careful political management of such programs did not prevent voters from ousting two seemingly popular and responsive state governments—partly due to corruption in the schemes' implementation—the relationship between economic reform and corruption began to be seriously rethought. The sense of urgency was reinforced when Prime Minister Vajpayee's governing coalition lost to Singh's Congress-led alliance in the 2004 national election amid an apparent wave of disgust among India's have-nots. The fear was no longer that corruption unduly impeded growth, but that it silted up the channels through which antipoverty resources were supposed to flow to those adversely affected by economic liberalization. Corruption thus threatened to render ineffective the ameliorative programs necessary to prevent antireform sentiment from coalescing into an effective political movement.

A Second Wave of Anticorruption Activism

In response to this shifting discursive landscape, anticorruption campaigners launched a second wave of activism. While the first wave (c.1995–2000) helped to blur the boundary between horizontal and vertical accountability, the second wave of activism (c.2001–2006) bridged divisions within the anticorruption movement itself, gaps that had hampered its effectiveness. Four such divides are discussed here.

1) The poor and the middle class. The first divide that the new wave of anticorruption activism began to bridge was between the poor and the middle class. First-wave anticorruption movements had not shied away from accusing middle-class groups of not supporting campaigns against forms of corruption that particularly afflicted the poor, or from blaming this failure of nerve on the middle class's desire to preserve its privileges. Middle-class people, in turn, blamed the poor for being unreliable allies in the struggle for better governance, too easily bought off with populist gestures. During the second wave of activism, however, *parts* of these two omnibus socioeconomic categories have sometimes been able to contain their mutual animosity long enough to work together. Cooperative instincts have been evidenced mainly among subgroups situated alongside the categorical border. This includes, from within the poor, not the truly destitute but the upwardly mobile "aspirational" poor, and from the middle class, not the prosperous end of this capacious category—in India the middle class is often synonymous with the economic superelite—but the vulnerable lower-middle class, many of whom are sole proprietors of microenterprises or low-level clerks in the public or private sectors.

A good example of how poor and middle-class people have begun to forge alliances to fight corruption is Parivartan, a New Delhi–based civic association formed in 2000 primarily by retired professionals. Their goal was to combat the corruption that was (and remains) rampant in the capital's public institutions. Parivartan originally focused on quintessentially middle-class issues, its first campaign targeting corruption in the income-tax bureaucracy. In India, only the comparatively wealthy are subject to income tax. Parivartan's methods also reflected the social profile of its supporters. Parivartan urged citizens to refuse to pay bribes solicited by income-tax officials and to report the details of any such solicitation to the association, which would assist in filing grievances against the officials concerned. Grievances would be communicated to higher-level income-tax officials, a technique effective only for an association brimming with retired civil servants and other well-connected professionals.

Within two years, however, Parivartan had begun addressing issues of more widespread concern, such as corruption-induced problems within Delhi's municipal electricity utility. But the service-delivery improvements that the group's initial complaints had generated were proving short-lived. Parivartan was learning the essential lesson that failing to expand the circle of beneficiaries from governance reforms undermines their longer-term viability, *even in middle-class areas where results may initially have appeared promising.* New political alignments and the natural turnover of officials tend to erode the original impetus for reforms. Parivartan's efforts to combat graft in public-service provision achieved far greater success when the group reached out to community-based organizations representing slum-dwellers, who faced far more acute service-delivery issues. The sheer numbers of slum-dwellers in Delhi, and their geographic concentration within certain electoral wards, attracted the attention of politicians eager to nurture "vote banks" within their constituencies. Parivartan gradually formed its approach around using the Freedom of Information Act that came into force in 2003 (and subsequently the stronger 2005 Right to Information Act). The group now helps poor people use these and various official-redress mechanisms to combat police harassment of street vendors, illegal slum-clearance drives, and irregularities in the supply of subsidized food. This has won Parivartan's activists valuable new allies in their daily battles for cleaner government.

Theories of democracy have long emphasized the key role played by an emerging middle class in both establishing and consolidating government by consent.[13] As they become increasingly prosperous and influential, middle-class groups are expected to find a political voice sufficiently autonomous to demand more accountable governance. Indeed, parts of India's rising middle class (whose members have been the main beneficiaries of economic reform since 1991) have begun to do what middle classes have historically done—namely, demand that public authorities treat them less arbitrarily. Others have played it safe, looking to fulfill their needs through private means rather than making enemies in the service of a losing cause: reform of India's public sector. The Parivartan example suggests that the urge to reform state institutions will founder without conscious efforts to overcome the differences that prevent poor and middle-class groups from collaborating.[14]

2) NGOs and people's movements. The second gap that the new wave of anticorruption activists has helped to close separates nongovernmental organizations (NGOs) from people's movements. Both types of association mobilize citizens to fight graft, but they have tended to remain aloof from one another. Indeed a good deal of enmity has characterized their relations in India since the 1970s. Within India's activist community, civic groups that are not "people's movements" are regarded as NGOs, a kind of lesser species of nonpolitical or even depoliticized social action. This perspective is best described as movement populism—an ideological orientation stemming from a belief that the more formal organizational forms embodied by NGOs fail to prioritize poor people's concerns and thus merely perpetuate elite biases. The origins of movement populism lie in the widespread discrediting of NGOs that took place in the early 1980s, when sections of the Indian left began to attack foreign-funded NGOs (and Indians who worked for or with them) as "agents of imperialism,"[15] and activist groups began avoiding the NGO label. The "movement" descriptor is a prized symbol of legitimacy for activists who believe that they are proposing radical alternatives to existing modes of political action. It is thus not surprising to find Parivartan, for instance, identifying itself with conspicuous emphasis as "*not* an NGO . . . [but] a people's movement for reinforcement of democratic values."[16]

In the late 1990s, many groups working to fight corruption tried to enhance their grassroots credentials by distancing themselves from the NGO sector, even though several NGOs were pursuing similar goals, in some cases through more or less identical means. During the second wave of anticorruption activism, however, at least one span of the ideological wall separating people's movements from NGOs was breached. Hybrid organizations emerged, borrowing elements from both types of association. The gradual evolution of several anticorruption groups whose movement credentials are beyond reproach has made this bridging of the NGO-movement gap possible.

NGOs working to combat corruption are, for the most part, eager to support like-minded movement groups, partly in the hope of associating themselves with a more radical form of civic engagement. NGO backing occurs informally—through the provision of meeting space, office help, transport, or accommodation—though often with systematic regularity. Rarely are distinctions made locally between prominent NGOs in a given vicinity and movement groups with which they may have forged durable, if informal, ties. In Rajasthan, the movement-oriented MKSS was closely linked to the Social Work and Resource Centre, one of the region's largest NGOs. The movement-like activities of veteran campaigner Anna Hazare's BVJA in Maharahstra were often difficult, if not impossible, to disentangle from the affairs of the Hind Swaraj Trust, an NGO that Hazare also helped to run. In Mumbai, the Rationing Kruti Samiti (RKS, or Committee to Save Rationing), a campaign to fight corruption in India's main food-subsidy program, stemmed from the work of (and relied on logistical support from) Apnalaya, an NGO that remained organizationally separate from the RKS. These NGO-movement partnerships represent a powerful combination. Even one of the NGO sector's most outspoken critics concedes that "when they have tied up with oppositional social movements," occasionally India's "NGOs have been able to transform political agendas."[17]

3) Civil society and the state. The third division that the new wave of anticorruption activism has at least partly transcended is between state officials and civil society actors (whether of the movement or NGO variety). It has already been noted that the MKSS and other organizations frequently relied on sympathetic bureaucrats to leak information helpful in exposing corruption. But in seeking to combat broader patterns of unaccountable governance in which corruption is a key component, civic groups have forged even more creative alliances with state actors. In some cases, alliances proved short-lived, as did the joint-monitoring program established in the 1990s between the RKS in Mumbai and the state-government official responsible for managing the city's food-subsidy program.[18]

Second-wave campaigners have sought models for state-civic engagement that are more durable and less likely to erode their hard-won autonomy. A notable example was the public-interest litigation that a coalition of activist and nongovernmental groups brought against the Indian government in 2000. The petitioners maintained that the government was not meeting its obligation to ensure that nutrition and food-subsidy programs were implemented as transparently and effectively as possible. The petitioners made specific reference to the stocks of food grains held by the Food Corporation of India and other government entities.[19] In a surprise "interim order" issued in 2001, the Supreme Court found that the government of India as well as several state governments had failed in their duties, and had in fact violated citizens' right to food, which the court located within the "right to life" provision of the Indian constitution.

While India's progressive jurisprudence has long been celebrated both at home and abroad, the record of court orders being implemented is far less impressive. In the so-called Right to Food case, however, the court's interim order specified what the activist-petitioners quickly recognized as a promising implementation mechanism: the appointment of a "food commissioner" who would monitor the actions taken by public authorities to comply with the Court's ruling. A vast array of government programs and departments came under the food commissioner's purview, and his office was empowered to undertake fact-finding missions to locations where government agencies were suspected of continuing to violate citizens' fundamental rights.

Activists have been criticized, in India and elsewhere, for relying excessively on litigation to right social wrongs. The charge, leveled with equal vigor by social-movement groups and right-wing critics of "judicial activism," is that court rulings are no substitute for effective political mobilization. The Right to Food case might well have been vulnerable to such an accusation had not the litigation spawned a fruitful ongoing collaboration between the food commissioner and activist groups seeking to combat corruption in the food and nutrition programs covered by the court's interim ruling.[20] In order to root out cases of official abuse in these programs, the food commissioner worked in cooperation with a far-flung network of activists that had been mobilized by groups involved with filing the suit. Through the investigative powers conferred on the food commissioner (a retired civil servant), activists gained access to documentation necessary to expose pilfering of resources intended for people suffering from acute food insecurity. The commissioner's reports led to further judicial orders, which kept the pressure on government agencies to improve their performance. The bridging of the gap between civil society and the state led, in this case, not to cooptation, but to ordinary people enhancing their capacity to oppose local manifestations of corruption.[21]

4) Activists and partisans. The fourth gap that has been bridged is between what might be termed the activist and partisan domains of anticorruption politics. The relationship between party politics and civic activism became a growing source of controversy as the second wave of activism began. The debate continues. One view is that activists trying to expose corruption should steer clear of opposition parties, which naturally seek to embarrass ruling-party politicians but are themselves compromised by corruption accusations leveled against their own members. On the other hand, is not exposing the misdeeds of state powerholders what democratic competition is all about? For anticorruption activists to avoid this central feature of political life is to register a huge vote of no confidence in the democratic process. Party politicians can help anticorruption campaigners by asking questions in the legislature, advising on investigative strategy, providing legal and accounting expertise, and using their vast networks of influence to pry information from leaky bureaucracies which, after all, are staffed by people from all parties.

An example from the state of Goa illustrates the complex relationship between partisan politicians and local efforts to expose corruption. In this case, anticorruption activism became enmeshed in clientelist politics, giving rise to what is best described as "anticorruption clientelism." As the 1990s came to a close, a resident of a village in northern Goa, less than ten miles from the state capital, sought to expose what he suspected were abuses by the elected village council. Citing Goa's 1997 Right to Information Act, the activist asked the council to supply financial records related to various development programs. When it refused, the activist complained to higher administrative authorities, including state-government departments. This produced no results either.

Only when he failed to elicit assistance from members of the party then in power in Goa—to which the allegedly corrupt chairman of his local council also belonged—did the activist turn for help to a state legislator from the opposition party. It was by invoking this powerful partisan patron, who clearly had an interest in embarrassing a village council controlled by the party then governing the state, that the activist finally obtained bureaucratic cooperation in his efforts to force the local council to divulge financial and administrative records. Following advice from his patron, the activist began framing his informational requests in ways that yielded more valuable data. In a departure from his earlier haphazard methods, the activist began grouping the information he sought into clearly demarcated categories—everything from the costs incurred by the council for the "disposal of dead bodies" to "expenses on stationery."[22] He was attempting to expose discrepancies between the council's accounts and the contractor's books much as the MKSS had done in Rajasthan. But in the absence of a people's organization to support him in obtaining and crosschecking the information, the activist had turned for assistance to a political boss.

This case demonstrates the way in which transparency reforms can create incentives for political collaboration that resemble a modified version of the traditional patron-client political relationship—ironically, one of the chief structural underpinnings of the very corruption that activists are trying to eradicate. Instead of being built around corrupt transactions (promises of special treatment in exchange for votes), anticorruption clientelism centers on the voluntary and mutually beneficial relationship between a local activist and a party politician. Politicians render assistance to activists' efforts to expose corrupt acts by the patron's political rivals, and in exchange, the patron stands to win credit within his party for any scalps claimed by activist-led investigations that he supported. Anticorruption activists implicitly reserve the right to turn against their patron if he or his party engages in corruption, just as the patron retains the freedom not to expend resources seeking out corruption within his own party.

Yet the Goa case also demonstrates the complications that arise in relationships characterized by "diffuse reciprocity." Over time, the activist-client's focus became influenced by his patron's agenda. The target of the information-seeking was increasingly the council's chairman rather than others (some from the patron's party) who were crucial accomplices. This fueled rumors that the activist's investigations were politically motivated, blunting their edge considerably. Still, the activist's work was regarded as having heightened popular awareness about the state's freedom-of-information legislation and various administrative procedures required to make it work. The success of the partisan patron, who went on to hold high office, motivated other aspiring politicians to engage in anticorruption clientelism—a phenomenon that bears watching over the next decade.

The activists who over the past dozen years have sought to curtail the everyday forms of corruption that afflict poorer Indians have not made much headway in immediate practical terms. Nevertheless, India's anticorruption campaigners have overcome formidable odds in redefining the public's role in holding governments accountable, as well as in bridging rifts within the movement that constrain its ability to fight corruption effectively. It is to this still-untapped reservoir of political energy that we must look for signs of India's continued democratic vitality. The entry of historically disadvantaged groups into positions of political power is a necessary but insufficient condition for the deepening of India's democracy. When corruption ceases to present the obstacle that it currently does to the provision of public goods, India's democratic transformation will indeed have penetrated to a deeper level. Civic engagement alone cannot bring about this transformation—but flexible alliances that empower people to expose corruption will remain essential to making the Indian state more accountable and competitive politics more inclusive.

NOTES

1. Christophe Jaffrelot, *India's Silent Revolution: The Rise of the Lower Castes in North India* (London: Hurst, 2003).

2. Kanchan Chandra, *Why Ethnic Parties Succeed: Patronage and Ethnic Head Counts in India* (Cambridge: Cambridge University Press, 2004).

3. Pratap Bhanu Mehta, *The Burden of Democracy* (New Delhi: Penguin, 2003).

4. Larry Diamond, "Advancing Democratic Governance: A Global Perspective on the Status of Democracy and Directions for International Assistance," unpubl. ms., 4, at *www.stanford.edu/ldiamond/papers/advancing_democ_%20governance. pdf.*

5. Diamond, "Advancing Democratic Governance," 13.

6. After Sanjay's death, Rajiv Gandhi, Indira Gandhi's other son and ultimately her successor, was thrust into the limelight along with his Italian-born wife Sonia. Rajiv was murdered in 1991; Sonia Gandhi is currently leader of the Congress party, which heads the United Progressive Alliance coalition government that took power following the 2004 general election.

7. "Question of Income and Expenditure," 3 June 1957, republished in Ram Manohar Lohia, *Rs. 25,000 a Day* (Hyderabad: Navahind, 1963), 17.

8. Rob Jenkins and Anne Marie Goetz, "Accounts and Accountability: Theoretical Implications of the Right-to-Information Movement in India," *Third World Quarterly* 20 (June 1999): 603–22.

9. Key conceptual distinctions are explained in Andreas Schedler, "Conceptualizing Accountability," in Andreas Schedler, Larry Diamond, and Marc F. Plattner, eds., *The Self-Restraining State: Power and Accountability in New Democracies* (Boulder, Colo.: Lynne Rienner, 1999).

10. Anne Marie Goetz and Rob Jenkins, *Reinventing Accountability: Making Democracy Work for Human Development* (New York: Macmillan/Palgrave, 2005).

11. The BVJA is analyzed in Rob Jenkins, "In Varying States of Decay: The Politics of Anticorruption in Maharashtra and Rajasthan," in Rob Jenkins, ed., *Regional Reflections: Comparing Politics Across India's States* (Oxford University Press, 2004), 219–52.

12. Mushtaq Khan, "Corruption and Governance in Early Capitalism: World Bank Strategies and Their Limitations," in J.R. Pincus and J.A. Winters, eds., *Reinventing the World Bank* (Ithaca, N.Y.: Cornell University Press, 2002), 164–84.

13. The *locus classicus* is Barrington Moore, Jr., *Social Origins of Dictatorship and Democracy: Lord and Peasant in the Making of the Modern World* (Boston: Beacon, 1966).

14. Other impediments are detailed in Rob Jenkins and Anne Marie Goetz, "Constraints on Civil Society's Capacity to Curb Corruption: Lessons from the Indian Experience," *IDS Bulletin* 29 (October 1999): 39–49.

15. See the article by Prakash Karat of the Communist Party of India–Marxist: "Action Groups/Voluntary Organizations: A Factor in Imperialist Strategy," *The Marxist* 2 (April–June 1984): 51–63.

16. This description is positioned prominently in the "About Us" section of the organization's website, at *www.parivartan.com*.

17. Neera Chandhoke, *The Conceits of Civil Society* (Delhi: Oxford University Press, 2003), 71.

18. Rob Jenkins and Anne Marie Goetz, "Civil Society Engagement and India's Public Distribution System: Lessons from the Rationing Kruti Samiti in Mumbai," Consultation Paper for the World Bank, *World Development Report 2004: Making Services Work for Poor People* (Washington, D.C.: World Bank, 2003).

19. George Cheriyan, "Enforcing Right to Food in India: Bottlenecks in Delivering the Expected Outcome—Focusing on Corruption and the Resultant Failure of Various Welfare Schemes," paper presented at the Second International Workshop of the ICSSR-WIDER/UNV Joint Project on Food Security, Helsinki, Finland, 12–14 October 2005.

20. See Jean Dreze, "Right to Food: From the Court to the Streets," at *www.right tofoodindia.org*.

21. Much of this interpretation emerged in the author's interview with N.C. Saxena, court-appointed food commissioner, New Delhi, 14 December 2004.

22. Letter from the activist concerned to the local council's chief administrative officer, 8 April 1999. Names withheld to preserve confidentiality.

10

BREAKING NEWS:
THE MEDIA REVOLUTION

Praveen Swami

Praveen Swami *is associate editor with the New Delhi bureau of* Frontline *and also writes for its sister newspaper,* The Hindu. *He is the recipient of the Indian Express–Ramnath Goenka Print Journalist of the Year Award for 2006, and the Prem Bhatia Memorial Award for Political Journalism in 2003.*

"A weekly political and commercial paper, open to all parties, but influenced by none," read the masthead of James Augustus Hickey's two-sheet *Bengal Gazette,* which commenced publication in Kolkata on 29 January 1780. In the two centuries since, India's mass media has succeeded in establishing itself as one of the most powerful institutions in the world's largest democracy.

Since 1989—when an investigation of defense payoffs by the journalists Narasimhan Ram and Chitra Subramaniam helped to ensure the electoral defeat of the government of Prime Minister Rajiv Gandhi—politicians and the public alike have become increasingly aware of the power of the media.[1] A concealed-camera sting operation conducted in 2001 by the weekly newspaper *Tehelka,* for example, helped to prompt India's federal criminal-investigation organization, the Central Bureau of Investigations, to bring charges for accepting bribes against former defense minister George Fernandes.[2] A welter of exposés, addressing everything from police misconduct to sexual harassment at the workplace, has since appeared on Indian television and on newspaper front pages. Journalists have also succeeded in placing the wrenching poverty that stalks much of the country at the center of political debate. Palagummi Sainath's work on indebtedness-related peasant suicides in western India, for example, compelled the government to initiate relief measures in the region.[3]

Yet significant challenges lie ahead. Recent decades have seen dramatic economic and social transformations spark a still-unfolding revolution in the reach of newspapers and television. A growing number of critics argue, however, that the very forces which set off the revolution may lead to its implosion.

From Empire to Emergency

India's mass media traces its origins to Hickey's *Bengal Gazette,* which specialized in colorful—and sometimes scurrilous—reportage on colonial high society.[4] Hickey's attacks on Governor-General Warren Hastings and his wife soon earned him the wrath of the East India Company. After a four-month term in jail, Hickey was sentenced to a fine of INR 5,000, which bankrupted the newspaper and forced its proprietor to leave India.

Christopher Bayly's seminal work on information networks in colonial India tells us that sophisticated communication networks predated the rise of the modern media.[5] Among the more notable of these institutions were the Persian-language letters issued by professional newswriters. Newswriters, who were formally accredited to the great courts of India, provided their clients with accounts of life in the great states of India, documenting the rise and fall of political favorites and the changing contours of influence. They also served a role remarkably similar to that of the *Bengal Gazette* or a modern tabloid, keeping "all India amused for years with a flow of dirty stories until a more severe morality intervened in the 1880s."[6] Indian bankers and traders, for their part, had similar communications and intelligence networks, which are known to have reached high levels of sophistication by the mid-seventeenth century.[7]

Hickey's publication, despite its limited reach and significance, flags the transition from these precapitalist institutions to the modern media. Hastings himself encouraged the founding of B. Messink and Peter Reed's *India Gazette,* a pro-establishment newspaper sympathetic to the East India Company; the *India Gazette* was soon followed by the *Bengal Journal* and the *Oriental Magazine of Calcutta Entertainment.* In 1785, the *Madras Courier* was launched in the city now called Chennai, followed six years later by the *Hurkaru* (named after the court newswriters). A decade later, Chennai had two more papers, the East India Company–sanctioned *Madras Gazette* and the unauthorized *India Herald.* The *Bombay Herald* launched operations in Mumbai in 1789. Within a year, a competitor called the *Courier* was carrying Gujarati-language advertisements, evidence that even at this early stage, the newspaper audience was not exclusively British.

For a variety of technological and cultural reasons, which are the subject of energetic debate among scholars, the printing press came late to Indians living outside the East India Company's coastal enclave. Between 1820 and 1840, however, Indian publications registered both growing circulation and influence. The Bengal intellectual Raja

Rammohun Roy, who led an important movement for social reforms that would later flower into the Indian national movement, launched a succession of journals that challenged the attacks on indigenous religions made by Christian missionaries. These included the Bengali-language *Sambad Kaumidi,* which launched in 1821, followed by the Persian-language *Mirat-ul-Akhbar* and the English-language *Brahmunical Magazine.* In 1822, the Mumbai businesssman Fardoonji Murzban launched the *Bombay Samachar,* which continues to publish in Gujarati.

This new media often found itself in an adversarial relationship with colonial authorities. The *Friend of India,* for example, intervened energetically in the debates over the Hindu practice of *sati* during William Bentinck's term as governor-general. As the East India Company's relationship with north Indian states began to deteriorate, the *Jami Jahan Namah* was charged by British representatives in Delhi of spreading slander. New papers emerged in regions as far apart as Lahore, Varanasi, Allahabad, and Kanpur, often with a marked anti-British stand. It would be mistaken, however, to overstate the impact of the new media. Bayly points out that these newspapers "in themselves did not create an information revolution." Rather, the new media "speeded up the velocity and range of communication among existing communities of knowledge. It helped transform some actors within the old ecumene into the leaders of a modern public, but it marginalised and subordinated others."[8]

In 1857, a massive rebellion against the East India Company transformed the structures of Indian political life. The failed rebellion led to the destruction of the states that comprised the precolonial order and paved the way for direct British rule. The coming of the British Raj interrupted the emergence of the modern Indian media, but did not derail it. British-owned newspapers hostile to Indian nationalism, such as the *Statesman* and the *Times of India,* occupied center stage. But powerful voices of resistance also began to emerge. *The Hindu,* founded in 1878, was to play a major role in promoting the cause of Indian independence. Its founders saw the need for an Indian-owned platform to challenge colonial domination. Seven years later, north India saw the emergence of the *Tribune* as an express challenge to the British-owned *Civil and Military Gazette.* The *Tribune* came to be an important platform for the freedom movement, defiantly reporting colonial outrages like the Jallianwalla Bagh Massacre in 1919 (also known as the Amritsar Massacre). The newspaper was closed down after the massacre, and its editor, Kali Nath Ray, was sentenced to two years in jail for his defiant proindependence polemic. As he commented at the time, "The holocaust at Jallianwalla Bagh showed off the British at their worst. They made us crawl on our bellies and shot us down as wild pariah dogs. That incidentally put a nail in the coffin of the British Empire in India. We had indeed come to the parting of ways."[9]

Large parts of the Indian media community, not surprisingly, viewed independence as a triumph. More importantly, the corporate, class, and ideological interests of newspaper proprietors closely coincided with those of the Indian state. Like the *Tribune* and *The Hindu,* for example, the proprietors of the *Hindustan Times* had an intimate relationship with the leading figures of the freedom movement. The proprietor of the *Hindustan Times,* Ghanshyam Das Birla, was a close personal associate and financier of Mohandas K. Gandhi. He was able to leverage his freedom-movement associations to advance the Birla industrial conglomerate's corporate interests after independence.[10] Perhaps predictably, the media developed, for the most part, a less-than-adversarial relationship with the new political dispensation in New Delhi. Although India's first prime minister, Jawaharlal Nehru, was not without his critics in the media, newspapers for the most part treated government with a respect bordering on deference.

Yet by the mid-1970s, growing strains in India's political life—and widespread disenchantment with the Congress party's regime—began to reflect itself in media reportage. In June 1975, Prime Minister Indira Gandhi declared a state of emergency and imposed full-scale press censorship. During an emergency, India's constitution enables the suspension of fundamental rights, including freedom of speech and expression; censorship, which in all other circumstances would be open to judicial scrutiny, becomes immune to legal challenge. Although the country had experienced emergency regulations during the wars of 1962 and 1971, censorship had not been imposed on either occasion. Indira Gandhi's regime, however, put in place a series of executive guidelines designed to make criticism of her government impossible. One of the instructions given to the censor was that "nothing is to be published that is likely to convey the impression of a protest or disapproval of a government measure."[11]

As the eminent jurist Soli Sorabjee writes, "anything that smacked of criticism of governmental measures or action was almost invariably banned, even if the criticism was sober and moderate."[12] Censors even arbitrarily blacked out quotations from Gandhi and Nehru when it appeared that these might be used to criticize the emergency regime. On occasion, the censors' decisions were farcical. The censorship board blacked out stories such as news that a former member of a royal family, Begum Vilayat Mahal, had been seen squatting on a railway platform in New Delhi; a report that an Indian film star had been held in London for shoplifting; and accounts of a meeting of wildlife authorities to consider granting a hunting license to a notable. News of large-scale official atrocities, not surprisingly, never made it to print.

Barring honorable exceptions such as the *Statesman* and the *Indian Express,* newspapers failed to mount even a limited challenge to the emergency declared in 1975. While individual journalists, particularly those involved in anti-emergency political mobilization, served time in jail, the media failed to mount a collective defense of press freedoms. Despite enormous pressures from the regime, India's courts did better. State high courts across the country struck down specific instances of indefensible censorship. Without the support of the media itself, however, these efforts were of little value. Lal Krishna Advani, who went on to become the deputy prime minister, acidly told journalists after Indira Gandhi's electoral defeat in 1977: "You were asked to bend but you began to crawl."[13]

For the Indian media, emergency rule proved to be a transformative experience. In the decades after, a new generation of journalists worked to erase the shame of that period by mobilizing in defense of press freedoms. An increasingly feisty and sometimes irreverent journalism was born, characterized by an adversarial relationship with authority. This new journalism coincided with a revolution in media reach and influence.

The State of the Media Today

During the first decades of independence, India's mass media had grown but slowly. In his magisterial work on the subject, Robin Jeffrey points to the multiple constraints that operated upon it.[14] Technological factors made printing in Indian languages expensive, while foreign-exchange shortages restricted access to both machinery and newsprint. As a result, both the production and reach of the mass media was limited. For an enterprise intended to destroy freedom of the press, however, the emergency rule of 1975 had a paradoxical outcome: It created widespread curiosity about the media and awareness of the need for a free press. Entrepreneurs now moved in to capitalize on this new climate, armed with technologies that made it easier than ever before to print in Indian languages.

Evidence of the revolution of the 1980s, so ably documented by Jeffrey, is not hard to find. Media production in India is now almost galactic in scale. In 2004–2005, the last financial year for which data is available, newspapers were published in 123 languages and dialects. The state of Uttar Pradesh alone produced 9,757 newspapers, magazines and periodicals, followed by Delhi with 8,194, Maharashtra with 6,913, and Madhya Pradesh with 4,210. Between April 2004 and March 2005, 1,948 new publications were registered with authorities, bringing the total to 60,413. Only four closed down.[15]

Successive studies by India's most authoritative poll of media audiences, the annual National Readership Survey (NRS), have shown that the reach of both print and broadcast media is expanding dramatically.[16] According to NRS 2006, Indian newspapers and magazines now reach some 222 million readers, approximately a fifth of the total population. Between 2005 and 2006 alone, more than six million new readers began

Table—India's Top Ten Newspapers

Newspaper	Language	2005 Readership	2006 Readership
Dainik Jagaran	Hindi	21,244,000	21,165,000
Dainik Bhaskar	Hindi	17,379,000	20,958,000
Eenadu	Telegu	11,350,000	13,805,000
Lokmat	Marathi	8,820,000	10,856,000
Amar Ujala	Hindi	10,469,000	10,847,000
Hindustan	Hindi	10,557,000	10,437,000
Daily Thanti	Tamil	9,445,000	10,389,000
Dinakaran	Tamil	1,485,000	9,639,000
Rajasthan Patrika	Hindi	8,651,000	9,391,000
Malayalam Manorama	Malayalam	7,985,000	8,409,000

Source: National Readership Survey, 2006.

to access newspapers or magazines. This is in stark contrast to trends in Japan, Europe, and the United States, where print-media reach has been in decline for several years.[17]

NRS 2006 estimates that a quarter of all Indians age 12 and over now read a daily newspaper. Two Hindi-language newspapers, *Dainik Jagaran* and *Dainik Bhaskar,* have more than 20 million readers each. Put together, India's ten largest daily newspapers have a combined reach of more than 126 million readers. On average, NRS 2006 estimates, the average Indian adult spends some 39 minutes each day reading newspapers and magazines, a substantial commitment of time that reflects the depth of public interest in media production.

Hindi-speaking states, home to the majority of India's population and often characterized as centers of economic and social backwardness, have seen energetic print-media growth. Five of the ten most widely read Indian newspapers are Hindi-language, a fact that may prove of no small significance to future political life in the region. Vernacular-language newspapers, in general, have expanded their reach. Between 2005 and 2006, the readership of all vernacular-language newspapers grew from 191 million to 203.6 million. By contrast, English-language newspaper readership remained static at around 21 million. While some English-language newspapers demonstrated growth in new markets, they also lost readers in others. While the *Hindustan Times* added 360,000 new readers in Mumbai during 2005–2006, for example, it lost ground across the Hindu-speaking states.

Newspaper-readership patterns also offer interesting insight into the changing character of information dissemination in India. Not one of the three largest English-language newspapers—the *Times of India* with 7.4 million readers, followed by *The Hindu* with 4.05 million and the *Hindustan Times* with 3.85 million—figures among the ten dailies with the greatest reach (see Table). English-language elites have historically had a critical role in shaping questions of policy, with the media functioning as an instrument for constructing and broadcasting this consensus. Yet the changing character of newspaper readership suggests that a wider public debate now feeds, informs, and places pressure upon decision making.

Policy makers in India have long understood the new realities that the NRS data documents. As Jeffrey writes:

> By the time the Narasimha Rao government came to power in 1991, there was a growing awareness, even in Delhi, of a fact that state politicians, especially in the south, had known for a long time: the Indian-language press had readers and influence. With his remarkable command over languages, Narasimha Rao seems to have been among the first to pay serious, regular attention to Hindi owners and editors. In 1993, the Delhi editor of *Punjab Kesari* expressed delight that the Prime Minister had begun to consult him. "He [the PM] was trying to convince *me*!" the editor said. "The politicians never used to do this sort of thing with Hindi editors." Today, it would be a foolish politician who did not keep the owners and editors of Hindi newspapers flattered and informed.[18]

What is driving the dramatic growth in newspaper readership? One obvious and plausible explanation is the expansion in literacy. As measured by the NRS, literacy in India expanded from 69.9 percent of adults in 2005 to 71.1 percent in 2006. As long as literacy continues to grow, newspaper reach is also likely to expand. Moreover, an enormous market of some 359 million literate Indians, 68 percent of them with Hindi-language skills, still do not access a newspaper. As Jeffrey perceptively observes:

> A newspaper is a cheap status symbol. For the price of a cup of tea, you can impress the neighbours. "What do you do if you are unemployed?" a Malayali friend used to say about Kerala in the 1970s. "You buy a diary and go to Trivandrum." The diary suggested you were an important person, and you bustled round the state capital, looking as if you were on the way to engagements. It used to be said of the grey, conservative *Daily Telegraph* in Britain that you didn't read it, but you bought it, because it made the neighbours think you were "deeper" than if you bought the lower-brow *Express* or *Daily Mail*.[19]

Broadcast media has expanded its reach in India even faster than print. In 2006, the satellite-television audience grew to 230 million, up from 207 million in 2005. Satellite broadcasters and the larger state-controlled terrestrial network now reach 112 million Indian homes. Of these homes, 68 million had access to cable and satellite television, up from 61 million in 2005. Interestingly, the southern states of Tamil Nadu, Karnataka, and Andhra Pradesh, where major political parties have holdings in the broadcast media, have the highest levels of both terrestrial cable and satellite reach. Significant numbers of households have shown the willingness to commit the not-insubstantial investments needed to fully capitalize on television. Sixty-four million homes had color sets in 2006, up from 58 million in the previous year.

Radio too has shown what NRS 2006 describes as "considerable resurgence."[20] Its reach is estimated to be similar to that of print, with between 23 percent and 27 percent of Indians tuning in to a station during an average week. One hundred and nineteen million individuals listened to radio broadcasts in 2006, up from 76 million in 2005. FM radio appears to have driven this explosion, and further growth seems probable. In early 2006, India expanded access to privately owned FM-radio stations by auctioning 338 frequencies in 91 towns across the country. By mid-2007, when the new stations will come on air, FM radio will have an additional potential audience of some 350 million people. Several major print-media organizations, including the *Times of India, India Today, Dainik Jagaran, Dainik Bhaskar, Malayalam Manorama,* and *Daily Thanti,* won broadcasting licenses in the auction, which fetched the Indian government 11 billion rupees.[21]

Outside of formal FM radio, there is some evidence that illegal community-radio initiatives are also proliferating. Mansoorpur village in Bihar's Vaishali district, for example, has a service run by a local radio-repair technician from his shack, offering a mix of pop music, news, and public-service content.[22] Given the low costs of the technology and its evident financial viability—the Mansoorpur station is claimed to have cost just one dollar to build and four dollars a month to operate, with revenues of forty-five dollars—such local initiatives could proliferate.

Print and broadcast media do not appear to face any significant threat from Internet-based platforms. For a country that has acquired an international reputation as a provider of Internet services, the growth of these new media within India has been relatively slow. Just over 9 million Indians logged on to the Internet at least once a week in 2006, up from 7.2 million in 2005. This figure represents just 1.2 percent of India's population over the age of twelve. The NRS findings on Internet access suggest that its growth has been far slower than expected, particularly in rural areas. The use of mobile phones to access information such as news or sports scores was somewhat more robust. Some 22 million individuals used such services in 2006, a number more than twice as high as in 2005. As Indian 3G mobile-services networks become available in 2007, growing numbers of young people may use these services, yet phones seem unlikely to pose a meaningful threat to either print or broadcast media in the foreseeable future.

Challenges for the Future

From its tentative origins in the late eighteenth century, the Indian media has flowered into a formidable institution, occupying a central role in shaping the destiny of the world's largest democracy. Mirroring the course of India as a whole, the media has overcome the multiple institutional, political, and economic challenges that faced it at the time of independence. But despite its enormous growth—or perhaps because of the factors that underpin that growth—India's media confronts challenges potentially more damaging than it engaged with at any point before or after independence.

Much Western commentary on the challenges before the Indian media has focused on its periodic skirmishes with state authority. *Tehelka*'s successful sting operation against defense corruption, for example, provoked a vicious government backlash that forced the publication out of business for some time.[23] After the publication of official documents that exposed incompetent conduct during the 1999 Kargil war, efforts were made to prosecute journalists (including the author) under the colonial-era Official Secrets Act.[24] India has also experienced an energetic debate over the government's occasional efforts at Internet censorship, which target overseas websites that are seen as seditious or inflammatory.[25] Although there have been some significant failures—notably occasional bucklings-under to terrorist threats in Punjab, the Northeast, and Jammu and Kashmir—India's media has for the most part demonstrated both the willingness and resources needed to resist coercion.[26] Unlike their counterparts during emergency rule, newspaper managements and journalists have mounted ferocious and successful challenges to government efforts to restrict free speech.

Two main challenges hang over the Indian media's future. These concern the media's commitments and values in the face of massive economic change that is transforming the ways in which news is produced and consumed.

The first challenge concerns whether or not the vernacular foundations of the new mass media will facilitate the demise of the secular-democratic values around which the Indian media's self-image has been built. These concerns were brought out in stark relief by the conduct of the Gujarati-language press during the anti-Muslim pogrom of 2002.[27] Dionne Bunsha has carefully documented the role of the Gujarati-language press in inciting violence in those areas where assaults on Muslims had not yet taken place. She records, for example, the front-page headline of the 28 February 2002 issue of the mass-circulated daily newspaper *Sandesh*, which called on its readers to "Avenge Blood With Blood."[28] Local television channels also often broadcast hate speech calling for attacks on Muslims. Bunsha points out that falsified accounts of Muslim attacks against Hindus were a leitmotif of this reportage.

As the scholar Paul Brass notes, "several of the vernacular media agencies in Gujarat became, in effect, part of the institutionalized riot system" of the Hindu right wing. In fact, Brass continues, vernacular

media have long played an important role in fueling communal violence in India.[29]

In this context, Arvind Rajagopal's work on the role of the media in
driving the Hindu-nationalist movement, a movement that provoked
the still-unfolding crisis in Indian secularism, requires careful consideration.[30] Rajagopal points to the linkages between the rise of the Hindu
right wing and the decision of the state-run broadcaster Doordarshan to
air a religion-based television serial, which registered record viewership.
Breaking ranks with a long tradition of prodevelopment soap operas
like *Hum Log,* Doordarshan's *Ramayan* serial placed Hindu myth at the
center of notions of the "nation." Its success spurred a larger debate in
the Hindi-language press on the role of religion in public life, which in
turn fed and informed the right-wing Bharatiya Janata Party's campaign
to build a Hindu temple at the site of a sixteenth-century mosque.

Rajagopal casts the debate that followed as one conducted in two
separate language-worlds, neither able to communicate with the other.
He finds that the filters through which English- and Hindi-language
journalists saw the temple movement were distinct. Whereas the English-language media represented the movement as a threat both to law
and order and to the secular state, the Hindi-language press was more
receptive to the movement's cultural nuance and idiom.

Through its representation of the movement, the English-language
press in a sense created the movement as it would become: closed, im-
placable, impervious to reason, and a challenge to the existing bounds
of legality—an embrace of religious fanaticism rather than the principles of constitutional democracy. Yet the Ram-temple movement was
plainly not a monolithic entity; it was composed of people with a range
of positions, from those critical of British-colonial inheritance or desir-
ous of more indigenous cultural influence, to the pious and devout, to
those who conceived of collective revenge against Muslims as a liber-
ating development.[31]

Parvathi Menon thus offers a powerful challenge to Rajagopal's vision of the Indian press as divided between "authentic-vernacular-com-
munal" and "colonial-English-secular" categories. Menon argues that
the ideologies, class interests, and political objectives of both individual journalists and media organizations were more important than
language and culture in shaping the terms of debate. She argues:

> To observers of and participants in the media coverage of the Ayodhya
> movement, the qualitative divide in the print media was quite simply one
> between reportage that was communal in its intent and choice of news, and
> that which was not. While it is possible that a larger section from within the
> Hindi print media turned into a Hindu media, and quite blatantly fabricated
> facts and data (of which Rajagopal offers several examples), sections of
> the so-called national English press were equally prone to reportage that
> was provocative, that relied on rumour, and that was sympathetic to the
> goals and the vision of the leaders of the Ayodhya movement.[32]

As Menon suggests, there is no *a priori* reason to believe that either a metropolitan location or knowledge of English renders individuals less vulnerable to the seductions of religious fanaticism. Noting that media content is shaped by "the manner in which social identities are fixed and defined as the basis for political interventions," Sukumar Muralidharan points to a "transformation of the content and tone of the Hindi language press over the decade-and-a-half of globalisation." Muralidharan writes:

> In 1991, the four most widely circulated Hindi newspapers earned the well deserved censure of the Press Council of India for their inflammatory—and in most instances, fabricated—coverage of the communal tensions arising from the Babri Masjid dispute. But with the communal carnage in Gujarat in 2002, these same newspapers were restrained, sober, elaborately attentive to the principles of fairness, and heavily critical of the institutions of governance that had failed to ensure security for the religious minorities. The media undoubtedly had reinvented itself over the preceding decade. But that observation would be little short of trite if it did not take into account the changing self-perceptions of the media audience. A constituency that once saw its identity in relatively narrow terms, had begun—as a consequence of political engagement through the decade—to see the essence of politics as engagement with other social groups and communities on terms of parity, within a common civic space.[33]

This insightful critique directs us to a larger problem in the scholarship. There has been little sustained attempt at multilanguage content analysis in Indian-media studies, in part because of the costs that such an enterprise would involve. As such, there is no way to empirically test the contention that Hindi-language media production, or its counterparts in other languages, constitutes a more narrow and inward-looking rendering of the world than its English or "national" counterpart. On the face of it, it would appear plausible that a substantial section of the audience for the new mass media may in large part constitute small and petty-bourgeois consumers who see religion and tradition as means through which the power of metropolitan English-speaking elites may be challenged. Indeed, a large body of scholarship exists that makes precisely this point. So far, however, a full empirical demonstration of the proposition has not been made.

What has been empirically demonstrated is that the class character of the new media's audience is producing a type of journalism that is distancing itself from the experienced concerns of millions of Indians. This is the second of the major challenges confronting India's media today.

On the basis of detailed content analysis of Indian-television production, N. Bhaskara Rao points to the disturbingly thin coverage of what he describes as "substantive issues crucial to a functional democracy."[34] Rao finds that almost two-thirds of news broadcasts between 2003 and 2005 concerned politics, crime, and sports; by contrast, issues

like healthcare, education, development, and the environment were as-
signed only two percent of the available airtime. In addition, news out-
put demonstrated a strong urban bias. He concludes:

> Some years ago, the news media was relatively more concerned about
> society, community and citizens. Today, they are preoccupied with mar-
> kets, consumers, voters and politics. Because of the market-driven media
> today, it is no longer journalists who determine the news priorities. It is the
> advertisers, market researchers and public relations people who determine
> the concerns and content-package of mass media. It is these forces who
> have become the "new gatekeepers" of news media.[35]

For at least the past decade, much debate in the Indian media has
centered around the impact that the slow erosion of the government's
commitment to prevent foreign ownership of the news media might
have on the structures of this "gatekeeping." Critics have contended
that foreign ownership will erode ownership-diversity by wiping out
smaller publications.[36] Yet, as Praful Bidwai notes, a process of
"Murdochization without Murdoch" is already underway, with or without foreign ownership; one example of this is India's largest-circulated
English-language newspaper, the *Times of India*. Amrita Shah describes
how a former cigarette-company executive was made the newspaper's
managing editor, eventually leading to the elimination of the core-
content position itself.[37] The *Times of India*'s circulation soared, pushing others to follow its emphasis of marketing over journalism. Bidwai
records:

> Three of the largest newspaper chains in India have put into practice, edito-
> rial policies and methods which characterize Murdoch's operation. . . . This
> silent "Murdochization" has transformed notions of what is acceptable as
> news and the range of views that are permitted expression. Serious analyti-
> cal writing is at a discount.[38]

Sainath, who is one of India's foremost journalists, also eloquently
describes the situation:

> The 1990s have witnessed the decline of the press as a public forum. This
> can be attributed largely to the relentless corporate takeover of the Indian
> press and the concentration of ownership in a few hands. Around seven
> major companies account for the bulk of circulation in the powerful En-
> glish language press. In the giant city of Bombay, with over 14 million
> people, *The Times of India* has a stranglehold on the English readership. It
> also dominates the Hindi and Marathi language press. *The Times* is clear
> and unequivocal in its priorities. Beauty contests make the front page.
> Farmers' suicides don't. Sometimes reality forces changes, but this is the
> exception, not the rule. Most other large Indian newspapers are eagerly
> following *The Times'* philosophy, inspired by the press baron Rupert
> Murdoch: a newspaper is a business like any other, not a public forum.

Monopoly ownership has imposed a set of values entirely at odds with the traditional role of the Indian press.[39]

India's new media, Muralidharan argues, "derives its profits not from delivering information of value to an audience, but from delivering an audience of value to the corporate advertiser."[40] Indian newspaper prices are among the lowest in the world; readers can purchase a month's subscription in some cities for as little as 30 rupees. In several cities, the cost of newspapers is in effect free, since readers can offset the subscription price by selling old copies for paper recycling. Given the enormous strains that such competitive pricing has imposed on publishers, news content is increasingly targeted at high-spending consumers. Muralidharan notes that the growth of the electronic media has been almost entirely underwritten by advertising rather than paid subscriptions, and that between 65 and 85 percent of newspaper revenues come from the same source. As a result, Muralidharan writes,

[The] media arena is not a competitive marketplace where information and ideas are allowed a free run so that the best among them rise to the surface. Rather, it is a carefully controlled environment to ensure the most favourable circumstances for advertisers to sell their wares to carefully screened and selected audiences.[41]

Even editors who support the liberalization of the Indian economy have become increasingly concerned over the growing control that advertisers wield over news content. Gautam Adhikari, the editor of the Mumbai-based newspaper *Daily News and Analysis,* notes:

[F]or a variety of reasons corporate advertisers have become a pillar of support in media economics. We do occasionally point to official corruption but rarely these days do we speak of cynical corporate manipulation or outright disregard of rules and propriety. On the contrary, we tend to glorify corporate chieftains as the heroes of our era. Their lives, their styles, are the stuff of modern legends. We have taken the late Deng Xiaoping's advice to heart, "To get rich is glorious."[42]

Muralidharan's concerns may be excessively stated: I have noted earlier that India's media played an important role in pushing poverty onto the stage of public debate, and that it has had enormous successes in fighting for official accountability. Yet the enormity of the challenge that lies ahead is unmistakable. The evolving character of capitalism in India indisputably propelled the media from a marginal actor to the principal agent of public debate. While there is little doubt that the growth of the mass media has rejuvenated institutions, cultures, and economic systems, its growing distance from its historic role as the provider of public information threatens to transform communities of citizens into islands of consumers.[43]

NOTES

1. "Developing a Paper for a New Reader," *The Hindu* (Chennai), 13 September 2003, at *www.hinduonnet.com/th125/stories/2003091300830500.htm.*

2. "CBI Missile Hits Fernandes," *Economic Times* (New Delhi), 12 October 2006, at *http://economictimes.indiatimes.com/articleshow/2143328.cms.*

3. Palagummi Sainath, "Where India Shining Meets Great Depression," *The Hindu,* 1 April 2006, at *www.thehindu.com/2006/04/01/stories/20060401007 31000.htm.*

4. Mubashar Jawed (M.J.) Akbar, "Open to all Interests, Subject to None," *The Hindu,* 29 January 2005, at *www.hinduonnet.com/2005/01/29/stories2005012903 091300.htm.*

5. Christopher A. Bayly, *Empire and Information: Intelligence Gathering and Social Communication in India, 1780–1870* (Cambridge: Cambridge University Press, 1996).

6. Bayly, *Empire and Information,* 70.

7. Mike Dash, *Thug: The True Story of India's Murderous Cult* (London: Granta Books, 2005), 126.

8. Bayly, *Empire and Information,* 243.

9. Varinder Walia and Neeraj Bagga, "Jallianwalla Bagh Revisited," *Tribune* (Chandigarh), 13 April 2006.

10. For a discussion of these linkages, see Stanley Kochanek, "Briefcase Politics in India: The Congress Party and the Business Elite," *Asian Survey* 27 (Berkeley: University of California Press, 1987), 1278–1301. Also see Leah Renold, "Gandhi: The Patron Saint of the Industrialist," unpubl. ms., 1999, at *http://inic.utexas.edu/ asnic/sagar/spring.1994/1.1.TEST_fn.html#fn38.*

11. Soli J. Sorabjee, *The Emergency Censorship and the Press in India, 1975– 77* (New Delhi: Central News Agency, 1977), 13.

12. Sorabjee, *The Emergency Censorship and the Press,* 27–31.

13. Kuldip Nayar, "The Foreign Hand," *Dawn* (Karachi), 29 June 2002, at *www.dawn.com/2002/06/29/op.htm.*

14. Robin Jeffrey, *India's Newspaper Revolution: Capitalism, Politics and the Indian Language Press, 1977–99* (New Delhi: Oxford University Press, 2000).

15. Registrar for Newspapers in India, *Press In India 2004–2005* (New Delhi: Ministry of Information and Broadcasting, 2006), 202–204.

16. National Readership Studies Council, "NRS 2006—Key Findings," India Audit Bureau of Circulations, 29 August 2006, at *www.auditbureau.org/ nrspress06.pdf.* The NRS is the largest survey of its kind in the world, with a sample size of 284,373 house-to-house interviews to measure the media exposure and consumer product penetration in both urban and rural India, as well as the esti-mated readership (not paid circulation) of publications.

17. For a summary of global newspaper-industry trends, see World Association of Newspapers, "World Press Trends: Newspaper Circulation, Advertising Increases,"

5 June 2006, at *www.wan-press.org/article11185.html?var_recherche= percent22world+Newspaper+congress percent22.*

18. Robin Jeffrey, "Breaking News," *Little Magazine* (New Delhi), 2003, at *www.littlemag.com/viamedia/robinjeffrey.html.*

19. Jeffrey, "Breaking News."

20. National Readership Studies Council, "NRS 2006—Key Findings."

21. "FM Radio Set to Explode as Bidding Ends," *Times of India* (New Delhi), 6 February 2006.

22. Amarnath Tewary, "The Amazing DIY Village FM Radio Station," BBC News, 24 February 2006, at *http://news.bbc.co.uk/2/hi/south_asia/4735642.stm.*

23. Navdip Dharial, "Scandal Website Reinvents Itself," BBC News, 10 October 2003, at *http://news.bbc.co.uk/2/hi/south_asia/3174460.stm.* Also see Tarun Tejpal, "For Whom the Bells Toll," *Seminar* (New Delhi), November 2001, at *www.india-seminar.com/2001/502/502 percent20tarun percent20tejpal.htm.*

24. Praveen Swami, "The Kargil Story," *Frontline* (Chennai), 10 November 2000, at *www.hinduonnet.com/fline/fl1722/17220240.htm.*

25. Reporters Without Borders, "India," at *www.rsf.org/article.php3?id_article =10750.*

26. For an analysis of these failures, see Kanchan Lakshman, "Analysing Reportage From Theatres of Conflict," *Faultlines: Writings on Conflict and Resolution* 8 (April 2001): 43. See also Press Council of India, *Crisis and Credibility* (New Delhi: Lancer International, 1991).

27. For a full account of the violence, see Dionne Bunsha, *Scarred: Experiments in Violence in Gujarat* (New Delhi: Penguin, 2005).

28. Dionne Bunsha, "Peddling Hate," *Frontline,* 2 August 2002.

29. Paul Brass, "The Gujarat Pogrom of 2002," at *http://conconflicts.ssrc.org/ gujarat/brass/.*

30. Arvind Rajagopal, *Politics After Television: Hindu Nationalism and the Reshaping of the Public in India* (New Delhi: Cambridge University Press, 2001).

31. Rajagopal, *Politics after Television,* 128.

32. Parvathi Menon, "A Message and the Medium," *Frontline,* 11 May 2001, at *www.hinduonnet.com/fline/fl1809/18090790.htm.*

33. Sukumar Muralidharan, "The Challenge to Media," *Seminar,* July 2005, at *www.india-seminar.com/2005/551/551percent20sukumarpercent20muralid haran.htm#top.*

34. N. Bhaskara Rao, "A Critical Review of Indian Television News Scene," in *Media Monitor South Asia 2005* (Lahore: South Asian Free Media Association, 2005), 41–42.

35. Rao, "A Critical Review of Indian Television News Scene," 43.

36. For a full account of the issue, see B. Sarkar, "Passing the Buck: The Issue of Foreign-Owned Newspapers," *Frontline,* 21 October 1994.

37. Amrita Shah, *Hype, Hypocrisy and Television in Urban India* (New Delhi: Vikas Books, 1997).

38. Praful Bidwai, "Whose Truth? Indian Media in the Global Village," *Humanscape* magazine, December 1996.

39. Sainath, "None So Blind as Those Who Will Not See," *UNESCO Courier,* June 2001.

40. Muralidharan, "The Challenge to Media."

41. Muralidharan, "The Challenge to Media."

42. Gautam Adhikari, "Corruption is Difficult to Prove in a Public Forum," *Daily News and Analysis* (Mumbai), 24 December 2006, at *www.dnaindia.com/ sunreport.asp?Newsid=1070904.*

43. As Prasun Sonwalkar notes, "how the Indian press and the elites balance commercial considerations with social obligations will influence not only the future of a vibrant and complex press, but also the contours of the world's largest democracy." "Murdochisation of the Indian Press: From By-line to Bottom-line," *Media, Culture and Society* 24 (November 2002): 830.

IV

The Economy

11

ECONOMIC GROWTH AND POLITICAL ACCOMMODATION

Aseema Sinha

Aseema Sinha is associate professor of political science at the University of Wisconsin–Madison. She is the author of The Regional Roots of Developmental Politics in India: A Divided Leviathan *(2005). This essay originally appeared in the April 2007 issue of the* Journal of Democracy.

What do the processes of market-based economic reform and globalization mean for democracy in India? Do they narrow or broaden the democratic prospect? Do they make democracy more or less secure? So far, fortunately, the answers to these questions appear to be positive. While Indian democracy possesses strong stabilizing features of its own, economic change and liberalization have served to reinforce and further stabilize democracy rather than undermine it, as some have feared would be the case.

Among those who warn of the baleful consequences that economic change might hold for democratic rule are Daron Acemoglu and James A. Robinson. They argue that democracy can find itself being undermined by elites who fear redistribution following mass political mobilization, by populist movements brimming with resentment toward institutions that seem to favor the rich, or in the worst case by both elite and mass hostility.[1] At first glance, India would seem to have the makings of such a trap for democracy: Absolute poverty remains alarmingly common in this vast society, and is now combined with the inequality-intensifying effects of economic reform plus the rising political power of "subaltern" classes that are now making their weight felt more forcefully than would have seemed imaginable scarcely a generation ago. Yet in India, the nature of the growth and the responses to it framed by the political elites appear happily to have made *both* elite and mass attacks on democracy less rather than more likely.

What accounts for this encouraging result? Karl Polanyi's observation (based on his reading of European history) that rapid and uneven economic change spurs political mobilization to soften its sharpest edges—

in the process shoring up rather than sapping democracy—may be one reason.[2] Then too, in contemporary India's case those who might most fear this mobilization from below—the rich—enjoy links to the global economy and the private sector that provide significant "exit" options. Thus the threat of a backlash by the rich (as glimpsed, for instance, in the protests against lower-caste–friendly "reservations" that broke out in the early 1990s and then again in 2006) grows less severe when wealthy Indians feel free to seek greener pastures abroad or in parts of the private economy that are but lightly touched by the state. The availability of such a safety valve in turn allows the state to respond to electoral and collective pressure from the mobilizing losers and the less well-off, thereby giving Indian democracy a salutary aura of responsiveness.

Along with the rich who know they can leave and the poor who know they can league, a third stabilizing force is the middle class that knows it is linked. India's bourgeoisie has ties to the West and the global economy that have only become stronger with economic reform and pro-Western policy shifts, leading to middle-class confidence, pro-democratic sentiment, and readiness to act as a buffer between the elites and the poor. These three mechanisms—leaving (or potential exit) by the elites, leaguing (or collective action) by the losers, and linking (to global patterns of prosperity) by the middle class—have subtly altered the balance of power among the dominant proprietary classes that Pranab Bardhan identifies in his classic analysis of India's political economy.[3]

Heterogeneity among the dominant classes still underpins India's democracy just as Bardhan noted, but portions of those leading classes no longer rely on the central state for subsidies and patronage. Instead, they look to the private and globalized economy and to their local state governments rather than to New Delhi. Moreover, the apparently weak coalition governments that India has had since the 1990s have proved to be a source of strength for democracy since these governments, given their very precariousness, respond readily to demands and pressures from the less well-off, thereby helping to forestall serious challenges "from below" to the democratic system.

The Realities of Economic Transformation

Any discussion of the changing nature of India's democracy must attend to the broader process of economic change that has been under-way for decades now and which provides a background to the current phase of economic liberalization that began in 1991. From about the mid-1970s to the mid-1980s, technological developments, changes in the productive activities and relative power of various classes, and rela-tions between public authorities and private capital all brought major shifts to the subcontinent. The technical and organizational advances in agriculture known as the Green Revolution allowed India to feed itself and even to export food. Many of the country's states became more aggressive participants in the growth process in the 1970s and 1980s, unleashing further changes with both local and nationwide effects.[4]

Two great themes in Indian social and economic life since the 1980s have been rapid economic growth and rising inequality. With the advent of fuller liberalization in the early 1990s, growth began to accelerate to a pitch seldom seen under similar circumstances anywhere else in the developing world. New groups of "winners" and "losers" came into being. Theoretically, widening gaps between the rich and the poor may impose tensions and stresses on a democratic system in two distinct ways: The rich may seek to make their economic advantages permanent by subverting democracy in order to seize political power for themselves, and the poor may seek the system's overthrow through violence. One may expect various elites to sabotage democratic institutions in order to stop market forces from taking away their rents, or to hijack political institutions in order to squeeze fresh rents from the newly liberalized economic environment. Although India's new rich have sought benefits from the state, they have not sought to capture it. And the poor have worked through rather than against democratic institutions to seek redress. This has happened not purely out of idealism, but in no small part because the rich now enjoy many options outside the state while the poor are too diffuse and divided to mount a full-scale antisystem challenge. Fortunately for them and for democratic stability, however, the weak coalition governments of recent years have responded readily to diffuse pressures.

In the 1980s, India's economy grew faster than ever—at times by rates approaching 6 percent a year—and in new patterns. Behind this accelerating growth lay an expansion and diversification of investment and economic activities. The most striking structural changes came in agriculture. Food production rose even as the share of annual Gross Domestic Product for which agriculture accounted dropped from 42 percent in 1980 to 24 percent in 2004. Over the same period, net agricultural production doubled, going from 96 million metric tons in 1980 to 180 million metric tons in 2000.

Figures such as these bespeak the success of the Green Revolution. The key was a more intensive application of capital and technology to farming. Yet this application did not proceed evenly throughout the country. Some parts of the country began growing enough not only to feed themselves but even to sell, thereby funding investments beyond farming. In some states—Punjab, parts of Uttar Pradesh, and Tamil Nadu—technical improvements in agriculture affected other sectors of the economy as prospering farms required more inputs, more processing infrastructure, and more construction. Rising incomes stimulated demand for goods and services, fueling industrialization in Gujarat, Tamil Nadu, Andhra Pradesh, Punjab, Haryana, and parts of West Bengal. Farmers invested in real estate, small-scale industry, and transport. "Class I" cities (with populations above 100,000) increased from 218 in 1981 to 393 in 2001. The number of medium-sized towns grew, with Tamil Nadu and Haryana experiencing the fastest rates of urbanization, according to the 2001 census. Nationwide, the number of "Class II" cities (those with populations of between 50,000 and 99,999) went from 270 in 1981 to 401 twenty years later. Likewise, the number of "Class III" cities (with populations between 20,000 and 49,999) went from 743 to 1,143 over the same period. Growth among these smaller cities broadened the base of economic transformation in India by creating more scope for the burgeoning agricultural sector to promote industry. The rising presence of Western culture and consumer patterns even in medium-sized towns and cities emphasized the expanding linkages with the West.[5]

Behind the numbers stand the human realities of economic transformation. Three developments in particular hold implications for India's democracy. The Green Revolution has created a new group of peasants with the means to turn toward city life and industry, and to invest in their children's education. As Staffan Lindberg notes, most agricultural households in Punjab "are becoming 'pluri-active,' standing between farming and other activities whether as seasonal laborers or small-scale entrepreneurs in the local economy. . . . Agriculture and farming [are] no more an all-encompassing way of life and identity."[6] The rise of a middle class with its roots in agricultural development has been evident not only in Punjab but in Tamil Nadu, Gujarat, and western Uttar Pradesh.[7] Maharashtra, Andhra Pradesh, and Karnataka have also seen similar expansions of an agrarian-rooted middle class. A few of the former states— Gujarat, Maharashtra, and Tamil Nadu—have also witnessed rapid industrial development.

Most importantly for democracy, urbanization around the big cities has transformed many small towns into cities and created new urban centers. Whole classes of once-agrarian people have undergone embourgeoisement. S.S. Gill describes the process:

> With the penetration of capitalist relations in agriculture, modern education has spread. Most of the Punjab villages have schools and some even have colleges functioning in them. Some of the capitalist farmers . . . are actually sending [their children] to urban centers to acquire better education. With this a large number of educated persons from rural areas have been coming forward to take up jobs in government and semi-government institutions. This has produced a distinct category of middle class intellectuals of rural origin.[8]

As is well recognized, urbanization and the urban middle class are powerful forces for democratization both in classical democratic transitions and in third-wave democracies. Moreover, the formation of business and commercial classes in many states—a regional bourgeoisie apart from national capitalist classes—has enhanced urbanization as well as linkages with regional political and party developments.[9] Sanjaya Baru notes:

> The process of agrarian change in many parts of the country has laid the foundations for capitalist development in the non-farm sector. This process has allowed a new generation of agrarian capitalists or other middle class professionals to make the transition to capitalist entrepreneurs . . . the latter seek political and material support from state governments and regional political parties. It is not surprising that regional parties . . . have been most active in States where regional business groups have been more dynamic and assertive.[10]

Various prominent regional parties now enjoy links to business groups in Maharashtra, Punjab, Andhra Pradesh, West Bengal, and Tamil Nadu. These ties have helped to consolidate two-party competition in many Indian states and have facilitated alternations in power, elite competition, and a more stable "pacted" democracy. Andhra Pradesh reflects this most strongly, with the Telegu Desam Party representing agrarian-rooted capitalist interests, and the Indian National Congress (Congress party) standing for more traditional economic interests. The logic of globalization means that each party must be consistently sensitive to the needs of local and foreign businesses, leading to a greater convergence on matters of economic policy across parties even at the subnational level.

After the market-friendly reforms of 1991, India's urban-industrial economy took off sharply, and overall annual GDP growth has been impressive ever since. From 2003 to 2006, it is thought to have averaged about 8 percent. Growth in the industrial sector has been less spectacular but stable at around 6 percent a year. Liberalization has also meant fresh patterns of growth and structural changes in the economy. Strikingly, the service sector has been at the cutting edge and has fueled much of the boom. This sector grew by 34.4 percent (in current dollars) over the last two decades, and now accounts for more than 50 percent of India's annual GDP.[11] By 2010, according to one projection, that figure may be almost 60 percent. This would "bring the size of India's services sector, relative to GDP, closer to that of an upper middle income country, while still belonging to the low income group."[12] Wages in the service economy have been surging at a compound annual growth rate of 23 percent yearly since 2000. Large parts of this service sector are linked to the global economy and underwrite the expansion of India's middle classes.

Winners and Losers

Many Indians have done well by the process of economic transformation that state-led industrialization first unleashed back in the 1950s and that economic liberalization has greatly accelerated since 1991. These winners could have sought to subvert state institutions for their own ends, but growing ties to the West and the global economy seem largely to have pointed them in other and healthier directions. India's professional and business classes have only become stronger with marketization and the country's recent "paradigm shift" toward a foreign policy that features closer links with the West generally and the United States in particular.[13] India's elites now have more educational and cultural links than ever to the West, while foreign trade accounted for more than a third of the country's GDP in 2004–2005. Moreover, the newest economic winners—the educated Indians who dominate the burgeoning information-technology (IT), service, and knowledge-based sectors—support democracy more strongly than do traditional business elites.

In the 1990s, politicians of many stripes began to send their children to the United States for higher education, setting the stage for a generational shift toward a closer embrace of Western and prodemocratic ideas. Large swaths of young people in India's cities express a desire to live and work in the United States. Travel to the United States and consumption of U.S. books, music, and films are now staples of Indian middle-class life. This consumption of U.S. popular culture implicitly promotes support for Western-style democratic institutions.

Most importantly, the greater "connectivity" that educated, middle-class Indians now enjoy makes them less inclined to try capturing the state for their own ends. Rising incomes allow them to rely on the private economy—generators, for example, in power-starved Delhi—rather than the state for crucial public goods. The late 1990s and early 2000s also witnessed Indian companies exploring opportunities in regulated markets such as those of the United States and Western Europe, further intensifying the network of human and economic connectivity with the outside world. Large Indian firms such as the massive Tata Group conglomerate and Reliance Communications began acquiring and interacting with U.S. companies. This trend gave rise to a pressure group in favor of good U.S.-India relations not only among the business community but also among the middle-class professionals who had found jobs carrying out many of the new global-market strategies. In 1999, for instance, the Confederation of Indian Industry—the country's leading business association—lobbied New Delhi to settle the Kargil conflict with Pakistan, as this small-scale shooting war along a remote but hotly disputed stretch of border between the two South Asian nuclear powers was threatening to harm India's relationship with Washington.

India's middle class is unlikely to support any radical critique of or challenge to the institutions of constitutional democracy. The pattern of India's growth since the early 1990s has created a solid middle class with a stake not only in the public sector but in the globally connected skilled and service sectors of the private economy as well. India's middle classes are educated, belong to the upper castes, and tend to favor the status quo. As such, they are hardly good candidates to form revolutionary alliances. With every year, their habits of travel, reading, schooling, work, and consumption give them closer ties to the West and its liberal-democratic institutions. Further, the natural divisions among them,[14] as well as between them and other class groupings such as manual workers, make any broad push to reshape state institutions quite unlikely.

Economic change has benefited many yet brought losses and new insecurities to some. Since the onset of liberalization, wage inequalities between occupational groups appear to have widened. In the 1990s, real agricultural wages grew by only 2.5 percent; since 2000, the salaries of middle managers in IT industries have risen by a compound annual growth rate of 23 percent.[15] Unemployment has risen as well, going from 6.7 percent among urban males in 1994 to 8.1 percent in 2004, and from 5.6 to 8 percent among rural males during the same period.[16] Within manufacturing, the number of workers employed in the formal sector has dropped despite high rates of overall growth, while employment in the informal sector has increased. From 1994 to 2000, formal-sector employment as a whole was stagnant, rising barely more than a half a percentage point per year throughout the latter half of the 1990s. Most of what job growth there was came in a handful of industries such as hotels, restaurants, finance, and insurance. Jobs in the informal sector, meanwhile, have continued to proliferate at higher rates—a trend that will probably only intensify in coming years. Although the informal economy creates jobs, the wages are typically low.

In the organized manufacturing sector, liberalization has been associated with an expanding wage gap that favors skilled over less-skilled workers.[17] This gap, which directly contributes to the growth of income inequality, also maps onto the widening gap that divides the service sector from the manufacturing and agricultural sectors of the economy. India's growing national economy is the fruit of a burgeoning service sector, technological improvements, and the skills of the populace. The large numbers of citizens who are unorganized, unskilled, and without knowledge of English are in danger of being left behind.

Magnifying these rising disparities are intensifying inequalities between regions. In India, where you live has much to do with the level of well-being that you enjoy. Economic growth has been concentrated in just a handful of the 28 states and 7 union territories. The most economically dynamic states are Gujarat, Maharashtra, Rajasthan, West Bengal, Tamil Nadu, and Karnataka, which together contain 38.8 percent of India's 1.1 billion people. In each of these states, annual growth is much higher than the national average.[18]

Disturbingly, multiple sources of inequality are reinforcing one another. Thus a slow regional or state-level economy compounds the misery of people who may already be suffering deprivations related to their gender and caste. A male head of household in the resource-rich but slow-growing state of Bihar on the Nepalese border, for example, not only earns less than his counterparts from all other states, but his wife is also likely to be the most deprived among women, and their children the most malnourished. As of 1991, fully 94 percent of the male residents of Kerala on the southwest coast could read and write. At the same time, the literacy rate among women from the traditionally lower (or "scheduled") castes in Bihar and the northwestern state of Rajasthan was below 10 percent (even reaching as low as 2 percent in some districts). Even if we remove an exceptionally developed state such as Kerala from the comparison, the disparities in well-being across states are vast. Although economic growth and prosperity offer no guarantee of positive spillover effects in other dimensions—signs of the abysmal treatment of women remain alarmingly common in the affluent neighboring states of Punjab and Haryana[19]—the data for low-income parts of the country show acute inequalities haunting almost every dimension of human well-being.

Rising Insecurities

One might expect that individuals, classes, and regions that perceive themselves as dogged by socioeconomic disparities and as net losers from life in the new and more freewheeling economic order would challenge the polity under which their interests have suffered. Yet that has not been the case, and one must ask why.

Part of the answer may lie in the sheer complexity and variation of economic and social life in a country the size of India. Academics and statisticians may report general trends such as the one toward growing urban-versus-rural income disparities or the rise in the Gini coefficient (a number showing the inequality of income distribution) across India since 1993. But the reality on the ground is that those on the wrong side of these trends do not form a single coherent, politically mobilized, and self-conscious class.

A major consequence of liberalization, informalization, the shift toward a technologically sophisticated service economy, and the concentration of growth in certain regions has been greater short-term to medium-term instability and insecurity in the lives of people whose resources for coping with such challenges are already thin. Thus preoccupied—and often toiling at precarious, low-paying, informal-sector jobs, perhaps while living in backwater regions or moving frequently in search of work—people who might under different circumstances see political organization as a solution to their problems are now too isolated to take collective action against the state.

Absent retraining and other forms of adjustment help that might qualify them for more stable and secure employment in the organized sector, such people are unlikely ever to escape the clutches of economic insecurity and the fear that disaster is just one mishap away. Those in the unorganized sector generally have no protection against the risk of illness, accident, or death of a breadwinner; earn little and sometimes even less than the statutory minimum wage; and have no regular, let alone secure, jobs.

Things are better in the formal sector, but insecurity is a rising problem there too. A new degree of labor-market flexibility spurred by globalization is causing more formal-sector jobs to resemble those in the precarious informal sector. A survey of about 1,300 manufacturing firms in ten states and both the public and private sectors undertaken by the Institute for Human Development (sponsored by India's Ministry of Statistics), found that while total employment went up by more than 2 percent between 1991 and 1998, most of the increase came in the form of jobs offered on a temporary, casual, contract, or other flexible basis.[20] As Rob Jenkins notes, "reform by stealth" in the field of labor policy continues, with a recent wrinkle being the introduction by employers of "voluntary retirement schemes" that are in fact far from voluntary.[21]

Because inequalities, impoverishment, and economic insecurities are so often localized, they can all too readily elude the grasp of the national news media and statistics-gathering systems. During the election year of 2004, for instance, there was little coverage of the impoverishment that many rural communities were suffering. The nonreporting of this story may partly explain the widespread expectation that the ruling Hindu-nationalist Bharatiya Janata Party (BJP) would easily retain power. When the BJP and its coalition narrowly lost the voting, even the top leadership and activists of the rival Congress party found their own victory a surprise.

Moreover, while there are ways of measuring poverty, outright joblessness, and other indicators of well-being or its absence, no measures can capture rising insecurities and vulnerabilities at the national or aggregate level. One must sift local histories and particular events— such as the 2003 riots against Biharis looking for railroad work in the extremely poor far-northeastern state of Assam—in order to gain insight into the problems and tensions that a declining sense of security and well-being can fuel.

Many other parts of the country yield an abundance of similar vignettes depicting rising insecurity and its malign effects. There is evidence, for example, that environmental despoliation and the dismal failure of state-sponsored antipoverty programs in the 1990s have left behind terrible misery in parts of Orissa. Even more worrisomely, the rising insecurity that has accompanied the decline of the once-mighty textile industry in Gujarat state and the nearby city of Mumbai in Maharashtra appears to have fed a potential for social unrest that Hindu-nationalist forces such as the BJP and Shiv Sena have learned to exploit.

The story of Ahmedabad, Gujarat's largest city and a town once known as the "Manchester of India" because of its huge textile industry, shows how economic insecurity can create fertile ground for local sociopolitical troubles. In the 1960s and 1970s, four out of every five people who had a job in Ahmedabad worked in the cloth mills. By the end of the latter decade, however, cloth-trade jobs had begun to dwindle. Rising employment in smaller-scale chemical and engineering concerns took up some of the slack, but this work was less steady.[22] Some displaced textile workers wound up toiling in the illicit local economy that revolved around the smuggling of alcohol, silver, guns, and drugs.[23] Many joined the Vishwa Hindu Parishad, its youth wing the Bajrang Dal, or other organizations dedicated to the militant promotion of Hindutva ("Hindu-ness") such as the Hanuman Sena.[24] In this fashion, the textile industry's decline and the informalization of former millhands arguably contributed to the bloody rioting that broke out along caste or religious lines in Ahmedabad in 1985–86, in Mumbai in the early 1990s, and then again in Ahmedabad during the first half of 2002.

While the Hindu-versus-Muslim conflicts that have plagued Gujarat and Maharashtra may be said to create especially difficult and dangerous circumstances in those places, one does not have to look too hard at the rest of India in order to find locales and communities that are struggling with rising economic disruption and vulnerability. There is the deep recession that grips the power-loom industry in Tamil Nadu; the crisis that has attacked the nationwide cooking-oil and oil-seeds industry since import tariffs were slashed in 1995 and then again in 1998; the collapsing crop prices and rising farmer bankruptcies and suicides that have beset the coffee and cotton growers of Kerala and Andhra Pradesh;[25] and the displacement of traditional fishing by commercial shrimp farmers in Kerala and Orissa. Widespread suicides by cotton farmers in Maharashtra, Karnataka, and Andhra Pradesh have been among the most tragic responses to the rising insecurities.

A related issue is that of transitional costs as people move from their traditional and more stable livelihoods into less stable, informal occupations. In many poor regions of India, seasonal migrations associated with informalization are masking the full effects of the phenomenon since migrants are by definition "moving targets" whose situation is harder for scholars and official fact-gatherers to study and measure. Yet there is no doubt that migration, while in its own way a socioeconomic "coping mechanism," also imposes social costs and increases social and political insecurities. The years 2003 and 2004 saw a rash of antimigrant riots in various parts of the country. And informalization, even if it does not spur migration, may mean longer working hours, less job security, lower status, and harsher working conditions.

Government Responsiveness

Those on the losing end of India's still-unfolding economic reforms seek not to challenge their country's democratic institutions, but rather to obtain redress by means of these very institutions. It must be said that from the point of view of political stability, the isolated situation of these "losers"—localized as they are within certain regions of a vast country— has been a help. But helping as well have been the preexisting stability of Indian democracy and the responsiveness that various coalition governments have shown since the 1990s. The ability of voters to change governments—not only nationally in 2004 but also in Andhra Pradesh the same year and Bihar a year later—may have restored many losers' faith in the democratic system. Latin American–style disenchantment seems less in evidence among Indians, except in parts of Assam and Bihar. The governments of the day, in New Delhi and certain key state capitals alike, have responded by modifying the design of economic programs in order to address the concerns of farmers, informal workers, and the unemployed.

While the earlier coalition governments of 1996, 1998, and 1999 had been generally responsive to the needs of diverse sections of society, 2004 marked a serious turn toward "reform of the reform." In July 2004, after the electoral victory of a coalition led by his own Congress party, newly appointed prime minister Manmohan Singh launched fresh policies that, by any reckoning, are seriously at variance with the spirit of the so-called Washington Consensus in favor of economic liberalization. This reflected the dominant view within the Congress party that its victory was a vote in favor of a more inclusive reform program. The National Common Minimum Programme identified seven priority sectors for focused attention: agriculture, water, education, health care, employment, urban renewal, and infrastructure.

Singh also announced a "New Deal for Rural India" encompassing the provision of free electric power to farmers in Andhra Pradesh; a minimal guaranteed-employment scheme; an emphasis on improvements in rural infrastructure; debt relief; and more public money for irrigation. "Inclusive growth" and the "common man" became important objects of economic policy after the alternation of power in 2004. While this discursive shift was itself significant, it is also striking that actual budgetary expenditures rose to reflect this reorientation of the reform program. There was a 21.4 percent increase in *actual* agriculture-related expenditures from 2003 to 2004, while health expenditures jumped by an enormous 187 percent and education expenditures by 26.2 percent with the new government in power. Importantly, these increases have been sustained in 2005 and 2006.[26]

These policy commitments and actual expenditures have prevented disenchantment with the reform program and created additional resources for stakeholders in the current government's policies. Many citizens' faith in the responsiveness of democratic institutions now rests in the hands of Prime Minister Singh and other officials who have been carried to victory in recent elections by voters' hopes for redress.

India's long-term success in holding regular elections, plus the increased participation by marginal communities that became so evident in the 1990s, together define the country as a successful case of what Atul Kohli calls "procedural democracy." The process of economic change that has been unfolding over the last several decades, and with even greater speed since the promarket and proglobalization policy turn of the early 1990s, has so far avoided arousing challenges to democracy either from above or from below. While local problems remain serious and could in principle spread to the point where they become significant on the national stage (something like this may have already happened in a limited way in 2004 and could help to explain the BJP's surprising defeat at the polls that year), the net effect of India's growth process so far appears to be one of democratic stabilization. There are, in short, plenty of winners, and the losers have not lost hope and turned to "antisystem" politics. Activists and idealists may bemoan the quality of Indian democracy, but the overwhelming majority of them are committed to using only peaceful, democratic tactics and institutions in order to advance not democracy's overthrow, but its reform. In India, democracy has become "the only game in town," aided and supported by processes of economic change despite the serious inequalities that those processes have brought in their train. If India's original adoption of democracy was a surprise in the eyes of modern social science, India's maintenance and deepening of democratic commitment in the face of sometimes-wrenching economic shifts may belong no less securely to the category of the unexpected.

NOTES

1. Daron Acemoglu and James A. Robinson, *Economic Origins of Dictatorship and Democracy* (Cambridge: Cambridge University Press, 2006), 321–22.

2. Karl Polanyi, *The Great Transformation: The Political and Economic Origins of Our Time* (Boston: Beacon, 1944).

3. Pranab Bardhan, *The Political Economy of Development in India* (Delhi: Oxford University Press, 1998).

4. Aseema Sinha, *The Regional Roots of Developmental Politics in India: A Divided Leviathan* (Bloomington: Indiana University Press, 2005).

5. For example, in the midsized city of Nagpur, Maharashtra, disco clubs, Western-style malls, and consumption of Western music and culture have become common.

6. Staffan Lindberg cited in Surinder Jodhka, "Beyond 'Crises': Rethinking Contemporary Punjab Agriculture," *Economic and Political Weekly,* 22 April 2006, 1535.

7. Ritu Sharma and Thomas Poleman, *The New Economics of India's Green Revolution* (Ithaca, N.Y.: Cornell University Press, 1993).

8. Cited in Jodhka, "Beyond Crises," 1535.

9. Sanjaya Baru, "Indian Enterprise," *Seminar* 449 (January 1997): 61–64; and "Economic Policy and the Development of Capitalism in India: The Role of Regional Capitalists and Political Parties," in Francine Frankel, ed., *Transforming India: Social and Political Dynamics of Democracy* (Oxford: Oxford University Press, 2000).

10. Baru, "Economic Policy and the Development of Capitalism in India: the Role of Regional Capitalists and Political Parties," in Frankel, *Transforming India,* 243.

11. Devesh Kapur, "The Causes and Consequences of India's IT Boom," *India Review* 1 (April 2002): 92.

12. Jim Gordon and Poonam Gupta, "Understanding India's Services Revolution," paper prepared for the IMF-NCAER Conference, 6–12 November 2003, 7.

13. C. Raja Mohan, *Crossing the Rubicon: The Shaping of India's New Foreign Policy* (New Delhi: Viking, 2003).

14. E. Sridharan, "The Growth and Sectoral Composition of India's Middle Class: Its Impact on the Politics of Economic Liberalization," *India Review* 3 (October 2004): 405, 415–20.

15. McKinsey Global Institute, *The Emerging Global Labor Market: The Supply of Offshore Talent in Services,* 2005, cited in Raghuram Rajan and Arvind Subramanian, "India Needs Skill to Solve the 'Bangalore Bug,'" *Financial Times,* 17 March 2006.

16. C.P. Chandrashekhar, "Unemployed in a Thriving Economy," *Frontline,* March 2006.

17. Rashmi Banga, "Liberalization and Wage Inequality in India," Working Paper 156, Indian Council for Research on International Economic Relations, New Delhi, 2005.

18. For example, annual growth (at constant prices) between 2002 and 2004 was 15.4 percent in Gujarat, 7.3 percent in Maharashtra, 22.3 percent in Rajasthan, and 7.4 percent in West Bengal. See *https://reservebank.org.in/cdbmsi/servlet/login.*

19. In some districts of Punjab and Haryana there are only 77 women for every 100 men. This low ratio springs from the growth of ultrasound-facilitated sex-selection abortions, a regionally specific preference for sons, and arguably, increasing dowry costs spurred by demands for consumer items such as cars and television sets.

20. Cited in Nagesh Kumar, "Indian Software Industry Development: International and National Perspective," *Economic and Political Weekly,* 10 November 2001, 4287.

21. Rob Jenkins, "Labor Policy and the Second Generation of Economic Reform in India," *India Review* 3 (October 2004): 340.

22. Shiv Sena also recruited its cadres from displaced textile workers in Mumbai. See Darryl D'Monte, *Ripping the Fabric: The Decline of Mumbai and Its Mills* (Delhi: Oxford University Press, 2002).

23. Sujata Patel, "Urbanization, Development and Communalization of Society in Gujarat," in Takashi Shinoda, ed., *The Other Gujarat* (Mumbai: Popular Prakashan, 2002).

24. Sujata Patel, "Corporatist Patronage in the Ahemdabad Textile Industry," in Ghanshyam Shah, Mario Rutten, and Hein Streefkerk, eds., *Development and Deprivation in Gujarat: In Honor of Jan Breman* (New Delhi: Sage, 2002).

25. P. Sainath, *Everybody Loves a Good Drought: Stories from India's Poorest Districts* (New Delhi: Penguin, 2002).

26. Agricultural expenditures (excluding fertilizer) rose by 31.8 percent from 2004 to 2005 and by 18.5 percent in 2006. A similar rise was evident for health and education. These figures have been calculated from budget documents that can be found at *http://indiabudget.nic.in*.

12

THE STATE OF THE STATES

Sunila S. Kale

Sunila S. Kale *is a research specialist at the Center for the Advanced Study of India at the University of Pennsylvania. She is a doctoral candidate in the government department at the University of Texas, Austin.*

The relationship of democracy to inequality is a complex one. For Jawaharlal Nehru, Indian nationalist leader and the country's first prime minister, the condition of economic inequality within the British Empire was the most urgent reason that India needed to chart an autonomous course; after independence, democracy leavened with socialism was meant to overcome inequality within the Indian national space.[1] Despite this early faith that democracy and economic planning could overcome inequality, multiple kinds of deeply unequal relations—economic, political, and social—persist in India. For many theorists of democracy, this inequality in all its forms endangers both political stability and the development of a meaningful democracy in India.[2]

There are multiple ways of conceptualizing disparities in India. Each of these has implications for how to go about studying and documenting inequality over time, as well as for crafting appropriate policy responses. A large body of literature on inequality in India approaches the subject from a *macro* level of analysis, comparing across either large administrative units, like states or groups of states, or across significant social categories like religion, caste, and gender. Another substantial corpus of work adopts a *micro* perspective, measuring inequality between individuals or households. In this essay, I propose that for the purposes of evaluating and understanding inequality's repercussions for India's political institutions, we also should attend to a third, or *mezzo,* level of analysis: persistent spatial inequality. Unlike other inequities, territorially defined inequality can generate demands for sovereignty, ranging from petitions for autonomy through the creation of new states to violent secessionist politics. Both the peaceful and the violent among these demands are proving increasingly consequential to Indian politics.

The complex relationships between intrastate economic inequality and political institutions seem to be articulated now in the demands for another round of states reorganization.[3] The first states reorganization, carried out partly along the principles laid out by the first States Reorganisation Commission (SRC), which was appointed in 1953, transformed the inherited British administrative structure into a new federal structure based on linguistic difference. Many of the new states created by this reorganization comprised various subregions that differed with respect to their cultural and political histories, land-tenure systems, and patterns of urbanization, industrialization, agricultural development, and social dominance. Disparities among intrastate subregions were only thrown into greater relief when they were brought into direct administrative contact with one another in India's new federal units. In some cases, the political and economic elites from lesser-developed regions feared being overshadowed by the power, organization, and wealth of elites from dominant regions, especially when the latter were also numerically preponderant. In many states, intrastate inequities have persisted since the 1960s, and it is in this context that we have to consider the myriad autonomy movements which articulate their grievances around imbalances in wealth and development.[4]

In one view, demands for autonomy represent the belief that a greater correspondence between the structures of governance and the population of the governed will lead to improved welfare outcomes. From another perspective, demands for autonomy are purely the product of politics: Regional political elites may realize that their greater fortunes lay in a bifurcated state, or politicians from existing political parties may either oppose or support these demands to shore up their own electoral bases and fragment their opposition. Evidence from India suggests that movements for autonomy are guided by both idealism and political pragmatism.

The next part of the essay surveys the academic studies and public policies that have addressed themselves to different kinds of inequality in India. While much has been written about both *macro* and *micro* inequality, less attention has focused on intrastate, or district-level, inequality. The section following looks at the federal-government initiatives that have over the years examined persistent spatial inequalities at the subnational level. The last third of the paper considers the connection between intrastate inequality and autonomy movements by surveying two of India's most vocal autonomy movements, which are in Maharashtra and Andhra Pradesh. In both states, disparities in development are important to these political conflicts, structuring how movement leaders frame the issues both to their supporters and to the central government.[5]

Inequality's Multiple Dimensions

Planners and politicians from independence onward recognized differences in patterns of development *between* states and formulated numerous policies to counteract these. Among the most important of these attempts, centralized investment allocation was meant to ensure that investments were dispersed throughout India, countering economies of agglomeration, or the tendency for firms to cluster. In addition, the Gadgil formula required that poorer-states' development plans be funded at a higher rate by the central government's Planning Commission than those of wealthier ones.[6] To create a more level playing field for industrialization, the policy of freight equalization adjusted the transportation costs for inputs like steel and coal to ensure that states without great natural-resource wealth could still be competitive.[7]

But as dirigisme has given way to the market over the last twenty years, scholars have debated whether the chasm separating wealthy states such as Gujarat, Maharashtra, and Punjab, from the "bimaru" (sick) states of Bihar, Madhya Pradesh, Rajasthan, and Uttar Pradesh, has widened or shrunk. Most studies demonstrate that interstate inequality is growing in India, as it is in Asia's other fast developing, populous country—China. [8] Typologies of Indian states into categories of high, middle, and low incomes suggest that while states' rankings have changed little over time, because low-income states are also those with the greatest population growth, poverty is becoming more geographically concentrated.

Interstate inequalities are also closely related to rural-urban inequalities because the states with the most rapidly growing economies are urban and industrialized, while those with sluggish growth remain primarily rural.[9] Over the last few years, the World Bank and other institutions have recognized the importance of regional inequalities for the long-term prospects of economic reforms and political stability, and have widened their lending priorities to include poor states like Orissa and Bihar rather than focusing exclusively on reformist, high-achieving states like Andhra Pradesh.[10]

Social forms of inequality—located in caste, religion, and gender—have been objects of both academic study and government intervention, including through governmental affirmative-action programs. Reservations on the basis of caste identity have a long history in India that predates independence. The constitution continued the practice by reserving spaces in public-sector employment and education for members of Scheduled Tribes (STs) and Scheduled Castes (SCs). In 1990, the Indian government extended reservations to members of Other Backward Classes (OBCs), a policy that led to a great deal of social and political conflict.[11] In 2006, another heated debate began about whether or not the government should further extend reservations to OBCs in India's prestigious professional schools.

In 2005 the government appointed a committee, known by the name of its chairman, Justice Rajinder Sachar, to examine the social, economic, and demographic position of Indian Muslims. The committee's sobering results show that Muslims as a whole are much more disadvantaged than non-Muslims on a host of social and economic indicators. Although the government has not yet formulated a policy response to the report, the findings have renewed public debate about how the state should intervene to improve the position of Muslims, or at least the poorest among them.[12] One controversial proposal would reserve educational and employment opportunities for Muslims, something that a few state governments (specifically, Kerala, Karnataka, and Tamil Nadu) have already done.[13]

Similar to caste and religious identity, gender also structures access to resources and power. The seventy-third and seventy-fourth amendments to the constitution devolve power to a third tier of village-level government, called *panchayati raj,* in which 33 percent of seats and one-third of the leadership positions in elected village councils are held for women. A national-level Women's Reservation Bill proposes similar reservations for women in elected bodies at the state and national levels. Advocates of the bill have tried over the last decade to maneuver it through Parliament without success.[14] Indian personal law—which governs matters such as marriage, divorce, and inheritance, and is based on religious affiliation—is also a key site for battles over gender inequality.

In addition to these *macro*-level analyses and policies focusing on interstate and intergroup differences, there is also scholarship on income inequality that examines rates of change in poverty levels over time. The data used to calculate poverty in India are nationwide surveys that track household consumption.[15] In these *micro*-level studies, in which the unit of analysis is the household as an individual consuming unit, economists and statisticians consider whether economic growth during the liberalization era has affected the rate of poverty reduction.[16] There have been two major foci of the debate: how to reconcile the results from the surveys conducted by the National Sample Survey Organization with the often conflicting results of national account statistics; and how to account for changes to the survey instruments over time that make temporal analyses more tricky. The sheer volume of material published about poverty in India during the 1990s is testament to how much attention is paid to this kind of income inequality.

Another related kind of *micro*-analysis tracks nationwide Gini coefficients to determine how inequality has been affected throughout various economic-policy regimes. On the whole, the results of these studies show no significant change from 1960 to the present.[17]

In 2004, India elected a new coalition government at the federal level—the United Progressive Alliance (UPA) headed by the Indian National Congress party (Congress party)—that has identified income inequality as a persistent problem and pledged to ensure that future growth will be more socially inclusive. To this end, the government passed the National Rural Employment Guarantee Act of 2005 (NREGA), which guarantees one-hundred days of unskilled employment to all adult members of rural households. All the country's districts will be covered within a five-year period, but in the first year, two-hundred districts were selected for implementation.

When thinking about the relationship between inequality, political institutions, and democratic stability, in addition to these foci of analysis, we must also consider inequality within individual Indian states, or *intra*state inequality.[18] Given that many states in India have populations larger than most countries of the world, there is good reason to look below the state level to the district, the primary administrative unit within Indian states.[19] Although not the focus of this essay, other *intra*-unit analyses look at disparities in wealth and power within caste and religious communities, which are arguably as important if not more so to development and politics in India as those between communities.[20]

Spatially concentrated, intrastate inequality has significant implications for democratic governance, development, and the stability of political institutions. State governments and bureaucracies, and below them administrators at the district and block levels, are important nodes of governance and sites of decision making in India's political economy, particularly in the all-important social (health and education) and infrastructure (power, irrigation, and transport) sectors. Decisions taken in these administrative units include the seemingly dry calculus that determines where new irrigation works will be placed, new roads built, further electricity transmission lines laid, and additional government hospitals and colleges located. But it is the accretion of geographic biases in these kinds of development decisions that is both determinative of and determined by the locus of political and economic power in a state as well as the unevenness in development outcomes. Given this, in order to understand how and why some regions of the country continue to lag behind others, it may be necessary to address the intrastate inequalities in power and resources that often lie at the heart of states' development paradigms.

The leaders of autonomy movements in underdeveloped regions are proceeding with at least some of these assumptions when they argue that the only way out of the trap of underdevelopment is by a radical reordering of political and bureaucratic structures. But even if the demands for new states fail, how and whether an existing state government will be able to carry out a development agenda may well depend on whether the state can incorporate previously disenfranchised populations, which are often geographically concentrated. Thus, for example, whether and how Orissa will be able to carry out a development program based on mineral-resource extraction and heavy industry will hinge on whether the communities that inhabit the most mineral-rich and simultaneously impoverished districts, which are often tribal communities, will oppose or comply with the state's agenda.[21] This is particularly true for large projects like dams and power and steel plants, since all these require the relocation of large populations and the conversion of farm-land for industrial use.

Intrastate Inequalities and Demands for New States

Over the years the central government has formed numerous commit-tees to investigate the causes of regional imbalance and propose ame-liorative policies. The earliest of these efforts was the Committee on Dispersal of Industries, formed in 1960, which used macroeconomic criteria to identify the hundred least-developed districts in India. This information was meant to feed directly into the Indian government's centralized-planning regime. The intention was not to stimulate agri-cultural development in these districts directly, but to facilitate all-around development indirectly by building state industrial enterprises. This was followed by the Wanchoo Committee Report in 1968, which determined a set of financial incentives to encourage industries to set up in underdeveloped districts and identify ways to overcome econo-mies of agglomeration. This same topic was revisited a few decades later by the Pande Committee Report in 1988. Other committees that investi-gated the problems of spatial underdevelopment were either partial in their geographic coverage or attempted to fine-tune the methodology of determining "backwardness," as the Indian government terms underde-velopment.[22]

More recently, the Sarma Committee was established by the United Front government in 1996 to synthesize a list of the one hundred most underdeveloped districts in India, delivering results in 1997. On this list are districts in the poorest states of India, including Bihar, Uttar Pradesh, Orissa, Madhya Pradesh, and the smaller states that were carved out of Bihar and Madhya Pradesh in 2000—Chhattisgarh and Jharkhand. An unexpected result of the survey is that ten districts on the list lie in one of India's wealthiest states, Maharashtra.[23] The one-hundred dis-tricts largely fit in two sizeable geographically contiguous regions, one in east-central India and the other in north-central India, suggesting that agroclimatic conditions that span state boundaries, as well as fea-tures of historical political economy, continue to impact the develop-ment patterns of the present.

Through various policy statements and programs like the NREGA, the current government has devoted attention to the problem of inequal-ity. The government's assessment of the Tenth Five-Year Plan, written in 2005, states that although "the issue of regional balance has been an integral component of almost every Five-Year Plan . . . the perception has been that regional imbalances have actually got accentuated, par-ticularly over the past 15 years." Furthermore, "Even the problem of intrastate inequalities has not been adequately addressed, with regional disparities persisting within all states (including the relatively prosperous ones)."[24]

Unlike the NREGA, which eventually will include all districts, the government's Backward Regions Development Fund (BRDF) specifically targets the poorest districts.[25] Announced in 2006, the program transfers funds directly to the *panchayats,* India's third tier of government. The BRDF initiative selected 250 districts. The list includes districts from every state, even though, as the Sarma Committee revealed, the hundred poorest districts are tightly concentrated in just a few states. Perhaps the change was due to political bargaining at the federal level, or perhaps it was made in recognition of the fact that some aspects of underdevelopment are relative, perceived only with reference to neighbors who form part of a community, such as a state.[26]

The number and scale of these initiatives as well as measures such as the various five-year plans indicate that the central government has recognized the spatial element governing underdevelopment. The government's efforts may also be an acknowledgement of the multiple consequences of persistent inequality. One is a strong impact on patterns of rural-to-urban migration; both sending and receiving regions are negatively impacted if the flow of migrants is overwhelming.[27] A more systematic analysis of intrastate inequality, one attuned to its political implications, also would investigate the relationship between districts that are included in government rosters of backwardness and those at the epicenter of autonomy movements.

Below we make a preliminary effort in that direction by looking at arguably the two most vocal current autonomy movements, those in Maharashtra and Andhra Pradesh. The hope of movement leaders is that, just as reservations were adopted to redress social inequality, the reorganization of states can be the solution to spatial inequality. In both states, inequities in the allocation of development funds are at the base of the autonomy movements. In both states, however, the movements have been most vocal and organized not in the poorest regions—Marathwada and Rayalaseema—but in the regions of intermediate development—Vidarbha and Telengana. While politicians from the two poorest regions publicize the grievances of their regions, they stop short of demanding autonomy.

In 2000, three new states were created in India: Jharkand (from Bihar), Chhattisgarh (from Madhya Pradesh), and Uttaranchal (from Uttar Pradesh). This federal reorganization came after a gap of several decades during which India's internal boundaries were fixed, and the political leaders at the center were seemingly unwilling to entertain change. The Congress party's position with regard to linguistic states shifted somewhat over time. During the colonial period, Congress support for language as the basis of administrative organization was manifested in its opposition to the subcontinent's first traumatic partition, that of Bengal in 1905,[28] and again in the 1920s when Congress adopted language as the organizing principle of its provincial units. After independence, however, the first commission that Nehru appointed to study this question, the Linguistic Provinces Commission (or Dar Commission, as it is known), warned in 1948 that for India to proceed down the path of linguistic states would endanger the country's very unity and stability.[29] Yet in the wake of state-level agitations across the length and breadth of India, the first States Reorganization Commission (SRC) implemented the linguistic federalism that would characterize the Indian polity for the next five decades. In the structure established by the States Reorganization Act of 1956, the much larger Hindi-dominant territories are represented by numerous states whereas other sizeable linguistic communities have one state each.

Although the SRC report provided a blueprint for the institutional changes that followed, not all the commission's recommendations were adopted. The commission supported a separate state of Hyderabad for the territories of the former Nizam (the preindependence, historical ruler of Hyderabad); instead, these districts were combined with the other Telegu-speaking districts of coastal Andhra and Rayalseema to form present-day Andhra Pradesh.[30] The first SRC also recommended that the regions of Vidarbha in eastern Maharashtra be considered for statehood; again, the decision was made to unite all of the Marathi-speaking districts together in a single state.

The current demands for statehood include some of those unsuccessful movements which have lingered since the first SRC, such as for a separate Telengana (which includes the territories of the Nizam's Hyderabad) and separate Vidarbha, as well as movements of more recent provenance. If language was the organizing principle of the first states reorganization, the advocates of a second reorganization argue that linguistic similarities can unify only to a point. Now the economic, social, and historical differences that have only become more rather than less acute since the first SRC should be the basis of a new federal logic.

A conservative estimate of the number of movements for separate states puts the figure at about eight,[31] while a more expansive estimate would number about thirty.[32] Since three new states were created in 2000, these demands have become more strident, and are often justified with reference to material deprivation. Agitators for a separate Vidarbha, in Maharashtra, for example, point to the spate of suicides among farmers in the Vidarbha region in 2005–2006 as evidence of the state's neglect of the region and the justification for their demands. The next section examines some of the current political contours and the history of two autonomy movements in Maharashtra and Andhra Pradesh.

Maharashtra

One of India's largest states (its population according to the 2001 census was approximately 97 million), the state of Maharashtra spans the Marathi-speaking regions of western and central India. The three main regions—Western Maharashtra, Vidarbha, and Marathwada—can be distinguished on the basis of both agroclimatic features and political-economic history. The districts of Western Maharashtra include the industrial lands surrounding Mumbai, the coastal areas stretching south of Mumbai, and the fertile agricultural lands in which sugar has come to be an important cash crop. [33] These lands were part of the Bombay presidency of the British Crown and were among the sites of colonial-era canal construction. Vidarbha, in northeastern Maharashtra, was part of the British Central Provinces, and contains rich lands for cotton production, which was the main input in first the Bombay textile mills and later the Lancashire mills. Marathwada, in the southeastern part of the state, was part of the Nizam's Hyderabad; the economy of the region was much more isolated from the national and imperial economies than Maharashtra's other two regions. Thanks to these and other differences, the three regions that were joined as Maharashtra in 1960 had very distinct rates and patterns of development. There were particularly noticeable differences in their levels of infrastructure development, much owing to colonial-era investments in railroads and irrigation works in the British territories that were underdeveloped in the Nizam's territories.[34]

In the earliest discussions about a united Marathi-speaking state in the 1950s, the leaders from Marathwada and Vidarbha were keenly aware of their disadvantage relative to the western districts in terms of existing wealth, but also, more dangerously, in terms of the distribution of political power and therefore development resources across the state. In 1953, the Marathi-speaking leaders of the three regions signed the Nagpur Agreement to guarantee that the two disadvantaged regions would have separate development boards, some parity in allocation of development funds, and equal opportunities for public-sector employment.[35] Despite these assurances, much of the spirit of the agreement was ignored for subsequent decades. Separate development boards, for example, were only created in 1994, after a gap of four decades.

Nearly three decades after Maharashtra was created, the districts of Western Maharashtra remained significantly more advanced in industry and agriculture than the districts of the other two regions.[36] Deep inequalities continue to exist across the three regions of the state. Of the ten districts that appear in the Sarma Committee's list of underdeveloped districts in 1997, three are in Vidarbha and the remaining seven in Marathwada. None are in Western Maharashtra. In the much longer list of districts selected for the NREGA, however, the regional representation of districts is quite different. Out of twelve districts selected for the employment scheme in its first year, six are from Vidharbha, three from Marathwada, and three from the rest of the state, which includes Ahmednagar, a district in Western Maharashtra that is rich in agricultural cooperatives and has given Maharashtra some of its most prominent political leaders.

   While not as underdeveloped as Marathwada, Vidarbha remains significantly less developed than Western Maharashtra. Even as the leaders of Vidarbha signed the Nagpur Pact with their other Marathi-speaking counterparts in 1953, significant sentiments in favor of a separate
Vidarbha remained. These sentiments have only grown stronger over
time, particularly in light of the significant disparities that developed
in the allocation of development resources. Western Maharashtra received—and continues to receive—disproportionate shares of resources
for irrigation development, rural electrification, agricultural-extension
services, and rural credit. The Maharashtra state government formed a
"fact-finding committee" in 1983, the Dandekar Committee, to investigate the disparities in development spending across the three regions.
The committee estimated the "backlog" in development spending, or
the difference between what should have been spent in a particular
region and what was actually utilized for development. Not surprisingly, the 1983 committee, and subsequent committees formed during
the 1990s, found the backlog in Marathwada and Vidarbha to be large
and growing over time. This was matched by lower rates of electrification, commercial bank lending, and literacy in Vidarbha and Marathwada
compared to the rest of the state.[37]
   Now there is some indication that as larger quantities of development
funds are generated from the open market rather than through state plans,
the state and central governments will be less able to mediate intrastate
inequities in development expenditure. One example is that the responsibility for irrigation planning and development now rests with the three
regional development boards, one each for Vidarbha, Marathwada, and
the rest of Maharashtra. Although the state plan devolves equal funds for
irrigation to these three boards, a much larger share of funds has been
generated by the Irrigation Development Corporations, which raise funds
through the sale of bonds and market borrowing. The Krishna Valley
Development Corporation in Western Maharashtra raised approximately
fifty times the amount of funds allocated through the state plan, whereas
counterpart irrigation corporations in the two poorer regions were much
less successful.[38] Thus, despite the existence of regional development
boards since 1994, intrastate inequities in development spending since
that time in Maharashtra have persisted and even deepened. As successive government attempts to remove intrastate inequities have failed,
the demands for a separate Vidarbha have grown stronger, supported
both by politicians and social-movement leaders.
   The issue of a separate state dominated the 2004 parliamentary elections in the region.[39] In editorials and interviews, Sharad Joshi, who
gained prominence as the leader of the farmers' movement in the 1980s
and who is also a member of India's upper house of Parliament (the
Rajya Sabha), suggested that Vidarbha's problems are the product of
the state's political economy. The terms of trade between cotton-rich

Vidarbha and the industries of Western Maharashtra always favored the latter, as did the division of resources between the two regions.[40] The solution in his view can only be for Vidarbha to separate itself from the rest of the state. Complicating the issue of elite support for autonomy are the more mixed views among the electorate. An opinion poll conducted by an Indian newspaper found that while only half the region's population is aware of the demand for a separate Vidarbha, only a little over a quarter is supportive of it.[41]

Andhra Pradesh

Like Maharashtra, Andhra Pradesh is composed of multiple regions, each with a distinct historical political economy. As mentioned above, the region called Telengana was the seat of the Nizam's Hyderabad, and contains the state's capital city, Hyderabad. The Rayalseema region, which includes the southwestern districts of the state, was ceded by the Nizam to the British and was administered as part of the Madras Presidency. Like Rayalaseema, Coastal Andhra Pradesh (in the eastern part of the state) also became part of the colonial Madras Province. Like Western Maharashtra, the districts in this region during the colonial period benefited from extensive irrigation investments in the late nineteenth and early twentieth centuries. As a consequence, the districts in Coastal Andhra Pradesh were well poised to take advantage of the Green Revolution policies of the 1960s, which further exacerbated the inequalities between this region and the other two. Rayalaseema, which is distinct agroclimatically from the coastal districts, neither benefited from irrigation development nor had natural-resource endowments that could be exploited.

The political conditions that led to the merger of all Telegu-speaking regions of India into the state of Andhra Pradesh were similar in some ways to those in Maharashtra in the 1950s.[42] The elites of the Telengana region were concerned that jobs and opportunities would be disproportionately captured by the more educated and wealthier from the coastal areas. To alleviate the concerns of the Telengana faction, and to facilitate the creation of a united Andhra Pradesh, the leaders of both regions came together in Delhi with Prime Minister Nehru in 1956 to sign a "Gentleman's Agreement." Although not legally binding, the agreement included provisions to safeguard the revenues collected in Telengana for that region, expand educational opportunities, and guarantee that public-sector jobs would be shared equally among the regions. To many in Telengana, however, the agreement was an insufficient protection. Under a strictly meritocratic system, the well-educated middle classes of the coastal districts had secured higher-ranked and better-paying government jobs than those in other regions—a fact that became clear soon after the new state was formed. Muslims concentrated in Hyderabad were also concerned that they would be lost amid a much larger Hindu population that would emerge from a united Andhra Pradesh. From multiple fronts, therefore, the agitation for the breakup of Andhra Pradesh began even before the new state was born.

The demands for a separate Telengana have now become more vociferous, and the debate has directly affected national as well as state-level politics. In 2001, Telengana-based members of the Telegu Desam Party led by K. Chandrashekhar Rao defected from the party to form the Telengana Rashtra Samithi (TRS), a party devoted to the cause of a separate Telengana. In the 2004 national and state elections, the TRS allied with the Congress party and became a part of the federal ruling coalition, winning twenty-six state assembly seats and five parliamentary constituencies. Largely in deference to its alliance with the TRS, in the draft of the National Common Minimum Programme that the Congress circulated to its allies just before the 2004 elections, there was an explicit mention of a second States Reorganisation Commission. Yet in the National Common Minimum Programme that the government announced after its election victory, no such mention was made, suggesting that political expediency was at the heart of the Congress party's support for this proposed new state.

The movement for a separate Telengana now has more widespread support than it did in the late 1960s. At least one observer of Andhra politics believes that the mass support for the movement stems not from affective ties to a Telengana identity, but from a pervasive belief that development of the region is not possible within an integrated Andhra Pradesh.[43]

A Second States Reorganization?

Is a major reordering of the federal structure in India's near future? The creation of three new states in 2000 intimate that national elites are much more open to a federal restructuring now than in previous decades. A second States Reorganisation Bill, drafted in 2005, is currently pending for debate in the Lok Sabha (Parliament's lower house). The bill's sponsor is Subodh Mohite, a member of the Shiv Sena party elected from the Vidarbha region. There is also much public debate about the issue of a second states reorganization, both in support of and opposition to the idea.[44]

Autonomy movements and economic underdevelopment are two separate issues that are linked together in only some instances, and states reorganization may be one way of countering some intrastate disparities in development. It is perhaps too early to gauge whether the three new states formed in 2000 have had more success in development efforts as independent states. Reorganization may be an ineffective solution if the greater resources that result are captured by a small elite rather than distributed widely; the effect might be an overall decline in welfare. Other measures to address intrastate inequality would require the creation or overhaul of institutions like state-level planning and finance commissions, and regional development boards. The central government could also play a greater role by expanding programs like the BRDF and other decentralized initiatives that bypass state governments and give funds directly to districts and *panchayats*.

Perhaps it is not surprising that the renaissance of state-creation movements is coterminous both with the decline of national parties in favor of a multitude of regional parties allied in coalition governments, and with the decline of centralized planning in favor of market pressures and competitive federalism. Each of these processes creates new incentives and pressures for federal fragmentation. In the era of coalition governments, the political parties that represent regional aspirations can come to occupy strategic niches from which to affect not just state but also federal politics, such as the TRS in Telengana.[45] Similar to the actors who worked for linguistic states in the 1950s and 1960s, these increasingly vocal and effective interest groups and political parties may see their brightest prospects in a newly organized federal system.

There is good reason to believe that in the first instance, the linguistic movements of the 1950s and 1960s represented the preferences of elite members of linguistic communities, who calculated that their greatest future opportunities would lie in large states that were drawn on the basis of language.[46] Indeed, the promise of employment within state institutions was one of the forces driving linguistic movements, and larger states would serve this purpose more effectively than smaller ones. Now, many fissures within linguistic communities that were evident but ignored in the 1950s are emerging as the vital forces shaping India's democratic, federal structure. Whether or not the pressures of regional inequality are addressed by the reorganization of states, the pressures may have reached a point where they must be addressed in some way. The challenge to India's federal structure is to answer these multiple calls for economic equilibrium in a way that maintains its long engagement with mediating the dangers of inequality to Indian democracy.

NOTES

For help in preparing this essay, I would like to thank Devesh Kapur and Christian Lee Novetzke.

1. Nehru's views are contained in numerous sources, including in his remarks to a meeting of the Indian Conciliation Group held in London in February 1936. This text is reproduced in a collection of Nehru's speeches from 1922 to 1945. Jagat S. Bright, ed., *Important Speeches of Jawaharlal Nehru* (Lahore, India: Indian Printing Works, 1945), 142–64.

2. Pratap Bhanu Mehta, *The Burden of Democracy* (New Delhi: Penguin, 2003). In a discussion of India's "culture of inequality," Mehta argues that the way that inequality permeates Indian social relations has serious consequences for the quality of democracy.

3. Another manifestation of the relationship between politics and spatially concentrated inequality are the revolutionary demands from groups such as the Naxalites. The Indian government classifies districts with a significant presence of groups espousing violent, revolutionary tactics, "extremist affected districts." In 2005, the Planning Commission listed fifty-five such districts that are included in a longer list of backward districts. Mihir Shah, "A National Authority for Rainfed India," *The Hindu* (Chennai), 19 April 2006.

4. Some of these movements for autonomy have been characterized by protracted violence, and have centered more self-consciously around notions of ethnic identity and cultural difference—for example, many of the movements in the northeast. Other contests have been fought more in the terrain of politics, and economic difference has been more explicitly at the heart of the conflict. This essay focuses on examples from this latter category of autonomy movements.

5. By looking only at two movements for autonomy, this essay speculates on the relationship between autonomy movements and inequality. A more comprehensive and systematic analysis of all such struggles for autonomy would yield a richer understanding of the phenomenon.

6. The formula is named after its originator, D.R. Gadgil, the deputy chairman of the planning commission from 1967 to 1971, who oversaw the Fourth Five-Year Plan. The Gadgil Formula removed much of the central government's discretionary power in the allocation of development funds, leaving it instead to a formula that took into consideration states' populations, relative incomes, and past performances.

7. Because resource-rich Indian states were in many cases the least industrialized, however, leaders of these states complained that by depressing their comparative advantage, freight equalization has actually perpetuated old divisions between industrialized and nonindustrialized regions.

8. For recent examinations of inequality in India and other countries, see Shubham Chaudhuri and Martin Ravallion, "Partially Awakened Giants: Uneven Growth in China and India," World Bank Policy Research Working Paper 4069, November 2006; and Branko Milanovic, "Half a World: Regional Inequality in Five Great Federations," World Bank Policy Research Working Paper No. 3699, September 2005. Available at *http://ssrn.com.* Often-cited examinations of India in particular include Montek S. Ahluwalia, "Economic Performance of States in Post-Reforms Period" *Economic and Political Weekly,* 6 May 2000; S.L. Shetty "Growth of SDP and Structural Changes in State Economies: Interstate Comparisons," *Economic and Political Weekly,* 6 December 2003; and Nirvikar Singh, Laveesh Bhandari, and Aoyu Chen, et al., "Regional Inequality in India: A Fresh Look," University of California–Santa Cruz Economics Working Paper No. 532 and U.C.–Santa Cruz Center for International Economics Working Paper No. 02-23, December 2002. Available at *http://ssrn.com.* This last paper contains a summary of several earlier studies of regional inequality, most of which concur that private investment flows drive the divergence in per capita state GDP.

9. India's phenomenal growth over the last two decades has been driven by the expansion of services located in urban areas. Manufacturing has remained stagnant over this period, and agriculture has declined.

10. World Bank, *Country Strategy for India* (Washington D.C.: World Bank, 2004), i.

11. The Mandal Commission was authorized in 1979 to investigate reservations for OBCs. Although the Commission produced its report in 1980, it languished for a decade before being partially implemented by the V.P. Singh government in 1990.

12. See Pratap Bhanu Mehta, "Separate but Unequal," *The Indian Express*, 18 November 2006.

13. Zoya Hassan, "Reservations for Muslims," *Seminar* 549, May 2005, at *www.india-seminar.com/2005/549/549%20zoya%20hassan.htm*.

14. Economists recently have begun analyzing the efficacy of reservations policies. See Rohini Pande, "Can Mandated Political Representation Increase Policy Influence for Disadvantaged Minorities? Theory and Evidence from India," *American Economic Review* 93 (September 2003): 1132–51; and Raghabendra Chattopadhyay and Esther Duflo, "Women as Policy Makers: Evidence from a Randomized Policy Experiment in India," *Econometrica* 72 (September 2004): 1409–43. Pande finds that reservations for STs and SCs at the state level have led to greater redistribution in favor of those communities. Raghabendra and Duflo, who investigate *panchayat* governance, find that women-headed *panchayats* invest more in certain kinds of infrastructure, like drinking water, that are more directly significant for women.

15. The Planning Commission, the institution charged with calculating the official poverty rate for the government of India, relies on the surveys carried out by the National Sample Survey Organization, which were intended to be carried out every five years but are often conducted at larger intervals.

16. Many of the original contributions to the poverty debate were published in the pages of *Economic and Political Weekly* throughout the 1990s and 2000s. Much of the spirit and substance of that debate is collected in Angus Deaton and Valerie Kozel, eds., *The Great Indian Poverty Debate* (New Delhi: Macmillan, 2005).

17. As an example, see Surjit Bhalla, *Imagine There's no Country: Poverty, Inequality, and Growth in the Era of Globalization* (Washington, D.C.: Institute of International Economics, 2002).

18. While not common, there are some studies targeted at the district level. Among those that are intrastate are Bibek Debroy and Laveesh Bhandari, eds., *District-Level Deprivation in the New Millenium* (Delhi: Konark, 2003); and Laveesh Bhandari and Aarti Khare, "The Geography of Post 1991 Indian Economy," paper published by Indicus Analytics, New Delhi, May 2002. The former evaluates district-level deprivation as measured against the Millennium Development Goals, and the latter constructs a gauge of regional economic performance using five variables: sales of transport fuel, sales of diesel fuel, bank deposits, bank credit, and cereal production. The authors use the regional classification used by the National Sample Survey Organization, which bundles together geographically contiguous districts within states (not cutting across states) that share certain agroclimatic features.

19. At the district level, the bureaucrat in charge—the district magistrate or district collector—is an officer of the Indian Administrative Service, and is responsible for administration and revenue. Law and order in India is also organized along district lines, with each district housing a superintendent of police drawn from the Indian Police Service. Most of the 310 districts that existed at the time of the 1951 census were adopted from British administrative divisions and the boundaries of princely states. In the intervening decades, districts have been subdivided, increasing the total number to just over 600. According to the 2001 census, the average population size of districts was 1.7 million, although the population of the largest district—Medinipur in West Bengal—is considerably larger at 9.6 million.

20. In Bihar, for example, the once seemingly hegemonic political formation of OBCs has subdivided further into Extremely Backward Classes and OBCs, a fracture that was a decisive factor in the state's most recent assembly elections in 2005.

21. I use the example of Orissa in particular because of a series of violent events in January 2006. While protesting the construction of a new steel plant by Tata Steel in the Kalinga Nagar industrial complex in the district of Jaipur, at least eight people from Orissa's tribal communities were killed. The conflict in Orissa, however, is not unique; there were similar protests against the construction of a car-manufacturing plant in Singur, West Bengal in December 2006 and January 2007.

22. There is a more comprehensive survey of these and other committees in Debroy and Bhandari, eds., *District-Level Deprivation in the New Millennium*, 12–17.

23. Excluding Delhi, Pondicherry, and Chandigarh—all three of which are small and mostly urban—Maharashtra has the second highest per capita net state domestic product, after Haryana in 2003–2004. Ministry of Finance, *Economic Survey 2005–2006* (New Delhi: Government of India, 2006).

24. Planning Commission, *Midterm Appraisal of the 10ᵗʰ Five Year Plan (2002–2007)* (New Delhi: Government of India, 2005), 505.

25. Many similar programs targeting "backwardness" preceded this one. Under the Tenth Plan, for example, the government started the Rashtriya Sam Vikas Yojana to give additional development funds to backward districts in each state. The districts from that program are also part of the BRDF initiative. Other development programs target specific categories of districts, such as the Drought Prone Areas Programme, the Desert Development Programme, and Extremist Affected Districts.

26. The allocation of funds for 2006–2007 is 37.5 billion rupees, a sum that is also promised annually for the Eleventh Plan Period (2007–2012). Each of the 250 districts is guaranteed 110 million; the remaining 10 billion is to be divided, half on the basis of population and half on the basis of territory. Unlike the resources from the NREGA, the BRDF funds are grants, not loans, and are devolved to the states as additional central assistance to state plans. Ministry of Panchayati Raj, *Backward Regions Grant Fund Programme Guidelines* (New Delhi: Government of India, 2007).

27. Migration is often a consequence of spatial inequality, as people from low-income and slow-growth regions migrate to high-income and rapidly growing areas of the country. Given the persistent and in some cases growing spatial inequality in India, some economists posit that India's current migration rates are actually much lower than expected. See Kaivan Munshi and Mark R. Rosenzweig, "Why Is Mobility in India So Low? Social Insurance, Inequality, and Growth," CID Working Paper 121, July 2005, Center for International Development at Harvard University, at *www.cid.harvard.edu/cidwp/pdf/121.pdf*.

28. Satish Kumar Arora, "The Reorganization of the Indian States," *Far Eastern Economic Review* 25 (February 1956): 27–30.

29. Other observers of India made similar pronouncements after linguistic reorganization was implemented. See Selig Harrison, *India: The Most Dangerous Decades* (Princeton: Princeton University Press, 1960).

30. For a firsthand account of the integration of the princely states, including the Nizam's territories in present-day Maharashtra and Andhra Pradesh, written by one of the bureaucrats who shepherded the process, see V.P. Menon, *The Story of the Integration of the Indian States* (New York: Macmillan, 1956).

31. An editorial following the states reorganization in 2000 identifies the following eight agitations: Purbanchal, Harit Pradesh, and Bundelkhand in Uttar Pradesh; Bodoland in Assam; Gorkhaland in West Bengal; Telengana in Andhra Pradesh; Vidarbha in Maharashtra; and Saursashtra in Gujarat. Devesh Kapur,

"Does India Need More States?" *The Hindu,* 21 August 2000.

32. Akhtar Majeed, "The Changing Politics of States' Reorganization," *Publius: The Journal of Federalism* 33 (Fall 2003): 83–98.

33. Some accounts further disaggregate Western Maharashtra into Konkan (coastal area south of Mumbai), Mumbai, Khandesh (districts north of Mumbai with large populations of Scheduled Tribes), and Western Maharashtra, and treat these three as distinct regions.

34. Manu Goswami details the ways in which the colonial regime relied on infrastructure ("state works") to physically mark its status as an imperial power in India. See Manu Goswami, *Producing India: From Colonial Economy to National Space* (Chicago: University of Chicago, 2004), 46–54.

35. K. Seeta Prabhu and P.C. Sarkar, "Identification of Levels of Development: The Case of Maharashtra," *Economic and Political Weekly,* 5 September 1992, 1927–37.

36. Prabhu and Sarkar, "Identification of Levels of Development," 1992. Of the nine districts that they identify as agriculturally developed in 1985–86, eight are in Western Maharashtra and one (Aurangabad) is in Marathwada. Of the ten industrially developed districts, seven are in Western Maharashtra.

37. Jasmine Damle, *Beyond Economic Development* (New Delhi: Mittal, 2001), 83–88.

38. Programme Evaluation Organisation, Planning Commission, *Performance Evaluation of Statutory Development Boards (SDBs) in Maharashtra* (New Delhi: Government of India, 2003), 47.

39. "Lok Sabha Polls to Clinch Issue of Statehood to Vidarbha," *The Hindu,* 16 March 2004.

40. Sharad Joshi, "Vidarbha—A Model Farmers' State?" *Business Line,* 10 December 2003.

41. "Who Wants a Vidarbha State?" *The Hindu,* 24 October 2004.

42. Much of the political history that follows is drawn from Duncan B. Forrester, "Subregionalism in India: The Case of Telengana," *Pacific Affairs* 43 (Spring 1970): 5–21.

43. C.H. Hanumantha Rao, "Statehood for Telengana: New Imperatives," *The Hindu,* 8 January 2007. The author is chairman of the Center for Economic and Social Studies, Hyderabad.

44. See for example, Rao, "Statehood for Telengana"; and Sidharth Sharma, "Creation of New States: Need for Constitutional Parameters," *Economic and Political Weekly,* 30 September 2003.

45. Although the TRS convinced the UPA to support separate statehood for Telengana *before* the elections, after the UPA victory, it became clear that the Congress would not act on that pledge. In protest, the TRS withdrew its support of the UPA and resigned its two cabinet posts in August 2006.

46. For the case of the formation of Andhra Pradesh, see Lisa Mitchell, "The Making of a Mother Tongue: Language, Emotion, and Collective Identity in Colonial and Post-colonial Southern India," Ph.D. diss., Columbia University, 2004, ch. 6.

INDEX